PERSPECTIVE DESIGN

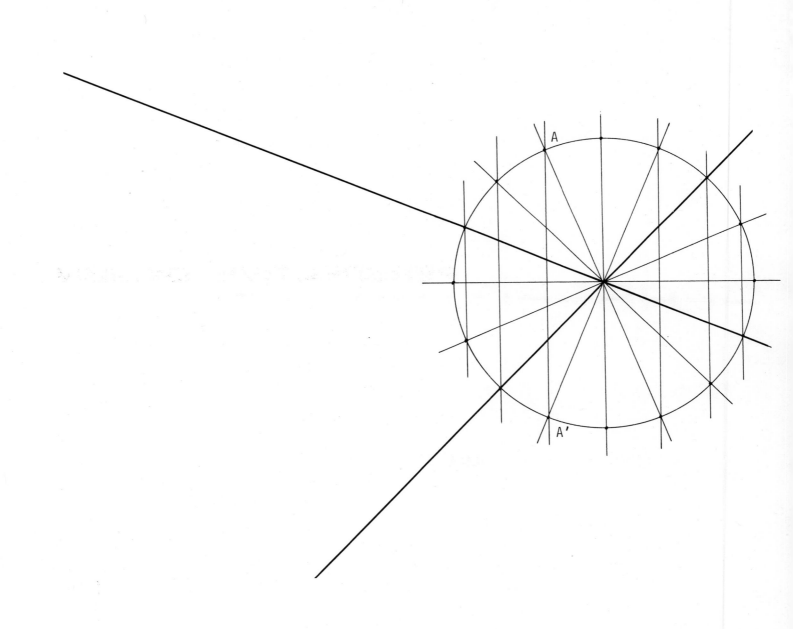

PERSPECTIVE DESIGN

ADVANCED GRAPHIC AND MATHEMATICAL APPROACHES

JOHN H. MAULDIN, Ph.D.

 VAN NOSTRAND REINHOLD COMPANY
_____ NEW YORK

Printed in the United States of America

Designed by Ernie Haim

Van Nostrand Reinhold Company Inc.
115 Fifth Avenue
New York, New York 10003

Van Nostrand Reinhold Company Limited
Molly Millars Lane
Wokingham, Berkshire RG11 2PY, England

Van Nostrand Reinhold
480 La Trobe Street
Melbourne, Victoria 3000, Australia

Macmillan of Canada
Division of Canada Publishing Corporation
164 Commander Boulevard
Agincourt, Ontario M1S 3C7, Canada

16 15 14 13 12 11 10 9 8 7 6 5 4 3 2 1

Library of Congress Cataloging in Publication Data
Mauldin, John H.
　Perspective design.
　Bibliography: p.
　Includes index.
　1. Perspective.　I. Title.
T369.M38　1985　　　604.2′4　　　85-3231
ISBN 0-442-26408-9 (pbk.)

ACKNOWLEDGMENTS

Appreciation is expressed to my wife and partner, Susan, for her patient assistance, to my mother for her encouragement, to Juan Espinosa for his photographic collaboration, and to Don Stone and the developers of the personal-professional computer for making possible the more effective testing and writing of the manuscript.

Contents

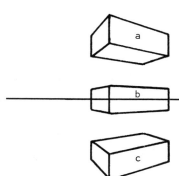

Introduction

Perspective as used in art or technical drawing has consisted of showing three-dimensional space in a two-dimensional picture, approximating the scene a human eye would see through a window. Human vision presents the world in a complex form of perspective altered by subliminal processing of the subject matter. Perspective is an intimate part of the way people view their surroundings.

This book is intended for artists, illustrators, designers, and architects who need a full explanation of modern approaches to perspective depiction of subject matter. The book may be used by graphic artists at any level of sophistication. Creative artists who are not now using perspective may find such use valuable in the future. Some artists who are already using perspective may have need of the book's more powerful and more accurate methods. Commercial and technical illustrators, generally

aware of the dramatic effect provided by perspective, may need further assistance with layout or other problems. The discussion of perspective here attempts to broaden the creative sphere of all artists and to provide practical help to technical artists in fields such as architecture, engineering drawing, and computer graphics. The ultimate goal is to place new theoretical tools and new approaches into the hands of artists of all kinds so that a solid foundation is laid for future developments in art, graphics, film-making, and many other areas of visual creation.

Two different but parallel approaches to perspective are presented in this book: first, graphic methods based on geometric construction; second (and closely linked to the first), a mathematical approach using calculation. The methods can be used for overall project planning, for drawing selected objects that may otherwise be difficult to depict or visualize, for sketching, or for a multitude of other uses limited only by the imagination and training of the artist. The mathematical methods are introduced in stages. The tools may be as simple as a ruler and square, to which a pocket calculator can be added, or they may embrace a computer, a plotter, and other specialized equipment.

Before any new mathematical approaches are presented, established perspective methods are reviewed and some misconceptions about them corrected. No one book could cover fully all aspects of historical and recent perspective; the graphic methods described here were chosen for their consistency and simplicity. The emphasis is both theoretical and practical, for a broad range of modern uses. Options for and restrictions on perspective must be thoroughly understood before either graphic or mathematical methods can be mastered. The intention is to lead artists to the frontiers of perspective as projected from art, computer graphics, and applied mathematics.

Readers with different purposes can pursue the study at different levels. Artists of all kinds can acquire additional techniques for showing depth. Practicing landscape artists can learn more about the behavior of objects in the distance and about illuminated surfaces. Still-life artists can deal directly with the perspective view of geometric forms. Figure artists can depict human forms under special conditions with greater accuracy."Realist" artists can study in precise detail how objects actually appear. Technical designers and illustrators can gain new freedom in creating effects and can learn to solve harder problems. Artists interested in abstract forms, particularly ones with underlying regularity,

can take advantage of the mathematical approach to perspective in pursuing new experiments. Computer-assisted artists can benefit from both the graphical and mathematical principles. Perspective must be well understood before graphics programs can be written, modified, or exploited fully.

The mathematical method used in this book presupposes that the reader has had a secondary-school education that included algebra and geometry. The first chapter includes an introduction for all artists on locating objects in space, using elementary and useful mathematical language. No mathematics is necessary until after the chapters on the graphic method. All terms and operations used— including trigonometric functions—are defined and explained to the extent needed. Some new but simple theorems are proved in the discussion and applied to artistic goals. Many projects can be carried out by means of a pocket calculator. Very ambitious work may require a computer (which is little more than a large, fast, and clever calculator). It is assumed that computer-assisted artists are already familiar with simple mathematical and graphic programming for their chosen machines. The perspective methods are presented ready for programming, and a few functional BASIC programs are given. The principal units of measure ("metric" or SI) are introduced, but the methods are independent of particular units and can be used with any units.

Many nontraditional references and procedures for perspective are provided. Information relevant to perspective, such as the behavior of illumination, is presented in detail (including physical principles) for both graphic and mathematical use. Some principles of perception are covered, but color theory is not. Symmetry, one of the many interesting mathematical topics relevant to art, is not covered except in regard to perspective problems. Composition, or picture design, is a large subject beyond the treatment of perspective; however, the tools provided in this book are directly necessary for overall planning of any artistic or graphic work that makes use of perspective. Technical drawing methods outside the field of perspective drawing are generally not included but left to the references.

Although precision and mathematics—features contributing to general competence in a highly technological culture—are emphasized, the fundamental goal remains to serve the creative artist. The discipline fostered here is intended to free and extend creativity rather than to restrain it. Perspective is a vast field, but the riches to be found with patient study can be very rewarding. The beauty inherent in mathematical description can complement in profound ways the beauty sought in the visual arts.

To aid the serious student of these methods, occasional study and practice questions are provided within the text, marked with the symbol Q. Figures and equations are also numbered for each chapter. The plates are grouped in one location. Footnotes for each chapter are collected at the back of each chapter and an alphabetical list of references is provided at the end of the book.

The reader/artist is invited to extend the ideas presented in this book as far as imagination can carry them. There is no replacement for a fundamental education in mathematics at the level presented (so much the better if it goes beyond, to calculus, complex variables, and matrix algebra). Knowledge of basic physics pertaining to artistic matters is also very valuable. The author further invites the reader to keep him informed of both progress and failures, and especially of possible errors and potential improvements in this material. If enough corrections accumulate and enough fascinating, new, and more precise material is suggested, a second edition will be considered. Please write in care of the publishers.

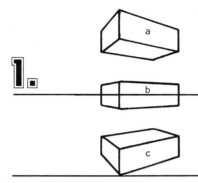

1.

Locating and Viewing
Objects in Space

The Nature of Our Three-dimensional Space

Three independent dimensions of measure, known commonly as width (or length), depth, and height, are required to describe or locate objects in the physical world. This law of nature is true regardless of our perceptions of the world. The three dimensions, however, require more precise definition before they can be used unambiguously. For example, confusion of length with width or width with depth must be avoided. When the common terms are used hereafter, they refer to the dimensions defined in figure 1-1; the viewer's location is imagined to be that of the human figure in the drawing. "Width" is measured across the field of view, "depth" is measured away from the viewer, and "height" is measured vertically. "Length" does not refer ex- clusively to any one of these three specific dimensions but instead has the general meaning of *extension*.

The name given to three-dimensional mathematical space whose properties closely match those of physical space as we ordinarily perceive it is *Euclidean space*. Important properties of Euclidean space include the following:

1. The three independent dimensions are measured at right (90°) angles to one another. (This property is called *orthogonality*.)
2. The three interior angles of a triangle add up to 180°.
3. Parallel lines exist, can be defined, and never intersect.
4. Space can be uniformly measured in incremental units that are of constant magnitude

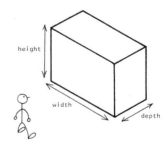

1-1. Three independent dimensions

1

and can be used in any direction. (For example, a centimeter stays the same size whether it is used as a measuring unit for width, depth, height, or any diagonal measure.)

Here, as later, all relevant mathematical and physical properties are presented explicitly so that the artist has the choice of using them or defying them in a knowledgeable manner—a privilege possible on paper but not in reality. Some basic rules are broken later in this book for illustrative purposes. Perhaps surprisingly, the postulated reality of our ordinary Euclidean three-dimensional space is in jeopardy. Work in physics and astronomy has found that each of the rules listed above is broken in nature at the largest scales and possibly also at the smallest scales.

Coordinate Systems

It is convenient to use a *coordinate system* to locate or describe objects in space. A coordinate system is a way of specifying in an orderly way three numbers that tell where an object is located with respect to each of the three dimensions. Any coordinate system requires a reference point or *origin* (O) where all three coordinates have values of zero. The location of O is at the point (0,0,0), where a zero is given for each coordinate.

In one simple coordinate system, the viewer's standpoint on the floor may be taken as (0,0,0), and the location of a nearby object—a light bulb, for example—may then be specified as 2 units north, 1 unit east, and 2 units up from the plane of origin (figure 1-2). These independent measurements in

the three dimensions can be made in any order, and the same point will be reached. Similarly, a rectangular desk 1 unit wide, ½ unit deep, and ¾ unit high, located with its bottom northeast corner at O, is described by the coordinates of each corner point. Going counterclockwise, the corners are at O, 1 unit W, 1 unit W and ½ unit S, and ½ unit S. The top could be described as ¾ unit in the up direction.

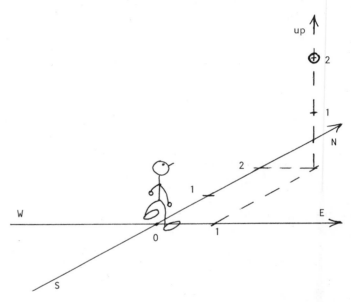

1-2. Compass coordinates

Several coordinate systems for three dimensions are widely recognized, including the following: the north-east-south-west or compass system, to which up and down must be added; the spherical coordinates on the earth's globe (latitude and longitude), to which altitude must be added; and the heading angle, radius, and altitude coordinates often used in flying.

Q1-1. Where is O for each dimension in the compass system? in the global system? What units of measure are commonly used for each? (There are a number of "correct" answers to questions such as these.)

Q1-2. Try to name another familiar coordinate system. Include or create all three dimensions.

Q1-3. For the "flying" system, show that each dimension is mutually orthogonal by considering how the coordinates are oriented for a particular object located in it.

Q1-4. Try to find a system of coordinates that does not have the dimensions at right angles (a permissible but rarely useful system).

For pictorial purposes, it is rarely convenient for the viewer to occupy the reference point (O). Instead, some point "internal" and of special significance to the subject matter is usually chosen as O. Often, O is the point at the center of the foreground of the subject, appearing at the bottom of the picture frame. The viewer may be standing on a lower level (the floor) at some distance from subject and picture.

Units of Measure

In the preceding examples, units of measure such as miles, feet, or degrees of latitude may have been suggested. For further work, metric units of length will be used. The principal one is the *meter*. One meter is nearly 39.37 inches or 3.28 feet. Metric units of measure are subdivided by tenths, hundredths, thousandths, and so on, creating numbers that can always be expressed as decimals. This is very convenient for calculation, as well as for measuring or laying out. One-hundredth of a meter is a centimeter (0.01 meter). Only meters (m) and centimeters (cm) are used here, although some rulers are also marked in millimeters (mm—0.001 m). For greater lengths, kilometers (km—1,000 m) might be needed. The conversions from metric back to English units are: 2.54 cm = 1 inch exactly; 30.5 cm = 1 foot; and 1.61 km = 1 mile.

Rulers measuring 30 cm are easy to find and are a necessity. A precision ruler for drawing is called a "scale," a term with other meanings. Unfortunately, 1-meter rulers (called "metersticks" and marked in cm and mm) are still considered scientific or educational equipment and are difficult to purchase locally. Artistic work usually involves a range of lengths from a fraction of a millimeter to several meters. Pictures are typically less than 1 m wide. Dimensions of artistic subjects vary from less than 1 mm (strands of hair) to tens of meters (small buildings) to many kilometers (outdoor scenes). Drawing astronomical objects (planets, galaxies) ordinarily does not require familiarity with larger metric units.

Architects and other artists who prefer to use English units should use measurements in decimal feet or decimal inches and not mix the two. Calculation and scaling with units and numbers expressed as decimals is relatively easy. There should be no need to convert any metric numbers used in this book; all diagrams are without scale so that they may be studied with any ruler.

Cartesian or Rectilinear Coordinates

For most work, a simple but precise coordinate system known as *rectilinear* (for right-angled) or Cartesian (after Descartes) is used. This system fits

Euclidean space. It is oriented according to a special alignment that is usually simplest for constructing pictures. The dimension for width is labeled x and measured across the viewer's vision. The dimension for depth is labeled y and measured in the direction in which the viewer looks straight ahead. The dimension for height is measured on a dimension labeled z. The x, y, and z dimensions or coordinates are shown schematically in figure 1-3. The x and y dimensions are always in a horizontal plane, called the xy plane. If the object or scene to be depicted has a floor or ground, it is natural for the z coordinate to have its zero value at that level. The reference point (origin) for x and y must be at the $z = 0$ level, but the exact location should be chosen on the basis of the subject matter, as discussed later. The basic lines along which x, y, and z are measured are called *axes;* each passes through the origin O at right angles to the other two.

It is essential to be able to recognize a right-hand coordinate system, and to distinguish it from a left-hand system. Otherwise, any calculation may produce false results. The right-hand rectilinear coordinates are so named because they can be made to match the fingers of the right hand. If the right hand is laid palm up and the thumb, first, and second fingers of the hand are stretched at right angles to each other, the thumb points in the x direction, the first finger points in the y direction, and the second finger points in the z direction (figure 1-4). The direction of pointing is important because in each dimension, measurement along the axis can be either positive $(+)$ or negative $(-)$ from the zero point. The right-hand fingers, when positioned as in figure 1-4, all point in the positive directions established by convention. Figure 1-3 shows (on two-

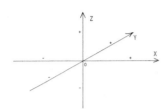

1-3. Rectilinear coordinates

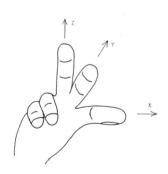

1-4. Right-hand rule for rectilinear coordinate systems

dimensional paper) a view of the three coordinate axes and their directions. It is of course impossible to show three independent dimensions in an unambiguous way on paper. Several different types of view can be drawn.

Q1-5. Test your left hand and see how many fingers point in the wrong direction when labeled as in figure 1-4.

The xyz system is used for measurements of real objects in three-dimensional space. This coordinate system cannot be used to locate views of those objects accurately in a picture. Other systems will be provided later.

The conventional way to write three coordinates is (x_1,y_1,z_1), with numbers in place of the algebraic symbols. The x coordinate goes first, the y coordinate second, and the z coordinate third. The notation (x_1,y_1,z_1) identifies a point in space whose coordinates have the values x_1, y_1, and z_1. These conventions are universal and compatible with calculators and computer programming.

For example, suppose reference point O is at the center of the square base of a 50-m-high Egyptian pyramid. The base is 80 m by 80 m (figure 1-5). The apex has coordinates (0,0,50) in meters. Proceeding counterclockwise from the positive x axis, the corners of the base are at (40,40,0), $(-40,40,0)$, $(-40,-40,0)$, and $(40,-40,0)$. A huge object has thus been fully described with five simple sets of numbers. It will be shown later that the perspective view can be found by simple calculations involving these few numbers. Drawing the pyramid by graphic methods could take more time than calculating and laying out the perspective.

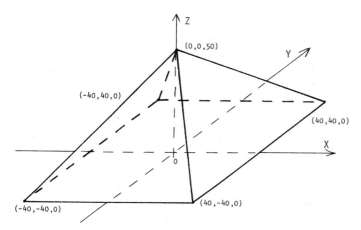

1-5. Rectilinear coordinates for a pyramid

Q1-6. Given a simple rectangular building 5 m wide, 10 m deep, and 20 m high, sketch each different way of showing it in *xyz* coordinates, choosing reference points and giving the coordinates for each corner (vertex) of the building. Even if this exercise is restricted to measuring width along the *x* axis, at least eight different ways exist.

Observers or Viewers

The observer or viewer of a picture is not usually within the picture and consequently is rarely at the reference point O. A relation must therefore be established between the viewer location (V) and O. For artistic purposes, the viewer's location is a special one, often intended to give the viewer the feeling of observing an actual scene from that location. The impression created at one viewing location may be different or unavailable at other potential viewing locations; the location chosen provides a certain framework and bias.

A human viewer naturally establishes a horizontal line called the horizon because in normal posture the person's two eyes are on a horizontal axis. The *x* axis is defined parallel to that horizontal axis. The picture a person sees while looking through two eyes is elongated horizontally and is less high vertically. The views through the two eyes do not overlap fully. Almost 180° of view can be seen horizontally, but less than 120° can be seen vertically (see figure 1-6). Picture framing replaces the wide oval field of view with a rectangular frame that is often elongated horizontally to match the human viewing field. Picture framing then helps reinforce both horizontal and vertical axes associated with the subject matter. However, the *xyz* coordinate axes cannot be directly related to the picture frame.

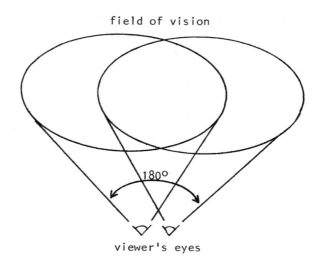

1-6. Field of vision for a human viewer

The vertical has special significance for earth-bound viewers. Gravity dictates the human upright form and provides a clue to the vertical. The horizontal axis of the eyes is then, by symmetry, perpendicular to the vertical axis of the biped. By convention, the z axis points in the vertical direction, but the positive direction is upward, opposite the pull of gravity. The direction the eyes look when at rest outdoors defines the third dimension (the y axis) at right angles to the other two. Thus, a person at rest standing on the ground establishes a natural rectilinear coordinate system.

Gravity provides many other clues to the vertical for pictorial subject matter—for example, in the way plants grow or structures are built. In some outdoor settings the actual horizon is visible, far enough away that it may appear as a straight line parallel to the x axis. The terrestrial horizon is not far enough away, however, to cause all objects to become infinitesimally small at great distances. A large ship on the ocean disappears below the horizon before it shrinks to nothing. Observed from a great height, the horizon of our spheroidal earth appears curved, with an accompanying change in our accustomed way of looking at large-scale scenes. It might be thought that a viewer standing on a smooth spherical earth and looking straight ahead (perpendicular to the vertical) would be looking tangentially to the earth's surface (figure 1-7). But the viewer

1-7. The earth's horizon (exaggerated scale: the earth is about 8 million times bigger than the observer)

would actually have to look slightly downward to see the horizon at which the line of sight tangentially grazes the bulge of the earth. Theoretically, this horizon is 4.37 km away from an observer who is 1.5 m (5½ ft) tall.

Q1-7. If feet had eyes, at what distance would they see the horizon on a perfectly smooth spherical earth?

The artist usually must assume that the viewer's posture defines the underlying coordinate system. Then, to design a picture, the artist must account for the three-dimensional relation of the viewer to the subject. If the subject matter is located around the origin of the xyz system, near $y = 0$, the viewer must be located at some negative y position (figure 1-8). The height of the viewer's eyes must be considered in connection with the various heights of the subject matter. The viewer's feet may or may not be on the same ground ($z = 0$ level) as the subject matter; the horizon appears at eye level, regardless. The symmetrical center of the viewer's vision establishes an $x = 0$ point. All of these natu-

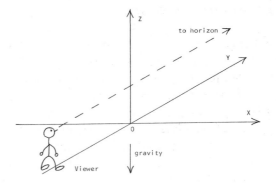

1-8. Relation of the viewer to rectilinear coordinates

ral assumptions must be fully understood for what follows, especially if the artist wishes to tamper with any of them. More specific conditions will be stated and used in later chapters.

Complex Objects and Outline Boxes

The description of subject matter would be complete if subject matter were limited to idealized boxes, bricks, rectangular buildings, and perhaps pyramids and thin poles. But all real objects have complex shapes. A real tree or person would be virtually impossible to describe with coordinates, even in approximation. Moreover, an object with complex shape may not appear much different in perspective from the way it appears in some other view. The presence of explicit or implicit straight lines in an object makes the perspective view more striking.

When used with a rectilinear coordinate system, *outline boxes* are a simple way to establish the locations and overall shapes and sizes of objects. Each object is imagined to be in a rectangular box (also known as a "regular parallelopiped" or a "rectangular prism"). Most objects have what are called *principal axes* (figure 1-9). One principal axis is assigned to the longest dimension of the object, and two others are assigned at right angles to it. The outline box should enclose the principal axes and should be aligned with the defining *xyz* system coordinates. Once the box is established, the (x,y,z) coordinates of its corners are easily obtained, and the object's location is thereby established in the *xyz* system.

Some objects, such as real buildings with slanted roofs, can be placed in outline boxes easily. Others, such as people and trees, fit poorly. The

fewer straight lines and flat or smooth surfaces an object has, the less easily the perspective view of it can be drawn or calculated, and the less it matters whether an accurate perspective view is shown. At a minimum, the object's location and height must be shown correctly, but it is not necessary to establish all three axes of the object. The axis representing the object's height can be thought of as a one-dimensional outline box; the object is replaced by a thin pole for purposes of locating it and finding the perspective view of its height. Later the full object can be drawn in the right place, using the established height to determine its other dimensions. If the object is a reclining figure, a one-dimensional box can represent the figure's length in whatever direction the figure is lying. If the principal features of an object consist of one or more parallel lines, the box is necessary only for locating the object; later methods can be used to establish its perspective.

One consistent corner of each outline box, preferably a front corner, should be defined as the reference point of the outline box. Then each box can be located by the (x,y,z) coordinates of its reference point P (figure 1-10). Even if there is only one principal object, however, the artist may not wish to locate its reference point P at origin O. When possible, the work can be simplified by orienting each box orthogonally—parallel to each other and to the *xyz* axes.

Filling Planes and Space with Tiles and Solids

Suppose that the subject matter is the *xyz* coordinate system drawn as a *grid* (figure 1-11), with lines spaced every meter so that the (x,y,z) coordinates

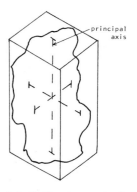

1-9. Outline box and principal axes of an object

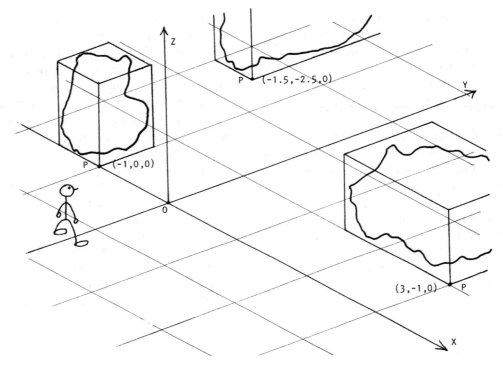

1-10. Outline boxes located in a rectilinear coordinate system

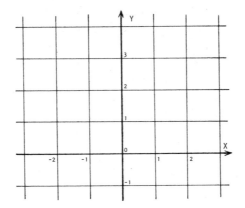

1-11. Square grid or coordinate system

at each intersection of grid lines are integers (whole numbers) in meters. In the ground plane, $z = 0$ everywhere. The grid is drawn on this ground (xy) plane, which looks like an unpainted checkerboard. For a picture of any complexity, this underlying grid can be imagined to exist; it will show the location of any object in the picture. In later chapters, the perspective views of grids are discussed. The appearance of the grid in perspective is a useful test of how the perspective of more complex objects will appear.

Just as an indefinitely large number of 1-m

8 PERSPECTIVE DESIGN

squares constitutes the *xy* grid, so can the *xy* plane be filled with *polygons* or *tiles* of other shapes. Tiling a plane is called *tessellation*. The tiles for a given tessellation (unless stated otherwise) are all assumed to be the same size and shape. Not every shape of tile works—another special property of Euclidean space. Squares, rectangles of any shape, equilateral triangles (figure 1-12), and regular hexagons (made from six equilateral triangles) complete the list of simple polygons that tile. These shapes have a high degree of symmetry. *Regular polygons* have all their sides and angles equal and have the highest symmetry. Within limits, many less regular shapes can tile.[1] Another term for a tile that describes the relation of the tile to the grid is "unit cell."

The subject of tessellation illustrates that there can be many different kinds of coordinate systems —for example, a triangular coordinate system with three axes at 60° angles, as shown in figure 1-12. None is as convenient as the square grid, unless the subject matter uniquely fits the geometry of another system.

If lines 1 m apart could be drawn in all three directions in space in the rectilinear coordinate system, the result would be a *lattice* filling all space (see plate 1). The three-dimensional analogy to tiling with squares is to fill space with 1-m cubes. Any parallelopiped (regular or "leaning") can also accomplish the task, but only a few unusual semiregular polyhedrons (solids) can be packed closely together. As is discussed in chapter 2 and later, examining the perspective views of cubes or rectangular boxes is an excellent way to test the behavior of perspective views set up by the artist. Surprisingly, the simple cube (or hexahedron) is rarely a unit cell or building block in nature, despite its many symmetries. The structure of real materials formed from atoms is based on different and more complex unit cells.[2]

Q1-8. The other four regular polyhedrons or Platonic solids, besides the cube, are the tetrahedron (four equilateral triangles for surfaces), octahedron (eight equilateral triangles), dodecahedron (twelve equilateral pentagons), and icosahedron (twenty equilateral triangles). Visualize or make several of one kind and verify that they do not pack together to fill space without voids. Holden's book *Shapes, Space, and Symmetry* describes the semiregular solids that do.

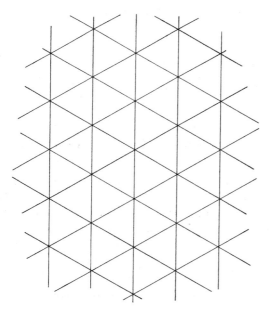

1-12. Triangular grid or coordinate system (also showing a hexagonal tessellation)

Sooner or later, every mathematical shape becomes important in art or technology and requires drawing. Nevertheless, artists are usually not concerned with filling space, except perhaps with buildings. The eye can see only surfaces—whether the earth's surface in a landscape or the surfaces of other solid objects. Open space is the most prevalent element in pictures. If the picture is thoroughly filled or "busy," many complex surfaces must be in view. The amount of filled space and the way it is filled affect the mood of the picture in subtle ways. Imagining the space as being filled with the underlying *xyz* lattice may aid the artist. (The notion that space is either filled or empty can be defied; see plate 2 and the discussion of fractals in chapter 10.)

The Basis and Goals of Perspective

Since the fourteenth century, when perspective viewing was formally discovered, the goal of perspective has been to imitate what the eye sees when looking through a window on the world and to retain the illusion of depth obtained thereby. The first methods of perspective used a transparent or translucent window (a ground glass screen or oiled paper, sometimes with a grid on it); the eye was positioned at a fixed observation point, and dots were traced where light rays from points on the object seemed to pierce the screen (figure 1-13). If the eye's line of sight was not used, straight light rays were simulated by a stretched string or a straight rod. Substantial improvements have been made in the original methods, but in essence they remain approximately correct.[3] The type of perspective

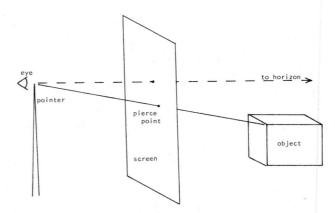

1-13. Perspective (Renaissance method)

that results can be called *rectilinear* because a flat screen is used, the screen is oriented perpendicular to the viewer's sight, and straight sight lines are used.

What appears on the screen is supposed to be the perspective view of the object observed, and therefore the screen shows the finished *picture* (perhaps after transfer to another medium). It must have boundaries called the *frame*. The view is a flat representation of part of the real world behind. The three real dimensions have been reduced to two in the picture. The depth (*y* axis) is compressed to zero, and the other dimensions are transformed with it. If it were not for practical limits, the eye could see—up, down, and to the sides—an indefinitely large amount of the universe within the framed picture. The picture constitutes a window on the universe and forms a "pyramid of vision," limiting the light rays that arrive from distant objects (figure 1-14).

The Latin roots of the term "perspective"

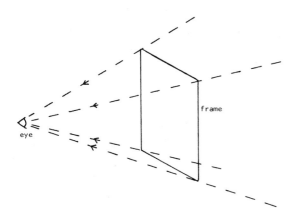

1-14. Picture frame—a window on the universe

mean "look through," and it is in this original sense that the term is used in this and all books pertaining to artistic methods. The term has acquired more general meanings outside the fields of art and graphics, and the casual user of the word may not realize it has a well-defined technical meaning for the artist. The term should also not be confused with "projective geometry," which is a branch of mathematics inspired by perspective drawing and first developed in the Renaissance.[4] It was eventually realized that projective geometry is non-Euclidean, since a perspective view of parallel lines shows them meeting in the picture. Various non-Euclidean properties appear in pictures formed by perspective methods, but it is beyond the scope of this book to explore those mathematical topics.

One reason for creating perspective views is to show what is not (and may never be) directly accessible to the observer. The window becomes canvas, paper, film, computer screen, or some other medium that stores visual information. But fundamen-

tal limits exist in physics and technology on recreating in a picture exactly what the eye sees. These limits are not due merely to limits in photography or in scientific understanding of human vision. Chapter 8 explores some of the difficulties that arise.

The use of perspective in art may have declined, but the technique has remained in the repertoire of most artists. Some older and some more recent artists have incorporated perspective into metaphorical statements, drawing attention to perspective as a way of perceiving. Since its inception, perspective has also influenced philosophy and the development of the classical sciences.[5]

There are many ways to change the perspective view. The viewer can move closer or farther from the fixed window or screen and see more or less of the world beyond. The screen can be tilted vertically or horizontally, or made larger or smaller. But once the perspective view is recorded as a fixed image, the viewer's flexibility is much reduced. Moving back and forth or sideways with respect to a painting changes little about it, compared to the same action in front of a window showing the same scene. (René Magritte illustrated this in several "window" paintings.) Information about the real objects is irretrievably lost after the chosen view is recorded. Holography preserves more depth information, at the expense of other visual information, but holography is a new technical method unrelated to perspective: the eye creates its own perspective when viewing a hologram.

The principal purpose of the perspective view is to give the illusion of depth to a picture in a realistic way. If the picture consisted mostly or entirely of unfamiliar objects that gave no obvious clues for depth perception, then using a perspective view might not help. Even a fairly obvious scene, such as a river winding across a flat landscape, might give insufficient or misleading clues as to the actual sizes and distances involved. Unaided by perspective methods, the artist must proceed with the design of the picture by guesswork, trying to obtain a result that looks acceptable. A map of the river transformed into a perspective view might yield a result that looks quite different. If a randomly wandering river is replaced with a regularly curving river (sometimes a more natural river), the regularity alone would give the viewer strong depth or distance clues. Alternatively, if scattered trees were added to the landscape in sizes that accorded with their distances, these clues might make an irregularly curving river very intelligible.

Showing Depth in Pictures

Other ways, independent of perspective, can be used to give pictures the illusion of depth, but their use in conjunction with perspective will enhance realism, especially when the subject matter lacks straight lines or regular features. The eye is very sensitive to most of these depth clues and will perceive them properly even when some conflict exists among the clues. The following list of nonperspective depth clues is given in the approximate order of their increasing ability to convey depth, but the order is hardly exact:

1. The viewer has foreknowledge (from experience or from verbal description) of the relative sizes of the objects.

2. A horizon is shown, or clues about the vertical are provided.
3. The color is lighter and less saturated in the "background" and in the lower part of the "sky."
4. Shadows are of consistent length and direction, and they fade properly.
5. A contrast in brightness is used at appropriate edges.
6. Distant objects are shown smaller and less distinctly.
7. Light is reflected or diffused onto one object from another; less reflection is evident on distant objects.
8. One solid object is put behind another, or awareness of hidden regions is promoted in other ways.
9. One of several identical objects is shown smaller than the others.
10. Similar kinds of objects are shown in regularly decreasing size, with the decrease occurring at the proper rate.
11. Use is made of human perceptual sensitivity to the rate of convergence of a series of object sizes or locations. (This is explained more fully in chapter 4.)
12. Hints of motion are provided, with the foreground seeming to move faster.

Except where perspective is concerned, no further discussion of these techniques is given in this book.[6] Generally, for the eye to perceive three dimensions, the eye-brain system must reconstruct three-dimensional information from the two-dimensional information provided in a flat picture. A circle drawn on flat white paper gives inadequate clues for three-dimensional perception, even if the artist intends the circle to be the opening of a short pipe. If a useful perspective view cannot be provided—for example, by moving the viewpoint to show part of the side of the pipe, or by moving closer to see inside—no sense of depth will be imparted by the picture.

Two other types of views used in technical drawing are helpful for showing depth. In an "oblique view" (used for figures 1-2, 1-3, and 1-5), two dimensions remain parallel to the paper and the third axis is oriented at a convenient angle. In an "axonometric view" (used for figures 1-1, 1-9, and 1-10), at least two axes are supposed to be at angles to the paper.

Modern Methods of Obtaining Perspective Views

The *graphic* method, using straightedge, pencil, and similar drafting tools, has evolved from the Renaissance methods of producing perspective views. This common method is covered fully in chapters 2 and 3, including the preparatory planning necessary for other, more advanced methods. The graphic method must be done on one large continuous sheet of paper (or equivalent arrangement). Beginners need a paper area that is about three times the area of the finished picture. Advanced drawing involves an almost impenetrable maze of construction lines, which may be simplified by the later calculation methods. Perspective has been limited in subject matter because of the tedious and complex graphic method, although early artists undertook rather ambitious buildings, plazas, arcades, and so forth, with many curves (see Descargues's book, *Perspective: History, Evolution, Techniques*). Twentieth century architecture, with a minimum of complex curves and an abundance of rectangular forms, has lightened the burden of the perspective artist using graphic methods.

Mathematical perspective by calculation is a new method. Although the mathematics is no more advanced than applications of trigonometry, little has been written about the approach. Computer programs for obtaining perspective views have been available for some years, but these are based on a mathematical approach different from the methods useful for the artist working on paper. Calculation can be used for the entire drawing, for planning one, for testing effects, for drawing specific objects or regions, and for other possibilities. Mathematical or numerical information about the objects is required beforehand, just as measurements are needed to set up the graphic method. The perspective of objects such as trees and mountains cannot be calculated in detail, but no viewer could detect small inaccuracies in the perspective of such complex subject matter. For subject matter based on regular patterns, the use of mathematics speeds the work substantially, while providing impressive accuracy.

Perspective by *photography* is a third method. Despite some claims to the contrary, the camera can make perspective views very precisely. A two-dimensional photograph presents an exact rectilinear perspective view, if the lenses are free from distortion and the film is flat. This does not mean that a scene will appear as the eye sees it. Our eyes are not flat windows: our retinas are curved, and our vision is very wide. An SLR camera with a "normal" (50-mm) lens has a field of view only about 40° wide. The camera can be used to solve difficult perspective problems, if the subject already exists or is accessible for photography. But for subjects that do not exist, for models that are too expensive to build, and for impossible viewpoints, the creative artist has plenty of freedom unchallenged by the camera.

Stereoscopic photography, a neglected art, uses two images taken from two different viewpoints, usually less than 1° apart. Each picture is a perspective, and a strong illusion of depth is obtained when each is presented to the proper eye for perceptual fusion in the brain. The same effect can be accomplished by drawing the two pictures.

In some ways, using two eyes hinders the illusion of depth when a person is looking at a single-perspective picture. Using two eyes gives more clues for seeing the picture surface itself and retards seeing "beyond" it. The human visual system is aware that when both eyes are making the same accommodation to see objects, the objects must be images on a flat surface. Moreover, both eyes cannot be put at the one viewing point for a perspective.

The Limit to Viewing—Infinity

Serious involvement with perspective brings the artist into close encounters with the nature of infinity. The simple perspective view of a railroad track extending toward the horizon shows that two parallel lines must meet at a *limit point* (figure 1-15). Instead of saying that they meet "at infinity," it is more meaningful to say that their limit point is infinity, or that they approach infinity. By its nature, infinity can only be approached, not reached. All lines, no matter in what direction they are drawn in Euclidean space, have infinity as their limit point if extended indefinitely. Infinity has a symbol (∞), but it cannot be treated as a number. Calculations such as addition, multiplication, and division cannot include ∞ as a term, and trouble may develop with algebraic calculations if a variable approaches ∞.

Q1-9. What is the largest number you can write down? What is the largest number your calculator will accept?

Similarly, an observer viewing an indefinitely large railroad yard of very long and uniformly spaced parallel rails would see a *limit line* (figure 1-16) in the distance. The limit line appears to be at

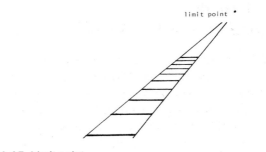

1-15. Limit point

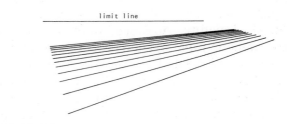

1-16. Limit line

the horizon, regardless of the angle at which the rails are viewed. If the earth were indefinitely large and flat, the horizon would be the limit line of all sets of lines. Another useful term is introduced in saying that the set of related lines in figure 1-16 approaches the limit line as an *asymptote*. The set of lines and its asymptote can be straight or curved. M. C. Escher created several prints illustrating limit points and lines; the lines were often neither straight nor simple.[7] One useful calculation given later in this book is the method of constructing a set of parallel lines in perspective, to fit a given situation. Drawing them with graphic methods could be more tedious and less accurate.

Many different possible choices exist for the rate at which the spacing of lines may approach zero. For example, the spacing could be halved at each step. The rates allowed in perspective are restricted. Guesses or simple patterns are not likely to look or to be correct. The rates shown in figures 1-15 and 1-16 were constructed for perspective by methods covered in chapters 3 and 4.

Finally, the notion of a *limit plane* can be of use to the artist. If an imaginary transparent vertical plane is placed on each line in figure 1-16, the planes will seem to accumulate in the distance at a limit plane placed on the limit line. Sets of planes are difficult to imagine, since they tend to hide each other. A more mundane example is to imagine rows of trees in an orchard. Each row defines a vertical plane. An observer will see in the distance a wall of trees near the limit plane. The rows have asymptotically approached a limit (and the tree heights have become indefinitely small, or "infinitesimal"). Artists must work with objects that obscure one another in the distance. Attention to the way they accumulate in the distance can make the perspective more convincing.

On the cosmic scale, space in our universe is non-Euclidean. Only locally is the rectilinear coordinate system accurate. Indefinitely long lines are not straight but curved and may form closed circles. No physical distances can approach infinity. These facts may be of interest to the "space" artist.

Notes

1. On tessellation, see Martin Gardner, "Mathematical Games," July 1975 and January 1977. For examples of tessellation in art, see Escher's prints as found in J. L. Locher, ed., *The World of M. C. Escher* and Bruno Ernst, *The Magic Mirror of M. C. Escher*.
   On the symmetry of patterns of tiles and other figures (including biological objects) in the plane and in space, see Hermann Weyl, *Symmetry*.

2. On lattices, regular and semiregular polyhedra, and patterns for making them, see Weyl, *Symmetry*; Magnus Wenninger, *Polyhedron Models*; Alan Holden, *Shapes, Space, and Symmetry*; Cyril Smith, "The Shape of Things"; and Harold Jacobs, *Mathematics: A Human Endeavor*.

3. For a pictorial history of perspective, showing many remarkable experiments over five centuries, see Pierre Descargues, *Perspective: History, Evolution, Techniques* (not to be confused with the seventeenth-century architect and mathematician Gérard Desargues).
   Perspective history is also covered in Fred Leeman, *Hidden Images: Games of Perception, Anamorphic Art, Illusion*; Alan and Judith Tormey, "Renaissance Intarsia: The Art of Geometry"; and Samuel Edgerton, Jr., *The Renaissance Rediscovery of Linear Perspective*.

4. Projective geometry, based on perspective but usually very abstract, was developed by Gérard Desargues and is introduced in Morris Kline, "Projective Geometry."

5. The metaphorical use of perspective is discussed in Radu Vero, *Understanding Perspective*. The philosophical and scientific implications of perspective are covered in Edgerton, *Renaissance Rediscovery*.

6. The use of color and illumination in perspective is covered in Vero, *Understanding Perspective,* and more generally in many art textbooks.

7. Limit points and lines are illustrated in Escher prints found (for example) in Locher, *World of Escher* and Ernst, *Magic Mirror of Escher*.

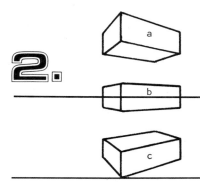

2.

Rectilinear Perspective by Graphic Methods

A person's study of perspective should start with investigation of the graphic methods for constructing a picture in perspective. Several methods, of varying difficulty, exist; the least troublesome are presented in this chapter. The appropriateness of a particular method depends in part on what type of view is being constructed. The types of views discussed here belong to the common form of perspective, which may be called *rectilinear*. The construction of the picture on a flat surface is one of its major characteristics. As views for various situations are shown, some will present seemingly distorted pictures of objects. This "distortion" is partly a failure of rectilinear perspective to create the type of view that best matches the eye. Chapter 8 on curvilinear perspective describes some alternative forms that offer less distortion.

A general nomenclature is used to name features throughout the book. Points are labeled with single upper-case letters. Lines may be identified by a single upper-case letter with a bar above it (for example, $\overline{H}$) or by a pair of upper-case letters with a bar above them (for example, $\overline{AB}$). Angles may be labeled as, for example, $\angle L, V, R$, where the middle upper-case letter represents the point at the vertex of the angle. Primes ($'$), double primes ($''$), and numerical or alphabetical ("alphanumeric") subscripts are sometimes used to extend the number of possible labels in a systematic way. Pairs or triplets of upper-case letters give symbolic abbreviations for terms and identify them as features in a diagram. A lower-case s suffixed to one or more upper-case letters indicates a plural.

Three Types of Perspective Views

While only one general form of rectilinear perspective exists, it traditionally has been distinguished

17

into three types according to the relative orientation of viewer and subject matter. In order for the distinctions to be made, the objects of interest must have or suggest at least one set of parallel lines or planes in their structure or arrangement. The type of perspective is then determined by whether the sets of parallel lines are in one, two, or three independent dimensions, and by whether any of these sets are aligned with the natural horizontal and vertical axes of the envisioned picture.

Assume that the subject matter consists of one object, such as a rectangular box, that has three mutually orthogonal sets of parallel lines delimiting its shape. The box could be an outline box or a more complex object. The geometric name for such an object is a ''rectangular prism'' or a ''regular parallelopiped,'' each name denoting that all angles are right angles and that edges and surfaces are parallel. All boxes used as examples here have these properties unless otherwise stated. Depending on the orientation of the box, one or more sets of its parallel lines will approach or converge toward limit points in the perspective view. The limit point for a set of parallel lines is usually called a *vanishing point* (VP) in graphics.

The classification of perspective views has traditionally been based on a count of the number of principal vanishing points. But the number of VPs has no definite and unambiguous relation to the type of view. Except in a casual sense, classification of perspective views as ''one-point,'' ''two-point,'' or ''three-point'' should be avoided. When this terminology is encountered, it may be interpreted as stating which type of view is being discussed; but it could also be referring to the number of VPs used in a picture's construction. A ''one-point'' view should not be presumed to contain just one VP, nor a ''two-point'' view just two VPs, and so forth.

The part of the drawing paper (or other medium) on which the final perspective view is to appear is called the *picture* and may have a *frame*. The surface of the paper represents a plane called the *picture plane* (PP). PP may be an infinite plane, but the picture must have a boundary. An assumption for this discussion is that the viewer has a simple relation to the picture plane. The picture is near eye level, the viewer looks straight ahead without movement, and the line of sight intersects PP perpendicularly near the center.

In the simplest orientation, the object (a box) has all three of its principal axes aligned with the three dimensions determined by the line of sight and the horizontal and vertical of the picture plane. The resulting view is called *parallel perspective* because the object has its front face parallel to PP (figure 2-1a). This type of view has also been called ''one-point'' because the parallel lines of the box that are perpendicular to PP converge to one VP at the horizon. This view is most often used to show interior spaces. The viewer does not necessarily have to be located so as to see the box in the symmetrical manner (''head-on'') shown in figure 2-1a.

In a more complex orientation (figure 2-1b), the box has only one set of parallel planes aligned with the axes of the viewer. The top and bottom faces are parallel to the ground and remain horizontal; the other faces are at angles to the picture plane. This type of view is called *angular perspective*. It has also been called ''two-point'' because two sets of parallel lines converge to two VPs. This view is the most common one used. It is more effective than parallel perspective, especially for exterior views, yet is not substantially harder to construct. For this view the object is rotated about a vertical axis with respect to PP, and the perspective is angular regardless of the location of the viewer. If the object is oriented parallel to PP and a method for angular perspective is used, the automatic result is a parallel perspective.

In its most complex orientation with respect to the picture plane, a box has no faces parallel to PP. The resulting view is called *oblique perspective*, a term that in some sources also refers to angular perspective. The word "oblique" by itself has other meanings in technical drawing. Another term for oblique perspective can be "aerial perspective." Oblique perspective should be thought of as a view tilted in all three independent ways that an object can be tilted (figure 2-1c). Each of the three sets of parallel lines determined by the edges of the box has its own VP; hence, the view has been called "three-point." Oblique perspective is an advanced

type, substantially more complex to construct than the other types, but the results can be very impressive.

The Viewer and the Picture Plane

Before one of the types of perspective views can be drawn, the exact location and orientation of the viewer (V), picture plane (PP), and object must be determined, specified, and laid out. The number of different arrangements for V, PP, and object is immense, and only general guidelines for making good choices can be stated. In this chapter no mathematical use of coordinates is made; instead, mechanical methods of measuring and laying out distances are used to establish locations and relationships. The artist may often be in a position to proceed in either direction—to choose the locations of V, PP, and object and then construct the perspective, or to specify certain arrangements desired in the perspective and then work back to find the locations for V and PP. When perspective methods are misunderstood or used too casually, the principal error often is to specify VPs without making them consistent with other requirements. Only the experienced artists will be able to start with VPs.

For the beginner at perspective, a sheet of paper substantially larger than the finished picture is needed. The paper should be oriented vertically so that the top two-thirds of it can be used for a plan view of the object and the construction area. Some room may be needed at the side for an elevation view. Figure 2-2 shows the initial arrangements. Only the lower third of the paper should be designated as the picture plane. Other regions of the paper will be used for other planes.

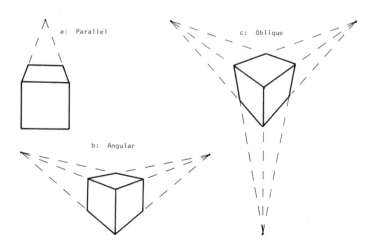

2-1. Three types of rectilinear perspective

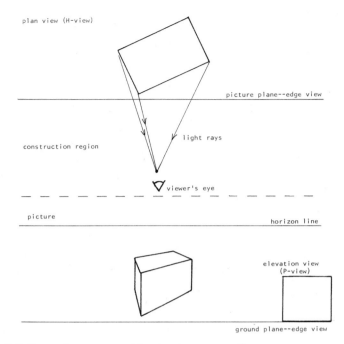

plan view (H-view)

picture plane--edge view

light rays

construction region

▽ viewer's eye

picture

horizon line

elevation view
(P-view)

ground plane--edge view

2-2. General arrangement for drawing perspective

feet. The artists may better visualize and connect the arrangements of figure 2-2 and 2-3 by realizing that rays of light must come from each exposed point of the object, pass through PP (as a screen), and reach the viewer's eye. The point at which each ray pierces the screen determines the perspective view of the corresponding object point.

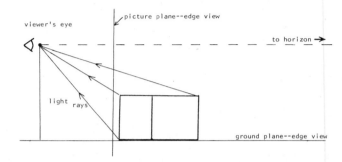

viewer's eye

picture plane--edge view

to horizon →

light rays

ground plane--edge view

2-3. Side view (from the right side) of the arrangement in figure 2-2

The object is usually placed behind PP, with one corner or surface touching PP if that is convenient for the artist's plans. The orientation of the object is shown in plan view in the top third of figure 2-2, and an edge view of PP appears as a line in the plan view. Here, as in later figures, the dashed line may be imagined as a fold in the paper between the horizontal plane of the plan and the vertical PP.

Somewhere near the center of the paper, V is placed. The position of V has a major effect on the view obtained. A side view of the relation of V to PP and object is shown in figure 2-3. Here, PP is seen only in edge view. For the present, the object is placed on the ground plane shared by the viewer's

Plan and Elevation Views

At least two consistent sets of information are needed about the object before drawing can proceed. Usually these take the form of a plan view and an elevation view. The *plan view* or "top view" shows all features of the object projected to a horizontal plane, whether or not those features are limited to one plane. Hidden lines are shown dashed or "broken." The plan view contains two dimensions of information and must be shown in the orientation desired for the final perspective view. If a plan drawing is already available, it can simply be taped in the desired location and orientation. The engineering graphics term for the plan view is *H-view,* where H denotes the horizontal plane.

The *elevation view* or "side view" is primarily needed to provide a third dimension for the object, giving information about the heights of features. The heights must be shown with respect to some reference plane, often the ground plane. The elevation view need not be a complete drawing. It can be as simple as a set of measurements of object heights. If a complete elevation view is used, it should include hidden lines and be a projection of the object to a vertical plane. The engineering graphics term for the elevation view is *P-view,* for profile view. Sometimes the frontal view (*F-view*) is used instead.

In engineering graphics, the set of plan and elevation views—or H-, P-, and F-views—is called a set of *orthographic* views, since each view is in a plane at right angles to the others. These views are obtained when an object in a box is projected to one, two, three, or even all six sides of the box. Hidden lines are shown dashed.

Every picture that shows a three-dimensional object by means of perspective or another kind of view could have been constructed from two or three orthographic views. Conversely, any two orthographic views that together reveal all hidden lines contain enough information to describe a three-dimensional object unambiguously. Orthographic views of objects are valuable because they show what are called "true views," in which all lengths in the view appear as "true" lengths. A ruler can be used to get the correct length, possibly with the application of a scale factor. In general, no lengths that appear in a perspective view are shown true length. Features that lie entirely in PP as seen in plan or elevation appear true length in the perspective.

The effect of placing the object's plan view in different locations with respect to PP is shown in figure 2-4. The object can be placed in front of PP, but this may bring it so close to the viewer that distortion becomes noticeable. There is theoretically no limit on where the object may be placed: the construction methods can still be carried out. Obviously, though, placing the object far behind PP makes it very small in the picture.

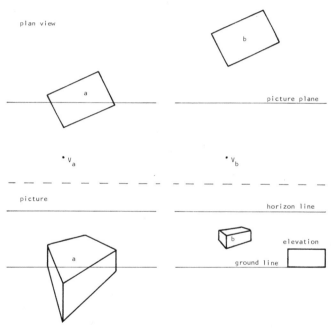

2-4. Comparing placement of an object in front of and behind the picture plane (viewer position is fixed with respect to the picture plane)

Locating the Viewer

The assumed location of the observer or viewer is crucial to the perspective. Two general positions are likely: either more than 1 m from a hung picture, or about 40 cm from a printed page. The artist can make only certain assumptions about the viewer—namely that the viewer generally looks straight ahead at the center of the picture while standing a reasonable distance away. The line of sight or *vision axis* (VA) must pierce PP perpendicularly. Other locations and attitudes of the viewer need not be planned for. A person looking at the picture from a location quite unlike the one planned by the artist will see distortions the artist cannot anticipate. The eye(s) of the viewer are assumed to be at point V (see figure 2-2). Another common name for this point is station point (SP); however, using SP may lead the artist to forget to keep a specific viewer in mind. Calling the point O (for observer) could lead to confusion with O as the origin point of a coordinate system.

The location of V should be determined first by considering its relation to the plan view and then by considering its relation to the elevation. With respect to the plan view (see the top third of figure 2-5), the better locations for V are those far enough from the object to make the angular width of the object less than about 35° as seen by the viewer. Putting V closer, to make the angular width larger, results in noticeable distortion. V can be placed very close, as shown, or even inside the object, but these strategies should be reserved for unusual effects.

Although putting the object far behind PP makes it appear very small, putting the viewer well in front of PP does not make the object appear much smaller in the picture. Instead, the whole picture, including its frame, becomes small. As V recedes from PP, the projection for perspective diverges

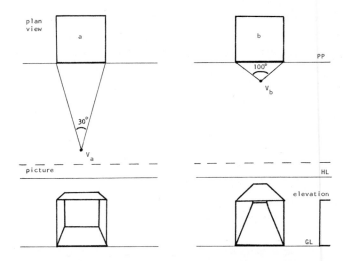

2-5. Changing viewer position, with a consequent change in angle of view (note that the size of the object in the picture does not change as the viewer moves closer; also note the effect on perspective as the viewer looks into the box)

less. A picture can be constructed for a distant V, and then observed close up. The apparent depth is reduced and the picture appears "flatter." If V were infinitely far away, there would be no perspective (and not simply because things are too small!).

When the viewer approaches the picture, a curious effect occurs. The angular size of any object behind PP appears to increase, but the space occupied by the object in the picture shrinks toward zero. When the eye touches PP, it is as if the viewer were looking through a pinhole in the picture plane. The whole scene is seen in a region of infinitesimal size on PP.

Q2-1. Try to diagram the relationship of V, PP, and object (in plan) and examine the preceding assertion. For a number of viewer positions, sketch the angular size of the object as seen; examine both the angular size and the intersection of the angle with PP. Note the difference between having the object touch PP and having the object located behind it.

PP could be placed behind the viewer. In this case, light rays from points on the object all pass through the point V and strike PP. The image of the object so formed is inverted, as if a pinhole camera had been used.

As an object grows smaller in perspective, regardless of the means used, the distortion of its shape is also reduced. This is not because the object becomes too small for distorted features to be apparent but because rectilinear perspective is more accurate to the eye when used in small regions. A good procedure for obtaining a large view with low distortion is to pull V far back for the construction. A large picture can be made by placing the object close to PP. The perspective effect is reduced, as will be seen later in the case of distant VPs. In actual use, the picture will be viewed much closer than point V, so a large view is obtained.

Figure 2-6 compares two different positions of PP—one close to V and one close to the object—while keeping the viewer the same distance from the object. In the former case, the object appears smaller because it is far from V. In the latter case, the object appears bigger because it is closer to PP; the greater distance of the viewer from PP is irrelevant. The object, a flat square, is seen from above at the same slant in both cases, as is shown in the side views in figure 2-6, but the angular size on PP is greater in one case. The shape of the object in the perspective view is the same in these two cases, a

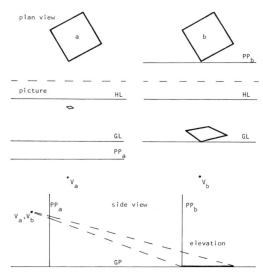

2-6. Changing the position of the picture plane while the viewer-to-object distance remains fixed (the object is a flat square; to save space, the construction region has been placed between viewer and object)

matter that can be proved later. (As an alternative to graphic placement, chapter 4 shows simple mathematical methods for calculating where to put the viewer.)

The viewer should be placed to obtain the best three-dimensional view. Just as presenting the object with its flat front face parallel to PP is not dramatic, placing the viewer so as to see only one face is not effective. Figure 2-7 shows three different vantage points, looking down on a flat square (a good way to test perspectives). View a, to the side of the object, shows mostly that side. View b, looking toward the corner with a slight bias toward the right side, is one of the best conventional positions. Although viewer V_b is looking head-on at PP, the

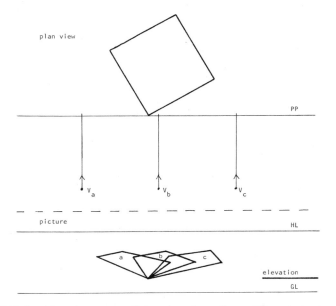

plan view

PP

V_a V_b V_c

picture

HL

a b c

elevation

GL

2-7. Looking down on a flat square from three different viewing positions

orientation of the plan view of the object provides a perspective showing a pleasing amount of two sides. View c shows only one side of the object, despite the rightward location of V$_c$. Because of the orientation of the object in plan view, other sides of the object are hidden. The effect of moving V to the side is not generally the same as that of rotating the object because the locations of V and object with respect to PP are changed differently in the two cases.

The angular height of the object as seen by the viewer should also be considered. Again, most distortion can be avoided if the angular height is less than about 35°. In figure 2-3, V must be more than a certain distance away to meet this requirement.

Since the requirement is not precise, it may not matter what tilt or orientation the object has at the time its angular size is estimated. If the object is shaped so that it is much taller than it is wide (such as a pole), V may have to be much farther away to satisfy the requirement. In this case, the angular width is small because of V's greater distance.

Viewer distance and height cannot be chosen independently. Once the distance in plan view has been decided, its effect should be checked in elevation view, preferably with a scale drawing such as figure 2-3. It may turn out that the viewer is being called upon to see the planned picture with excessive angular width vertically and must be moved back.

The Ground Plane and Ground Line

For best viewing, it may be desirable to place V higher than the object's top, as shown in figure 2-3. If the object and the viewer stand on the same *ground plane* (GP), this condition is met for objects shorter than the viewer (less than 1.5 m or 5½ ft tall). For a high object, V must be raised to see the top. The effect of varying a moderate-sized object's location above a fixed ground plane on which the viewer stands is shown in figure 2-8. The top, the bottom, or neither is seen. For construction purposes, the elevation view of the object must include measurements made from the ground plane.

For very small objects, both object and PP must be brought very close to V. In reality, the eyes cannot focus closer than about 30 cm (1 ft), so PP cannot be brought closer than that, but scaling can be used to expand a tiny object to fill the picture. To see the object's top, V must be higher than the

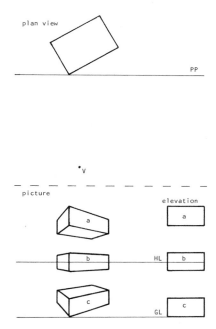

plan view

PP

•V

picture

elevation

a

HL b

GL c

2-8. Perspective of a rectangular box located above, in, and below the viewer's line of sight

viewer stands on the floor at a level far below GP, and GL may appear near the bottom of the picture (figure 2-9b).

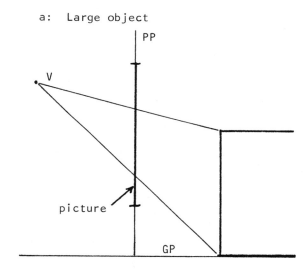

a: Large object

PP

V

picture

GP

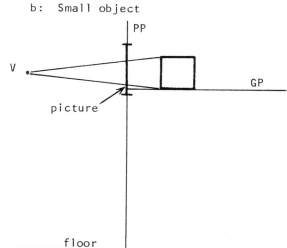

b: Small object

PP

V

GP

picture

floor

2-9. Framing the picture for large and small objects

top in the elevation view. The ground plane for small objects must be raised.

Generally, the ground plane (GP) must be associated with the object, not with the viewer. The *ground line* (GL), where the PP intersects the GP, is not necessarily the bottom boundary of the framed picture; it may be lower or higher. A human-size object may share its ground plane with the viewer's feet, but pictures are usually hung so high that GP intersects PP below the bottom frame. If the object is large and resting on the floor, the entire object may still be visible if placed far enough behind PP (figure 2-9a). If the object is small, the

Scaling and Framing

Consideration of human height with respect to object height usually determines the scale of the picture. Scaling, if any, must be done in plan and elevation prior to constructing the perspective. The picture is assumed to be full size, so the paper, canvas, or other medium must be as big as the final picture is to be.

By convention, objects that are too large are scaled down by the scaling 1:n, where n is the scale factor. If a 20-m-tall building is to be shown 0.5 m tall in a drawing, the scale factor is 20/0.5 or 40, and the scaling is 1:40. If a 1-cm bolt is to be drawn 30 cm long, the scaling is 1:0.0333 (which can also be written 30:1). The same scale factor must be applied to all lengths in the plan and elevation unless special effects are desired. Only the lengths that lie in PP are shown true length after scaling. All other lengths are smaller (except for parts of the object in front of PP). Measuring instruments called "scales" (available in versions for engineers and architects) make rescaling convenient, as no computation is required for standard scale factors. (The engineering term "dimensions" is not used here to denote lengths, to avoid confusion.)

The desired picture frame size is determined by considering how far from the viewer the picture is to be displayed (no closer than 30 cm). Then the field of view to be filled is considered. Unless constrained, the viewer tends to step back until no more than about 60° of the field of view is filled by the picture. For a 1-m-wide picture, the viewer would stand about 1 m away. If the picture is 1 m high, its center would be 1.5 m above the floor, and the bottom frame would be 1 m above the floor. Changes, such as tilting the head, and ways to cal-

culate these arrangements will be discussed later. If a large picture is planned, scaling may be used to reduce both human height and picture size temporarily for planning, as in figures 2-2 and 2-3.

The Horizon Line

The *horizon line* (HL) appears only in the perspective view, as a horizontal line at the height of the viewer's eye. At risk of some confusion, it may be considered an edge view of the plane in which the plan view is drawn (the H-plane). When the viewer stands on GP, HL is about 1.5 m above GP and GL, whether or not features on GP are visible in the picture. Figure 2-8 showed the effect of varying the location of the object above and below HL.

Objects taller than 1.5 m protrude above HL, whether they are near or far, provided the viewer stands on their ground plane. If a tall object is to be shown, even in the distance, the elevation view may have to occupy much height on the paper. Only practice and experience (perhaps with calculation) can teach the artist how to plan these sizes for the desired effect.

The horizon line is part of the finished picture even if it is not explicitly visible. It may be hidden by landscape or objects, or it may be "behind" an interior view. The limit point of all straight lines parallel to the ground is on HL. The limit line of all lines parallel to PP is HL. Because of the very gradual curvature of the earth, HL is perceived as straight by the viewer.

The Center of Vision

The *center of vision* (CV) is the perspective view of point V. It is a point on HL showing where the vision axis pierces PP. In figure 2-10, CV is located in plan by projecting V to find the pierce point with PP and then projecting to HL in the picture. For best effect, CV should not be allowed to fall on a front edge of an object. CV should fall in the region that is of greatest interest in the picture. In a picture planned with CV to the side of some object, that object will appear distorted when looked at directly but will appear normal when CV is looked at instead.

The viewer normally expects CV near the center, and subject matter must be arranged to satisfy this expectation. In the absence of other influences, the viewer approaching a picture will first gaze at its center. Special features or an influential or asymmetrically placed vanishing point may lead the viewer to look elsewhere. Most persons, when first gazing at spatial subject matter such as a picture, unintentionally shift their eyes to the right. In right-eyed, right-handed people, the eyes favor the right field of view because the brain uses its right side for processing spatial information. A review of classical art will show repeated accommodation of this rightward tendency in the principal subject matter.

When HL is placed very high or low in a picture, V must be located correspondingly so that CV occurs on HL. Although features in the picture may lead the viewer to vary the location of CV, the artist planning the picture should assume one CV.

Locating Vanishing Points

A vanishing point (VP) is located by using the axiom that a set of parallel lines converges toward a limit point. In figure 2-10, the orientation of the plan view indicates that an angular perspective will be constructed. The plan view establishes two sets of parallel lines at right angles, so two VPs must exist toward which perspective views of these lines converge. VPs are found by constructing lines from V parallel to each of the principal directions in the plan view. These constructed lines will pierce PP at points labeled L and R. When these points are transferred to the picture region, the corresponding points on HL are the VPs, labeled VPL for the left one and VPR for the right one. These VPs are located on HL because the object is oriented with its top and bottom faces parallel to the ground plane. If the box were tilted, the VPs for its edges would be above or below HL and an oblique perspective might have to be constructed.

A 90° angle exists between lines $\overline{VL}$ and $\overline{VR}$ only because the object itself has a 90° angle connecting the edges for which the construction was made. If the object were made of planes intersecting at a different angle, the location of the VPs would employ that different angle between $\overline{VL}$ and $\overline{VR}$, producing a different VPL and VPR. Figure 2-11 shows the location of the VPs for the angular per-

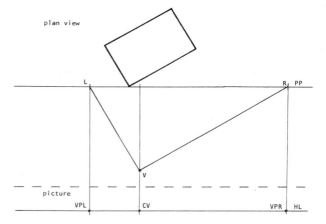

2-10. Locating the vanishing points for a rectangular object in angular position

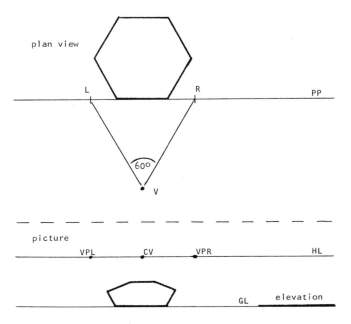

2-11. Locating the vanishing points for a flat hexagon, and viewing the object in perspective

spective of a hexagon. Moving V does not change the construction angle; it only changes the location of the VPs.

Adjusting the angle between VPL and VPR (∡L,V,R in figure 2-10) produces other-than-normal views, similar to the effect of changing lenses on a camera to wide angle or telephoto. Construction or calculation of these will be given later. The normal view of 90° used to construct VPL and VPR should not be confused with the angular width of field obtained with a "normal" camera lens (about 40°). The angular field of view in perspective can appear as wide as the artist wishes to arrange it, using wide paper and a close viewer position. Or the field may be narrow, based on a distant viewer position and VPs outside the picture frame.

Some of the illustrations given in this book appear distorted because they were designed with a close V so that the VPs would remain within the picture frame for purposes of demonstration. If these illustrations could be viewed close up, they would appear less distorted. For a viewer at the proper position, the angle of view between VPs would become 90°. For the reader's eyes to be at the suggested 40 cm from a book page, the page would have to be ridiculously large (about 80 cm wide) to accommodate both VPs.

Q2-2. Obtaining proper V position from the V position shown in the plan views, test for reduction of distortion by viewing the various figures of this chapter from that position.

For distant viewer locations or for an extreme angular view (one face of the object almost parallel to PP), one of the VPs is likely not to be on the paper. Either more paper must be added for construction or the methods described in chapters 4 and 10 must be used. In the extreme case, as the object face approaches parallelism with PP, one VP will move toward infinity and the other toward CV, giving a parallel perspective.

Q2-3. Sketch in plan view the case when V is very far from PP, showing that the VPs must recede outward along HL.

Regardless of the type of perspective, CV can be a VP for any object lines that happen to be perpendicular to PP. Auxiliary VPs for an object with other sets of parallel lines are also likely. The diagonals of a grid such as a chessboard would be found to have VPs—one for each set of diagonals. Although the diagonals have not been drawn, the viewer will see them as regular features that converge in the distance. The VPs for the diagonals may be more prominent than the VPL and VPR used for construction. Objects with parallel lines aimed above or below HL, such as the edges of a simple pitched roof, have auxiliary VPs not on HL. Chapter 3 covers the location of VPs for such features.

Finding and Constructing the Perspective View of One Point

Once the correct perspective of one point of an object is found, the method can be repeated numerous times to show the entire object. Procedures to make the process more efficient will be discovered along the way. Since two points define a straight line segment, only the two end points of any straight line segment need to be constructed. The method given in this section involves traditional construction techniques; all sizes are presumed to be available in plan and elevation. To accelerate the process, sizes can be established with a ruler in places where true sizes can be used.

The essential tools are a long and very precise straightedge, a large square, and soft and hard pencils. Very thin, light construction lines should be used, since the work will become crowded. Darker pencil should be used to make the final results stand out. It is usually necessary to label points in the plan and elevation and on the perspective to keep track of the work. Projections down or across the paper

should be aligned perpendicular to or parallel to HL and GL, respectively. Some means of drawing parallel lines is needed, either two large 30° triangles or a drawing machine. A more tedious method is to use a ruler to measure the spacing for each parallel line.

As a general rule, the figures accompanying this and later methods of construction show different aspects of the construction with different line thicknesses. The thickest lines show the outlines of objects under discussion (or views of them). Lines of medium thickness show planning and layout lines —lines necessary for working but omitted from a final picture. Thin lines are used only for projection in construction and would be nearly invisible or removed from a finished picture. Occasionally, lines of one thickness may serve several purposes.

The construction should start with a front corner point of the object (a rectangular box), preferably one that lies in PP. Point A on the plan view in figure 2-12 lies in PP but is not on GP in the elevation view. For illustrative purposes, the object is chosen to be above GP. A construction line may be used to bring A straight down into the picture, where its location is determined by the elevation of A projected across to the picture. For this point, which was in PP, no use of VPs is needed. In choosing later points for construction, the artist should work from front to rear and from base to top.

Point B, a rear corner, can be used to illustrate the full method for angular perspective. Prior to construction, a viewer at location V was established as shown in figure 2-12. Viewer height is conveniently above the top of the object in elevation, and the location of HL in the picture is thereby determined. The VPs appropriate to the object were also

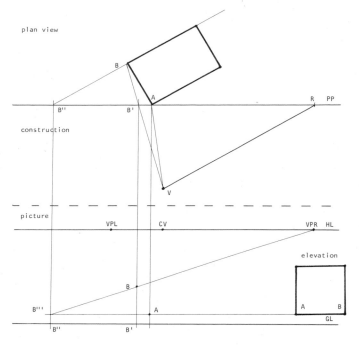

plan view

construction

picture

elevation

2-12. Constructing the perspective view of two points of a rectangular box, starting with the point in the picture plane

constructed on HL in the picture. This could have been done by placing a square with its vertex on V, aligning it parallel to the object faces in the plan view, and noting the points L and R where the square intersected the edge view of PP. VPL and VPR are located in the picture by projecting straight down from L and R.

Using prime labels (B′, B″, and B‴ for B) during intermediate construction steps, the procedure for finding the perspective view of B is as follows (see figure 2-12):

1. Connect V to B in the plan view, and find the pierce point B′ in PP.

2. Project B′ down to GL, and place another point B′ to label this line $\overline{B'B'}$. The perspective of B will be somewhere on this line.
3. Choose one VP for further work, either VPL or VPR. (VPR is used here.)
4. In the plan view, construct a line containing B parallel to line $\overline{VR}$ to pierce PP at B″. This line would have VPR as its vanishing point in the perspective view.
5. Project B″ down to GL, and place another point B″ to label this line $\overline{B''B''}$.
6. From the elevation view, project B across to intersect line $\overline{B''B''}$. The intersection point B‴ is the pierce point in PP of a line containing B aimed toward VPR.
7. In the picture, project B‴ toward VPR, intersecting line $\overline{B'B'}$ along the way. The intersection point is the perspective view of B and should be labeled B.

Completing the Perspective View

The seven-step procedure above is continued for other points of the object to complete the perspective, as shown in figure 2-13. The front edge of the box appears true size because it touches PP. As the end points of each line segment are determined, the finished line segment should be drawn darker to keep track of the work. VPL can be used to aid the work, reducing the number of points that must be plotted using the full set of steps. In this simple example, all line segments in the picture either converge to a VP or are vertical. Generally, using one VP or the other allows easy and accurate plotting of points. Both VPs may be used to plot some points. Experience is the artist's best guide.

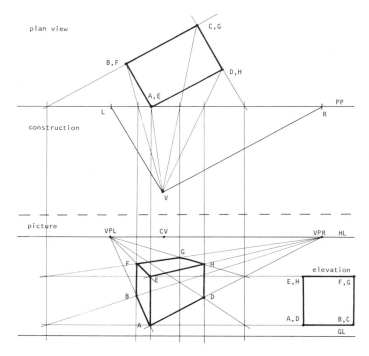

2-13. Completing the perspective view of a rectangular box

Q2-4. Redo figure 2-13, using VPL to reduce the work to plotting four points (two easy, two harder).

Q2-5. Use VPL to locate point B and show that the same location is obtained.

When some of the object is located in front of PP (in the plan view), the direction of projection in step 7 should be reversed, going from the VP toward the viewer. The perspective view will appear to be in front of PP.

For the case of parallel perspective, CV is the only VP for step 3. In step 4, the point is simply projected down to PP to find its pierce point. The projection is continued down for step 5. Figure 2-14 shows some details of the method for the parallel perspective of an object located on GP and behind PP.

The general procedure for these steps in angular or parallel perspective is to bring distant object points forward to PP, use the elevation data to establish true locations, and project these back into the picture. Because picture points must have two coordinates in order to be located, two separate projections are needed to locate each point; each projection uses a different set of original measurements from plan and elevation.

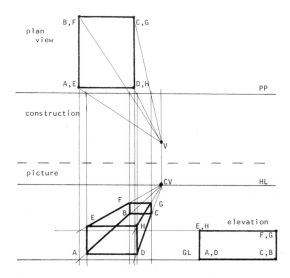

2-14. Constructing the parallel perspective of a hollow box viewed off-center

Q2-6. Check the construction of figure 2-6 to see how the projections of points were done. Note that steps 2 and 5 were followed, although the direction of the projection from PP to reach GL was reversed.

Once the artist gains some proficiency, the construction layout can be made more compact. The picture may be constructed in the region between the viewer and the plan view. If two sets of construction lines are laid on top of each other, however, work on any but the simplest objects can get too confusing. Often, complete construction lines need not be drawn, since their only purpose is to locate points in PP and on GL. The straightedge can locate points as follows: place it against a sharp pencil point in one position; move the pencil point to another position (for example, to a pierce point);

and rotate the straightedge around the pencil point to make the projection. Errors of placement are also reduced by this means.

The method presented here is called the "measuring line" method, since lines are used to bring points to PP so that their locations can be measured. A less easily understood method (not covered here) is the "measuring point" method, in which lines are rotated to PP. Another method, using projection to PPs in both views ("double projection"), is described later.

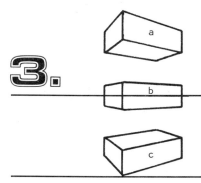

3.

Applications of the Graphic Method

The ability to plot points and locate vanishing points enables the artist to show an object in perspective. The following general applications and examples of methods extends this ability to cover any situation. The emphasis is on perspective; assistance with geometric construction and drawing can be gained from other sources.[1]

Lines and Planes

A study of the effect on lines and planes of being transformed from orthographic views to a perspective view can serve to familiarize the artist with many properties of perspective. Obviously, straight lines remain straight in perspective, and flat planes remain flat. Horizontal (x-direction) and vertical (z-direction) lines that are parallel to the picture plane (PP) remain horizontal and vertical, respectively, in perspective. But ''depth lines'' (also horizontal but parallel to the y axis) are transformed into diagonal lines in the perspective.

A set of parallel lines has been found to converge toward one point—a vanishing point (VP)—in the perspective view. At whatever orientation the set of lines appears in the plan view, the set converges toward VP. In the case of lines parallel to the picture plane, VP is indefinitely to the left or right in the picture, and the lines retain their appearance of parallelism in the picture. This discussion has not yet assumed that the set of parallel lines is *coplanar* (lying in one plane, as in figure 3-1a). A set of lines piled in three dimensions, as if they were a pile of poles, appears parallel in the plan view and yet is not coplanar (figure 3-1b). This set still has one VP. In addition, two or more lines may appear parallel in orthographic views but not be truly par-

33

allel. Figure 3-2 shows two lines that appear parallel in both plan and elevation views; yet a front view reveals them to be *skew* (neither parallel nor intersecting). Proper labeling of points along the lines allows the perspective view of them to be found using any two of the orthographic views.

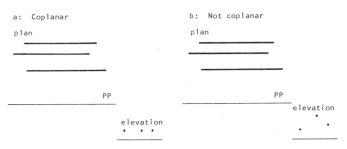

3-1. Sets of parallel lines—coplanar and not coplanar

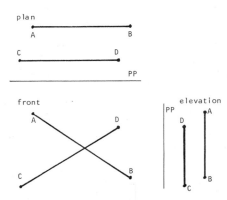

3-2. Three orthographic views of two skew lines

Q3-1. Assume a suitable V and PP for figure 3-2, and construct the perspective view of the skew lines. Note: (a) the points labeled on the lines are consistent in all views; and (b) no common VP is suggested by the lines. The work must be done using

carefully labeled points like the ones shown. VPs for the work, if used, may be found independently of the subject matter.

Lines that are not parallel either are skew or intersect somewhere. Intersecting lines define angles. Two intersecting lines also define a plane. In this section, the intersecting lines are confined to a horizontal plane. The point of intersection is a point that may be shown in two views and may be found in a perspective view. The angle may appear different sizes in the views and in the picture. In figure 3-3, $\angle ABC$ is shown true size in the plan view; it appears to be 180° in the elevation, and it appears smaller in the perspective picture. The elevation reveals that the lines lie in the ground plane.

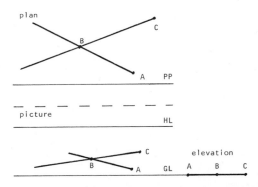

3-3. Intersecting lines defining an angle and a plane (in this case, a horizontal plane parallel to the ground plane)

Q3-2. Study the angle as shown in elevation in figure 3-3 until you are comfortable with that view. For intersecting or skew lines, visualization may be aided by orienting two pencils in space to represent the lines and by viewing them from various positions.

The fact that two intersecting lines define a plane may aid in finding the perspective view of a plane. Simply find the perspective of three points that define the intersecting lines; then draw the lines through the three points. The behavior of the plane is suggested by the lines. The fact that two intersecting lines define a point has already been used to construct perspective views of points.

A set of coplanar parallel lines that are equally spaced is valuable for establishing regularity or performing measurements in the perspective view. The set of parallel lines shown in figure 3-4a divides the ground plane into equal parts along the x axis, as if a ruler were laid along PP. Their equally spaced pierce points are called *measuring points,* located along GL as a *measuring line* in PP. A more distant horizontal line such as $\overline{AB}$ is then divided into equal parts that are smaller, showing smaller spacings in perspective. A diagonal line such as $\overline{CD}$ is divided into parts of apparently diminishing size, good for measuring in that direction.

A way to measure distance in depth "into" the picture (along the y axis) is also needed. A set of equally spaced parallel lines in the ground plane can be defined indefinitely far in the y direction in the plan view of figure 3-4b. The limit line of this set of lines is HL in the picture. Any line, such as $\overline{AB}$ or $\overline{CD}$, that is marked in equal parts in the plan view appears to be marked in segments of regularly decreasing size in the picture. The lines $\overline{AB}$ and $\overline{CD}$ in plan view can be thought of as rulers laid on the ground plane. In perspective they are foreshortened, and $\overline{AB}$ measures depth along the ground plane. An efficient way to lay out parallel lines in perspective (equivalent to providing a "depth ruler") is described below.

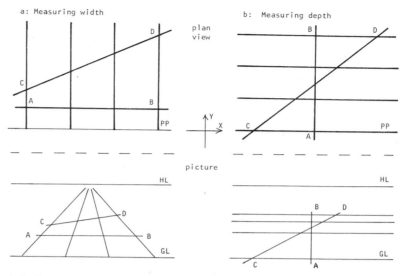

3-4. Sets of equally spaced parallel lines in a horizontal plane, measuring distance across and into the picture

Suppose that the line is extended from GL to HL, and that it ends at a VP, as shown in perspective in figure 3-5. Line $\overline{A_1VP}$ must be the diagonal of some square or rectangle in the foreground. Extend the sides of the rectangle (which appears trapezoidal in perspective) to CV. Point A_1 is at one corner. Then the top of the rectangle must be a line parallel to HL and intersecting $\overline{A_1VP}$ at point A_2. Since the rectangles are all identical (in a plan view) and are to be placed as regularly as tiles on a floor, there must be another diagonal through VP which passes through A'_2 and crosses the next rectangle. It establishes the next top at A_3, and a line parallel to PP may be drawn through it. The process is repeated with a diagonal through A'_3 to establish the top of the next rectangle, and may be continued indefinitely until as many lines parallel to PP are

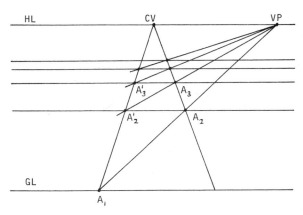

3-5. Constructing equally spaced parallel lines in perspective

obtained as needed. In plan view, the lines would be regularly spaced; thus, they establish a perspective "ruler" extending into the background. Their spacing seems to become closer and closer as HL is approached. The VP for diagonals that mark off space is also called a "measuring point."

Another way to subdivide depth is shown in figure 3-6. In this method, a base line (preferably GL) is marked with equal spacings. A depth line is drawn from each measured point to CV. From point A_1, a diagonal to a VP is chosen. At each point where the diagonal intersects a depth line, successively at A_2, A_3, and so on, a horizontal line can be constructed. The set of parallel lines so constructed are the perspective view of an equal-spaced set in GP.

These procedures may be carried out with any VP, any CV, any height of viewer, and any shape of rectangle that meets the preceding conditions. If the perspective view of a square is used, a square grid is formed. The diagonal VP then corresponds

to the 45° diagonal of the squares. For a given viewer position, the simplest way to start a square grid is to use the desired square in plan view and follow the procedure for constructing the perspective of it. The square should be in GP unless the grid is needed elsewhere. Further uses of the grid, and examples, are given later.

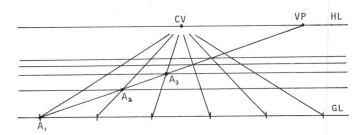

3-6. Alternative method for constructing equally spaced parallel lines in perspective

The construction for figures 3-5 and 3-6 was done in parallel perspective, with line segments parallel to HL. If the VP is to the side (VPR, for example), and if the line segments—instead of being parallel to HL—are to have another VP (VPL, for example), an angular perspective is indicated (figure 3-7). The initial spacing and the VPs are set by the first quadrilateral formed. Further spacings can be found either by extending lines from VPL to equally spaced measuring points on GL (A_1, A_2, . . .), or by locating VPD—the vanishing point for the diagonal of the quadrilateral. Further diagonals from VPD then intersect PP at a different set of measuring points (B_1, B_2, . . .). The first quadrilateral must be postulated by sketching or found by perspective

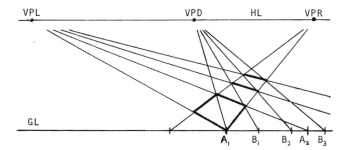

3-7. Constructing equally spaced lines in angular perspective

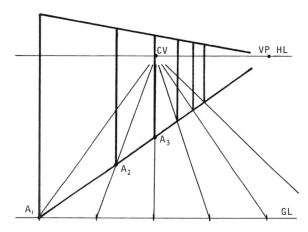

3-8. Dividing a vertical plane (a wall) into equal sections

construction from the plan view of a rotated rectangle. If a square is used, the result is the beginning of a square grid, rotated in perspective. The grid, whether or not square, may be continued by adding more lines to figure 3-7, using equally spaced measuring points.

Q3-3. Try to reconstruct the plan and elevation views that must have led to the pictures shown in figures 3-5, 3-6, and 3-7; such reconstruction verifies that these procedures are in accord with the seven basic steps for finding the perspective of points.

A vertical plane may be similarly subdivided into rectangles for measurement or other purposes. Consider the thin, transparent, flat wall shown in perspective in figure 3-8. Its base is a diagonal line from A_1 to a VP. Its top edge must also approach the same VP. Let the distance $\overline{A_1A_2}$ be the desired unit distance on the ground. Use the procedure for figure 3-6 to lay out additional unit lengths into the distance. Vertical lines from each point A_1, A_2, A_3, and so on, will then subdivide the vertical wall. The diagonals for each wall section are explored next.

Inclined Lines and Planes

To introduce the concept of a *vertical vanishing point* (VVP), consider the problem of finding the perspective of a simple pitched roof like the one shown in figure 3-9. Because of the viewer's height above roof level, both sides of the roof are visible. The sides of the roof appear to converge to VVPs located above and below HL. The locations of the VVPs may be best understood by considering the vertical projections of the roof lines onto the ground plane, in the plan view. Because the roof edges are parallel in the plan view, their projections approach VPR in the picture. When the roof lines slant upward, the projections of these lines onto the ground still approach VPR. Therefore VVP is directly above or below VPR on line $\overline{UU'}$. For a given slope, as shown in the elevation view, the corresponding VVP above or below HL has a definite height. If the roof of figure 3-9 were flattened, the VVPs would

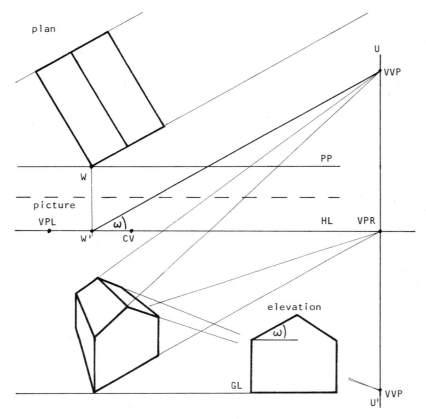

3-9. Finding the vertical vanishing points for slanted planes (planes of a roof)

approach VPR on HL. If the roof were made extremely steep, the VVPs would recede far above and below HL.

Whether the VVP for a given slanted surface is above or below HL depends on its tilt with respect to HL in the elevation view. One way to find the height of a VVP begins with noting that the vertical plane containing the slanted roof line in the plan

view of figure 3-9, when rotated into alignment with PP, shows the angle of slant true size in PP. The axis of rotation goes through point W, whose projection down to HL is W′. If the angle of slant ω (omega), shown in the elevation view, is duplicated in the picture plane with the vertex placed on HL at W′, the extension of the slant intersects the line $\overline{UU'}$ at VVP. To understand this procedure, the reader must realize that the sheet of paper containing the picture is as large a depiction of PP as is needed to carry out constructions. Line $\overline{UU'}$, HL, all VPs, and ω are shown in a "front-view" plane, which is PP.

Alternatively, the information from plan and elevation can be used to construct the perspective of at least one slanted line before the height of VVP is determined. VVP lies where an extension of the slanted line intersects $\overline{UU'}$ directly above or below the VP. In chapter 4, the means of calculating the location of such VPs is given. The plan view must be used to determine the VP to which the VVP belongs. Slanted lines may seem to indicate a VVP above a given VP when in fact some other VP must be used.

A road going up and down a series of jagged hills, making abrupt turns along the way, has a series of VPs above and below HL, as shown in figure 3-10. To see the road going downhill, the viewer must be high enough to place HL above the highest elevation the road reaches. Arbitrarily placing these VPs creates an imaginary landscape—one that does not necessarily follow the "rules" that nature follows when hills are arranged and eroded. Making the road follow real terrain requires plan and elevation data for the terrain; this subject is covered in

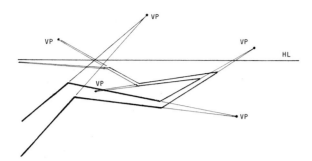

3-10. Various vertical vanishing points used to construct a road wandering over hills

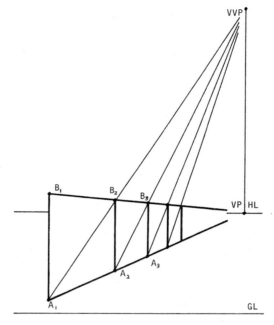

3-11. Using a vertical vanishing point to divide a vertical wall into equal sections

the discussion of topographic perspective (chapter 6).

The vertical wall shown in figure 3-8 could have been marked off by means of diagonals for each section. These diagonals have a VVP located directly above or below VP. If the diagonal $\overline{A_1B_2}$ is extended, it identifies VVP's position above VP, as shown in figure 3-11. It also establishes the next vertical line. A new diagonal from A_2 locates the next vertical at B_3 as it is extended to VVP. The process can be continued until as many equal wall sections as needed are marked.

A flat surface may have two different VVPs. Consider the tilted rectangle in figure 3-12. It is not parallel to GP or PP. To find its VVPs, examine the projection of the rectangle onto GP. One pair of sides in the projection indicates VPR, above which VVPR can be found. The other pair of sides shows where VPL and VVPL are located. The height of VVPL and VVPR were determined by using an elevation view (not shown) and carrying out the usual perspective construction. More detail must await the discussions of oblique perspective.

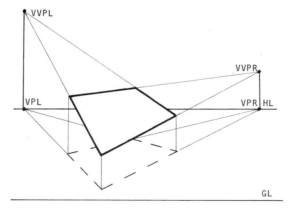

3-12. Plane surface with two different vertical vanishing points

Objects Formed of Lines and Planes

The perspective for line segments, squares, rectangles, and hexagons has been discussed. The procedure for other *polygons* composed of straight line segments, whether regular or irregular, is hardly different. For figures that are regular and have an even number of sides, one or more sets of parallel sides exist which then have VPs. These VPs may be different from the VPs established in angular perspective by the viewer's location. For example, in figure 3-13, a regular hexagon is viewed so that five different VPs occur: VPR and VPL, to which no sides converge; and one VP for each pair of sides. The view is rather distorted because V is placed so close that all VPs appear inside the picture frame. The locations of the VPs for the hexagon can be found by constructing lines from V to PP parallel to each side in plan view. The perspective of the figure may be drawn by plotting five points by the normal seven-step procedure and using the VPs to complete the work. Any figure with an odd number of sides may have as many VPs as it has sides. That they are VPs may not be apparent when only one edge converges to each VP, but they may be used for construction. A more symmetrically placed hexagonal grid is shown in perspective in plate 3.

A solid such as a tetrahedron is formed of planes (in the tetrahedron's case, four). The planes are oriented at various tilts with respect to GP, and the edges of the solid have VVPs. Few other solids have perspectives more challenging to construct than a tetrahedron's. In figure 3-14, the elevation view need show merely the height of the apex; the exact width of the base as seen from the side is irrelevant (and may be difficult to find). All neces-

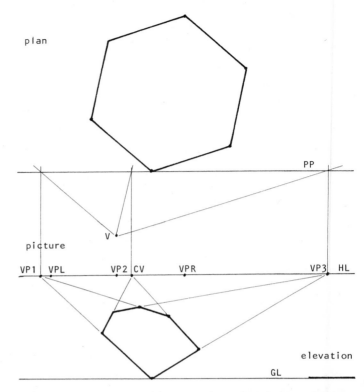

3-13. Regular hexagon viewed so as to create three new vanishing points

sary construction lines have been shown. Placing point D at the center in the plan view causes the solid to be regular. It might be thought that angles quite difficult to construct or draw have been determined in the picture from rather simple information in the plan and elevation. However, the height of the tetrahedron had to be calculated before the elevation could be shown. The problem was one of analytic geometry.

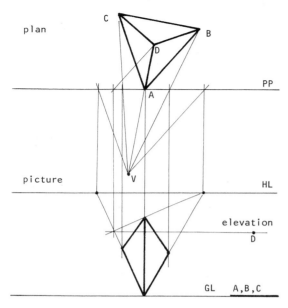

3-14. Perspective of a tetrahedron

Q3-4. Try to find a VVP for one of the edges of the tetrahedron.

It is often useful to know or to plot the center of a triangle. While at least four different centers can be defined for a triangle, the usual one of interest is the *centroid*—the "center of gravity," as if the triangle were cut from uniform material and balanced at that point. A *median* is constructed from the midpoint of each side to the opposite vertex. All three medians intersect at the centroid.

Q3-5. Draw a plan view for a triangle, and find the center. Test this procedure on any pentagon.

The center of any regular polygon may be found by constructing two diagonals across the fig-

ure, cutting it into two identical parts in two different ways. The center is at the intersection of the diagonals.

Q3-6. Draw plan views for a regular hexagon and a regular octagon, and find the centers.

Centers for solid regular figures may be found by the same principle of symmetry; however, the practical work is difficult. The simplest procedure is to find the center in both plan and elevation and plot the perspective as if the plan and elevation centers were a single point. Irregular objects (except triangles) do not have geometrically defined centers. Nonetheless, every object has what may be called a center of gravity. If the object is imagined to be constructed of uniformly dense material, whether sheet or solid, the useful center is the point from which the object could be hung and remain motionless (in equilibrium).

Q3-7. As an illustration of the subtlety of centers, consider finding the center of the tetrahedron in figure 3-14. Point D is the center in the plan view. But if the center for the elevation view is to be found, additional views of a triangular side must be drawn, or use must be made of the fact that the center of a regular (equilateral) triangle is at one-third of the distance from the base to the top. Plot the perspective of the center.

Circles, Ellipses, and Arcs

Many objects of interest have features such as circles, arcs, and other curves. Even in the case of circular arcs, considerable difficulty is presented to the perspective artist. A circle viewed from other than the true view (front view or "head-on") appears elliptical, although the mind is quite agile at interpreting any elliptical curve as a circular arc. To an observer gazing head-on at the center circle of a row of identical circles, all seem unquestionably circular. Yet careful observation of the circles far from the center of vision—those seen through the "side" of the eye—reveals that they actually appear elliptical. For good perspective, circles must be drawn as properly shaped ellipses in order to give the viewer the illusion that they are circles. The eye is quite sensitive to the required shape of the ellipses, and small errors may destroy the illusion. The CV is also critical. A viewer who looks elsewhere than the planned CV, as often happens, will see ellipses improper for that direction of gaze and therefore will not see them as circles.[2]

Q3-8 Carefully draw a straight row of several uniformly spaced identical large circles. Place the viewer (in plan view) in front of the center circle. Draw tangent lines from V to each side of each circle. Examine the apparent widths of the circles that the viewer at V would see in PP. Do they get larger or smaller as the viewer looks to the sides? Examine also the angular width of each circle that the viewer sees.

The descriptive properties of an ellipse are shown in figure 3-15. It is symmetrically bisected by a major axis $\overline{AB}$ and by a shorter minor axis $\overline{DE}$. Ellipse shape is described by its *eccentricity* (*e*). Elongated ellipses have values of *e* near, but less than, 1. As a circle is tilted farther from the viewer in perspective, its apparent eccentricity approaches 1. The value of *e* increases rapidly with the tilt. An ellipse that resembles a slightly flattened circle has *e* = 0.5. Rounded ellipses have values of *e* near zero, a circle being a special form of ellipse with *e* = 0. Figure 3-15 represents a circle viewed at a 35° slant, giving an ellipse with *e* = 0.81. A circle seen in edge view appears as a totally flat ellipse—a line segment with *e* = 1.

An ellipse also has two points called *foci* (plural for *focus*), which can be used to construct it or for other purposes. The focal points F are near the center C if the ellipse is circular and near the "ends" if it is very elongated. One defining property of an ellipse is that a string attached from one F to any point P on the ellipse and then to the other F is of constant length, regardless of the point.

A conceptually simple but technically tedious procedure for rendering the perspective of a circle is to plot it point by point—labeling several dozen points on the plan and elevation views and plotting them all. The result of connecting all the points in the proper order should be an ellipse. Many circles and circular arcs can be represented by a rather small number of judiciously chosen points, enabling this procedure to be carried out with less work.

In figure 3-16, the circles in the plan view are enclosed in squares. Each square is then bisected by horizontal, vertical, and diagonal lines so as to establish points at which the circle is tangent to the square and four other points easily plotted. The center is also established. In the perspective view, the squares appear as trapezoids or quadrilaterals with the ellipses inscribed.

The view in figure 3-16 is for a viewer located symmetrically in front of the center circle. For the circle located to the left of the center circle, the

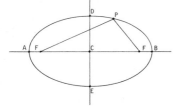

3-15. Properties of an ellipse

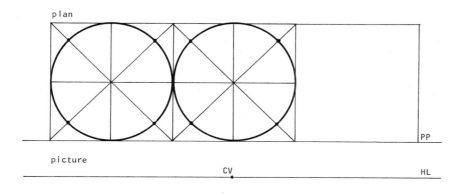

plan

picture

CV

HL

PP

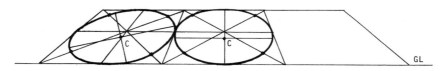

GL

3-16. Perspectives of centrally viewed and angularly viewed circles compared

construction results in a distorted trapezoid (a quadrilateral) to the left in the picture. The ellipse clearly has it axes tilted. Thus the simplest perspective view of a circle can result in a tilted ellipse bounded by an irregular figure. Neither the center (C) of the ellipse nor its axes would be aligned with any of the construction lines or points. The artist can estimate, by symmetry, the major axis and center. The center lies near the plotted center of the circle; sometimes it is so close that little error results from estimating its position.

It may be somewhat unexpected that the shape within the trapezoid or quadrilateral is an ellipse; a

mathematical proof verifying this result is given in chapter 6. In some other types of views (such as isometric), a circle also appears as an ellipse. Any standard procedure for constructing an ellipse requires at a minimum that the center of the ellipse be found. The center is not provided during the perspective construction. In the perspective in figure 3-16, the center of the circle is not the center (C) of the ellipse. The major axis of each ellipse has been added to the picture, not constructed. It intersects the minor axis at some point ''in front of'' the perspective view of the center of the circle. Although of no use for drawing the ellipse, the center of the circle is likely to be needed for other construction work. It can be automatically located during the process of constructing the lines that determine the ellipse.

The ellipse may be drawn by freehand arcs through the tangent points and the four diagonal points, or a "flexible" curve can be used. Various portions of a French curve can be matched to the plotted points. The fourfold symmetry of the ellipse should be used to advantage: the same portion of the French curve can be used for four different parts of the ellipse (turning it over for two of them). The curve should be aligned with the points of tangency to the enclosing quadrilateral and with other portions of the curve already drawn. It is hard to avoid a lumpy appearance. No part of a French curve produces a truly elliptical curve, and the eye notices small defects in curvature once the whole ellipse is formed.

A compass may be used to approximate the ellipse with suitable arcs if the eccentricity is low. Since standard procedures for drawing ellipses require information not available in perspective views, the artist preferring to approximate an ellipse with arcs instead of by plotting points had best use trial and error. A light sketch of the ellipse that fits the trapezoid can be examined for its symmetry and the major axis sketched in. The minor axis is the major axis's perpendicular bisector. Then two points can be found on each axis for the compass point. Suitable arcs can be drawn to approximate both the rounded "ends" and the flatter "sides" of the ellipse, staying within the bounds of the trapezoid. This method does not give an accurate shape if the ellipse is elongated. The available procedures for constructing the points for drawing the arcs are unnecessarily complex and also noticeably inaccurate for elongated ellipses.

Ellipses can also be constructed with templates, pins and string, or other instruments.[3] Templates are available in sets (in metric or English units) with various sizes of major axis for each of several shapes. Shapes are designated in degrees, representing the angle at which the viewer would have to look at a circle in order to see the particular shape of ellipse. A large set of templates is needed to handle most drawings that arise; even so, the largest major-axis size offered is usually only about 15 cm. The true angle of view is usually not shown in the plan or elevation, and a special view has to be constructed if the angle is to be measured (chapter 6 shows how to obtain it mathematically). Only the tilt of a circle near the vision axis corresponds closely with the designated angle of the ellipse to be used near CV in the picture.

If a drawing is to consist of one or more identical circles in perspective, the artist may want to work backwards. Obtaining an elliptical template of desired size and shape (or making one by plotting an ellipse on cardboard as described in chapter 6), the artist can design the perspective around the template. The plan or elevation view, a circle, can readily be constructed from the picture if required.

The graphic method sometimes needed to find the center and axes of an ellipse follows. (An accurate drawing of the ellipse must already be available.) In figure 3-17, any two parallel lines L and M are drawn across the ellipse. The segments within the ellipse are each bisected, producing points A and B. The center C is at the bisection of the line $\overline{DE}$ drawn through A and B. (If $\overline{DE}$ turns out to intersect the ellipse too close to its "ends," try an-

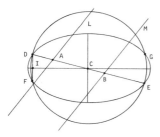

3-17. Method for finding the center and axes of an ellipse

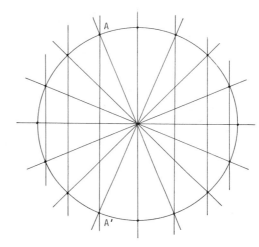

3-18. Locating points on a circle prior to contructing its perspective view by the strip method

other pair of parallel lines to improve accuracy.) Using C as center, a circle of radius $\overline{DC}$ is drawn. It intersects the ellipse at four symmetrically located points, D, E, F, and G. Line $\overline{DF}$ is constructed and bisected at I. The line through I and C is the major axis. The line through C and perpendicular to the major axis is the minor axis.

Other methods for constructing the perspective of a circle are the strip and grid methods. The grid method is covered later on for the general case of any irregular curve. The strip method begins (figure 3-18) with dividing the circle into sixteen or more equal sectors, by means of lines through its center. Each pair of sector lines is connected by a line, such as the one through AA'. Parallel strips of variable width are formed. The sixteen points around the circumference are plotted by the usual rules into the picture. All the strips have the same VP. The points must be connected freehand or with a French curve. Unfortunately, there is no enclosing trapezoid to enforce symmetry and tangency unless a square is included in the plan.

Circular arcs, such as those defining some arches, may be in a vertical or other plane. Enough of the circle and its enclosing square must be shown in plan or elevation to plot the necessary points in

perspective. In figure 3-19, the arch is represented by semicircles. The full enclosing squares with diagonals are needed to identify the shapes of the ellipses in perspective. They are shown for both the front and the back of the arch, and only their construction lines are made visible in this figure. The major axes of the ellipses do not have a simple orientation, but do have a VVP. The parts of the ellipses needed to represent the arch are then drawn where visible. They are not easy to draw, since they are only parts of asymmetrical halves of whole ellipses.

Caution must be used in deciding whether arches or other curved features consist of one or more circular arcs. More complex curves may have been used. Noncircular curves must be treated as irregular curves, which are discussed later.

Any perspective view of a circular feature should be examined for its effect. Especially trou-

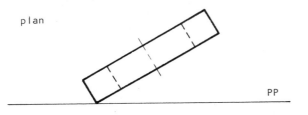

plan

PP

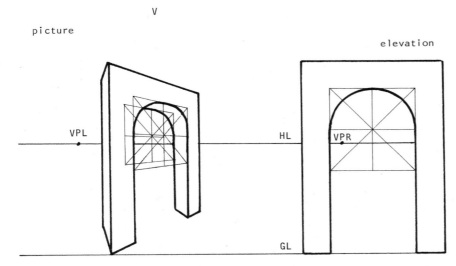

V

picture

elevation

VPL

HL

VPR

GL

3-19. Constructing the perspective of an arch

blesome are the ends of cylinders, which look incorrect when the cylinder is not near CV. Circles, cylinders, and even rectangular objects tend to appear wider at the sides of the field of view. This is not an illusion; it is the result of rectilinear perspective that has been correctly done but then is incor-

rectly viewed, making its inherent distortion more apparent. If the viewer could be constrained to look only at CV from the proper distance, a circular or any other regular object would appear properly shaped as seen through the corner of the eye. The reader may test this notion on any perspective drawing in this or other books that appears distorted. When the eye is located exactly where V was designed to be (usually too close for clear vision in the case of a book illustration), the distortion is much reduced.

Some sources[4] recommend altering the perspective for circular or cylindrical features by constructing a portion of a PP perpendicular to a line to V for each object. Each object would be drawn as if V looked directly at it. While this may be effective with a mural consisting of a uniform row of columns, for example, it works well only for particular locations of V and in other situations may harm the overall perspective. Some parts of the picture grow incompatible with other parts as actual space is lost in some places and created in others.

Spheres and Other Curved Solids

It may seem contrary to intuition that the rectilinear perspective of a sphere is not a circle in PP unless the center of the sphere is on the vision axis. This assertion is demonstrated graphically in this section and is discussed mathematically in chapter 6. Looking at spheres raises a dilemma similar to the one encountered when looking at circles and cylinders. A sphere would appear as a circle if the viewer looked directly at it without the intervention of a PP. But if the viewer is looking at a PP, spheres to the sides appear wider as the points at which the lines of sight tangentially touch the spheres move around the bulges of the spheres. To an observer looking at the center of an array of spheres, those far from the center (and seen out of the corner of the eye) appear ellipsoidal to some degree. Pirenne presents photographs of the effect in *Vision and the Eye;* the effect is small even in extreme cases. That spheres should be drawn as ellipses and not as some similar shape in perspective requires proof. The effect on shape occurs for any rounded forms, such as those of human figures. Contrary to circles and cylinders, off-center spheres ought not to be represented by ellipses. Since the viewing distance cannot be fixed, distortion is more obvious.

A simple procedure for drawing the perspective of a sphere is shown in figure 3-20. The sphere is imagined to be in a cubical outline box, and the box is drawn in perspective. A vertical slice is made through the center of the sphere in plan view, and a horizontal slice is made in the elevation view. The horizontal slice forms a circle that can be plotted as an ellipse using the method described for figure 3-16. The ellipse indicates the edge of the perspective of the sphere at its greatest side-to-side width. The top and bottom of the sphere in perspective are found with a vertical slice of the sphere, giving a circle in PP.

Only when the center of the sphere is so close to the vision axis that CV lies inside the outline of the sphere in PP can its shape be approximated with a circle. This is the case shown in figure 3-20. Under these conditions, the largest error likely to be made is a very small percentage of the size of the outline. The approximating circle has its center at the center of the horizontal ellipse (point C in figure 3-20). The sphere in its outline cube is tangent to the centers

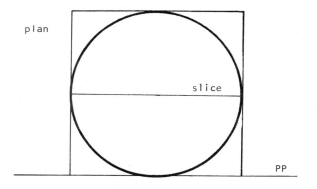

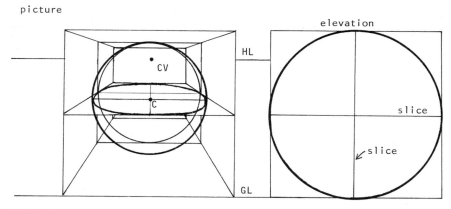

3-20. Constructing the perspective of a sphere near the center of vision

of all six sides of the cube. These points of tangency are obscured by the bulge of the sphere that lies in front of them, as seen by the viewer.

A sphere can be displaced from a central viewing position in only two ways. The center (which is the best feature of the sphere to use for locating it)

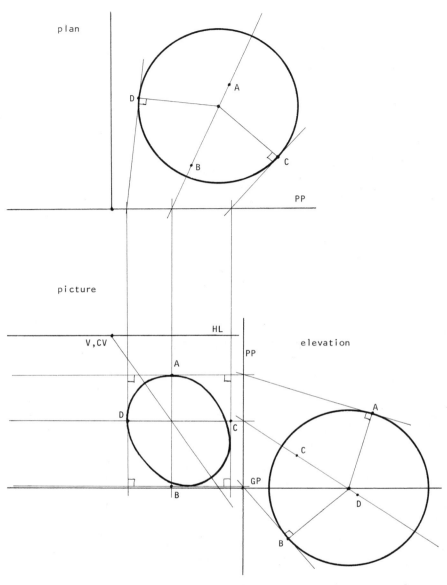

plan

PP

picture

HL

V,CV

PP

elevation

A

D

C

GP

B

A

C

B

D

3-21. Constructing the perspective of a sphere viewed asymmetrically

can be to either side of CV, and it can be above or below HL. Figure 3-21 shows the more challenging problem of drawing the perspective of a sphere which is both to the right in plan view and below HL. The procedure to be used involves perspective projection from both plan and elevation. This double projection method is used extensively for oblique perspective later. An alternative procedure involves enclosing the sphere in an outline cube and finding the perspective of the cube and of slices of the sphere within.

Since a sphere defines no VPs, no VPs can be used, and the process of locating corresponding points becomes more complex. The least difficult way to locate points on the sphere is to consider lines of sight from V to the sphere's edge. (These lines of sight do not necessarily create points of tangency.) The picture of the sphere is obtained by locating where these lines intersect PP. The "width" of the sphere in PP is different from its "height," producing an elliptical shape. Even for extreme viewing points, the shape does not differ substantially from circular. The major axis of the elliptical shape is at an angle to HL. Again, the perspective is being constructed for a viewer at V, looking at CV. If the viewer's vision axis could be moved to the center of the sphere, PP would rotate accordingly, and the sphere would appear circular.

For viewer locations that are close (angular size greater than about 35°), or for sphere locations more than about 45° from the vision axis, the bulge of the sphere in plan and elevation views hides the points located on it by means of tangents. The reader can best visualize the situation by constructing a simple model with two diverging straight rods fastened to a ball and examining it from all orientations. The points of tangency are difficult to locate and plot in the general case because they can be found correctly only in special plan and elevation views. The viewer sees them at the edge of the sphere, but they do not appear that way in orthographic views. The plane containing V and the points of tangency must be parallel to the xy or yz plane in order to show points of tangency truly on the edge of the sphere. Rotating the views to this position is necessary to define the points of tangency; then the points must be returned to the views shown in figure 3-21. Four auxiliary views must be constructed to plot the points of tangency, but the points are rarely needed. They do not, in general, define the sides of the rectangle, and the rectangle can be found by the simpler procedure previously mentioned.

The asymmetrically located sphere is represented in figure 3-21 by circles in plan and elevation in their desired positions. V must be the same distance from PP in each view, and it is least confusing to put V for each view at the same point (the same goes for CV). Lines of sight from V reach the apparent edge of the sphere at points A and B in elevation and at points C and D in the plan. A and B lie in a plane containing V that is seen in edge view in the plan. C and D lie in a plane containing V that is seen in edge view in the elevation. Each of these planes also includes the center of the sphere. Since neither of these planes is parallel to the xy or yz plane, none of the points A, B, C, and D are tangent points. The location of points C and D in the elevation view can be found by realizing that they must be the same distance from PP in elevation as they

were in plan. Similarly, the location of points A and B in the plan can be found by measuring how far they are from PP in the elevation.

Once A, B, C, and D have been located in both views, the perspective can be constructed. Lines from V to each point in both views are constructed to locate pierce points in PP. Each pierce point is projected down or across to find an intersection in the picture, thus locating the perspective of A, B, C, and D. Points A and B indicate the height of a rectangle that delimits the perspective of the sphere. Points C and D delimit the apparent width of the outline of the sphere as seen in PP, and therefore they indicate the width of the rectangle.

The major axis of the ellipse to be drawn in the rectangle must aim at CV, from considerations of symmetry. A line is drawn from CV bisecting the rectangle (not necessarily corner to corner). Given this major axis, only one shape of ellipse can be constructed in the rectangle. It describes the outline of the sphere in perspective. The points of tangency that result from viewing the sphere lie on this elliptical outline but generally are not at its extremes. If the viewer's eye were situated at the same distance above CV that V is from PP in the figure and were then to look at CV, the elliptical shape, seen obliquely out of the corner of the eye, would appear circular!

Q3-9. Try to draw the perspective of the sphere for figure 3-21 by the outline box method.

Q3-10. Rotate the plane containing V and the center of the sphere to a position parallel to GP in figure 3-21. Find the new view of the sphere in plan and locate the points of tangency where the viewer sees the edge of the sphere. Plot these points in elevation and rotate the plane back to the correct position. Do the points of tangency appear at the edge in elevation? (Note: the rotation must be done about an axis parallel to PP.)

Constructing perspectives of some curved solids involves examining how the solid could have been created by a series of circles or by rotating a polygon around an axis. The circles' midpoints or the rotation axis defines an axis of symmetry for the solid. A cone can be thought of as a stack of circles of decreasing size or as the result of rotating a triangle around one edge. More complex solids may consist of intersections of planes or cubes with simpler curved solids. The perspective of each element is obtained separately, in its proper place. Judgment must be used in removing some lines that should be "hidden," as discussed later.

Irregular Curves and the Use of Grids

Any curve that can be expressed mathematically, such as a hanging cable, can be plotted relatively easily using later mathematical methods; alternatively, it can be treated as an irregular curve. Irregular curves can be plotted in perspective only point by point, using as many points as necessary to preserve the accuracy desired. Reasonably detailed information about the curve must be available in the plan and/or elevation views. The method that brings order to the work consists of laying a grid over the given irregular curve, a process also called "graticulation."

Figure 3-22 shows a grid with large units and an irregular curve to be plotted. The grid should be oriented as simply as possible—preferably parallel to PP. The grid sections need systematic labeling. The first step is to construct the grid in perspective. Then points on the curve can be located by the section they are in and by their location (usually in quarters of a unit) within the sections. Locating should be done with reference to either x or y grid lines but not both simultaneously. The process of estimating positions between grid lines is called *in-*

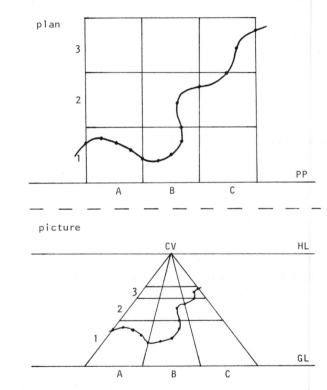

3-22. Perspective of an irregular curve constructed by the grid method

terpolation. In the picture, the correct section is found by label, and the locations of several points within that section are estimated. Distances between points nearer the viewer are larger than those between points farther from the viewer. Experience improves the artist's judgment.

Grids may be vertical or tilted if necessary. They should be square, with the grid lines equally spaced and at right angles in the plan or elevation view. Grids should have large units rather than small ones, to avoid unnecessary crowding and confusion of lines. The unit spacing should correspond to a metric or other unit of measure if possible. A special form of grid called a "topographic map" has the elevation data provided either at each grid intersection or by means of contour lines. The perspective of the grid itself indicates the nature of the view being designed and shows the degree of distortion. The grid is helpful to the artist in locating objects in the picture or in judging their proposed locations.

Q3-11. Draw the perspective of part of a grid in a plane that is neither vertical nor horizontal.

Oblique Perspective

The effect of moving the center of vision to the left or right has been discussed. Different perspective views are obtained because either the viewer has moved sideways or the picture orientation has changed. In figure 3-23, the viewer may move from position 1 to position 2 to see a different picture. (Recall that when CV moves, a different picture of the fixed subject matter is constructed; CV does not merely slide along an existing picture surface.) If the viewer stays at position 1 and looks at the posi-

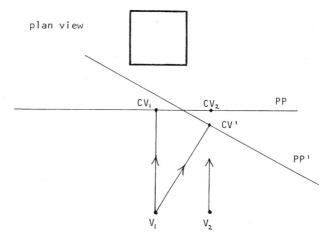

3-23. Viewing an object obliquely

tion CV_2, PP must be rotated to meet the line of sight perpendicularly at CV'. Again the perspective changes because the fixed object has a different relation to the new PP. It should be clear from figure 3-23 that the same pictorial result is not obtained in these two different cases, either.

Instead of changing the direction of view sideways or rotating PP about a vertical axis, these changes can be done vertically. The viewer can look up or down at an angle. For the new picture to be obtained, PP must be rotated about a horizontal axis so that the line of sight pierces PP perpendicularly. Alternatively, the viewer can stand higher or lower to see the object differently. Figure 3-23, if examined sideways, illustrates these changes. The principal change of interest is the tilting of the view and of PP. This new orientation of PP requires a third type of perspective—oblique (three-point). With respect to conventional orientation, it is as if the viewer were in the observation bay of a tall building, looking perpendicularly through windows tilted downward at the landscape below (sometimes called an "aerial" or "bird's-eye" view). Indeed, the viewer could stay on the ground and look downward through a tilted PP, but the objects seen might be ones on the ground near the viewer's feet rather than the more distant ones intended.

The same changes in viewpoint apply to a viewer standing at the base of a tall building and looking up (sometimes known inelegantly as a "worm's-eye" view). The viewer might expect no oblique perspective to be involved. But if the picture frame through which the viewer looks is tilted correctly and the building is viewed through it (figure 3-24), PP is no longer parallel to the sides of the building. Vertical lines appear to have a vanishing point in the sky, an effect not seen in the previous types of perspective. Plates 1 and 2 show oblique perspectives, with convergent vertical lines and convergent horizontal lines. ("Oblique perspective" should not be confused with the term "oblique views" used in technical drawing.) In an extreme case, V looks straight up. PP is parallel to the ground and CV is at the zenith, toward which all vertical lines converge. The perspective may then be oblique, angular, or parallel, depending on the subject matter.

Although the need for oblique perspective is most apparent in cases involving a tilted view of a normally oriented object, oblique perspective is also needed when the orientation of the object behind PP is changed by two or three rotations. These rotations of the object with respect to PP are automatically implicated when tilted views are used. Therefore, all discussion here assumes that the object has been rotated. One rotation of an object

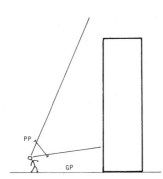

3-24. Viewing a tall object obliquely

about a vertical (z) axis, as has been shown, requires the use of angular perspective. Two rotations, most typically about the z and x axes, give the object an angular orientation and tilt the top and bottom surfaces (figure 3-25). Rotation only about the x axis also produces this tilt, but the methods of angular perspective turned sideways can be employed. Rotation about all three axes produces oblique perspective, too. The third rotation, about the y axis, makes the object lean over, as shown in figure 3-26, and is the least likely orientation to be encountered.

Oblique perspective requires more complicated construction methods, but the effect can be very rewarding. The restrictions on setting it up are less obvious, especially with regard to finding the correct vanishing points. The mathematical approach that starts in chapter 4 is especially helpful in setting up or carrying out an oblique perspective. The series of steps given for angular and parallel perspective, sometimes known as the "measuring line" method, must be replaced by one of two new procedures. The principal one discussed here involves using appropriate plan and elevation views to illustrate the rotated object, and then finding picture points from the combined use of these orthographic views. This "double projection" method was used for the asymmetrically located sphere and could have been used for angular perspective. The other method, sometimes called the "measuring point" method, is covered in Giesecke, French, and other sources. It uses unrotated plan and elevation views but rotates measurements made from them. Since the latter approach represents a more drastic departure from the procedure for angular perspective, only the former approach is covered here.

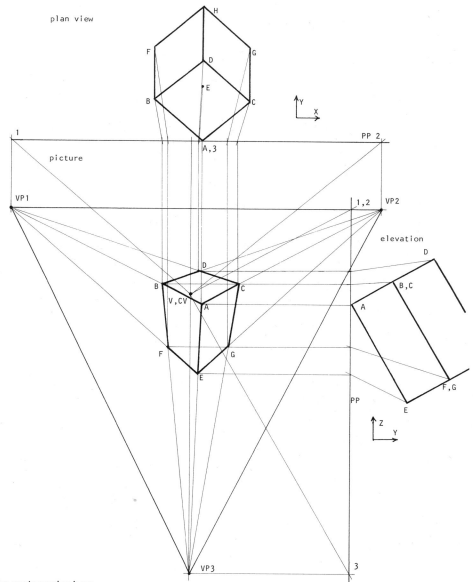

plan view

H

F   G
    D
  E
B   C

Y
X

1   PP 2
        A,3

picture

VP1   1,2   VP2

                                    elevation

        D   D
    B   C   B,C
    V,CV A   A
    F   G
        E   F,G
                                E
                        PP

                            Z
                            Y

VP3   3

3-25. Oblique perspective of a rectangular box
rotated 45° around the z axis and 30° around the x axis

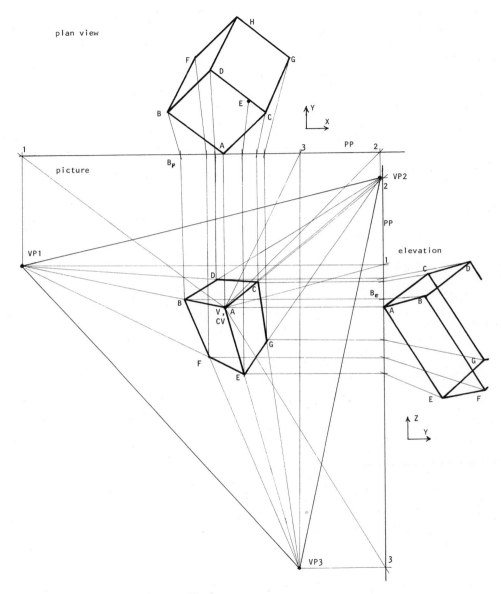

plan view

picture

elevation

3-26. Oblique perspective of the box shown in figure 3-25 after a third independent rotation of 15° around the *y* axis

54

A rectangular object that can act as an outline box can be used to illustrate the method. Three principal VPs exist, one corresponding to each principal axis of the box. The box shown in figure 3-26 has been rotated 45° about its front edge (around the z axis), has been tilted forward 30° (around the x axis), and has had its bottom point slid to the right along GP (by means of a 15° rotation around the y axis). The simplification to rotations about only the z and x axes is shown in figure 3-25, where the 15° y-axis rotation has been omitted.

Starting the method is perhaps the most difficult step. Rotated views of the object must be obtained in plan and elevation, as in figure 3-26. Technical drawing methods can be used for rotating simple views. If the artist proceeds one view and one rotation at a time, the reorientation of the box is relatively easy. The same points are the same distance from PP in each view. A front view may be temporarily needed.

Next, a viewer position must be chosen. The line of sight still intersects PP normally. PP, again seen in edge view, is added to the elevation view, and the elevation is placed so that the viewer can see both plan and elevation from the same point V. V must be the same distance from both PPs. The object may or may not rest on GP (GP is omitted from figure 3-26). The construction of the picture must be done in the same region occupied by the final picture. V and CV appear in the picture region.

The object as seen rotated in plan and elevation does not usually exhibit right angles. The right angles of a box no longer appear to be 90° when viewed at a tilt. The box instead appears as a parallelopiped in both views. All edges that should be parallel do appear parallel, making some construc-

tion work easy. The construction of lines parallel to box edges to find VPs must follow the box edges shown. To find the VPs, lines are drawn from V parallel to all box edges in both views. The angle of view between any pair of VPs is never 90°. Three pierce points, labeled 1, 2, and 3, are obtained in both PPs, and these are extended down and across to obtain intersection points. VP1 lies at the intersection of the two pierce points 1; the other two VPs are found in like manner.

The three VPs can be thought of as the vertices of a triangle that becomes useful later. This triangle is also the outline that would result if a plane parallel to PP were sliced through an indefinitely large box. Each side of the triangle is the horizon line that results if the three sides of an infinitely large box are viewed in perspective. The three-rotation oblique view produces a tilted, asymmetrical triangular arrangement of VPs. The two-rotation oblique view (see figure 3-25) is constructed by the same procedure, but two VPs turn out to be aligned horizontally, and the triangle is oriented without tilt.

The actual position of V is directly outward from CV in the picture. The point V (and CV) shown in the picture is therefore the downward projection of V onto the picture. The picture region is also a "front view" of the construction work. Ordinarily, V and CV should not be aligned with the top front corner of the object, but figure 3-26 uses a simplified case. Figure 3-25 shows the construction for a less centrally placed CV. Since the viewer normally looks at CV in PP, an HL exists with CV on it, but this HL may not be seen and need not be used for construction. GL is located in accord with wherever the elevation shows GP to be.

Points of the object may now be plotted. Point

A happens to plot where V and CV are located. For other points, the usual procedure of constructing lines from V to the points is carried out. For point B, pierce points B_E and B_P are found in the PPs. These points are extended across and down, respectively, to locate an intersection at which B is plotted in the picture. This procedure must be continued for all needed points before shortcuts can be employed. Any line segment whose extension approaches a VP can be drawn from a plotted point. The VPs could also have been found, perhaps less accurately, by plotting more points of the box until its edges indicated their locations in the picture. All parts of these procedures should be done extremely accurately because errors in point locations accumulate. Critical point locations should be checked by using redundant procedures; even so, small discrepancies are likely to remain.

If more room is desired for the construction—perhaps to avoid having VPs fall within the plan region, creating confusion—two different views of V can be used. Each V must be the same distance from its PP. CV occurs at the intersection of vertical and horizontal lines containing these Vs. Determining all further points, starting with the VPs, must involve transfer of locations vertically or horizontally so that all distances are measured with respect to CV instead of with respect to the Vs. More work is necessary.

If the VPs happen to be given—perhaps because the desired shape of a rectangular box has been postulated in the picture—the needed viewer location can be found. Figure 3-27 shows the triangle formed by the three VPs. The three VPs and CV are not independent of each other. If any three of these four points are known, the fourth can be

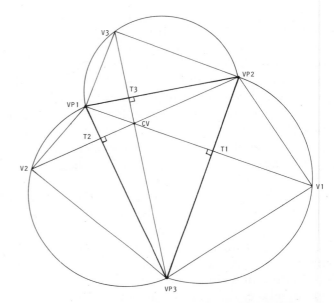

3-27. The vanishing point triangle for oblique perspective

found by construction. If CV is not known, it can be found by drawing an *altitude* from each VP to intersect the opposite side of the triangle perpendicularly at T1, T2, and T3. CV is at a center called the "orthocenter," which is not to be confused with several other possible centers of this irregular triangle.

To find the location of V above CV, draw a semicircle on the outside of each of the triangle's sides, using an arc from the center of each side. Extend the perpendicular lines through each T-point to intersect each semicircle at V1, V2, and V3. These points are the same as would have been obtained by placing right triangles in the semicircles. The right triangles are shown "true view" (all sizes and angles true size). For V a given distance above the picture, each of the distances $\overline{V1,T1}$, $\overline{V2,T2}$, and $\overline{V3,T3}$ is the distance from V to the corresponding line $\overline{VP2,VP3}$, $\overline{VP1,VP3}$, or $\overline{VP1,VP2}$. If figure 3-27 is visualized as showing the corner of an infinite box, V is above the corner. If each right triangle were rotated about its hypotenuse to bring the three vertices together, they would meet at V above CV. In principle, the location of V above PP has been found, but either additional construction or trigonometry is needed to find the actual distance. The mathematical procedure is given in chapter 4.

Q3-12. Choose one distance, such as $\overline{CV,T3}$, from figure 3-27. Form a right triangle with legs $\overline{CV,T3}$ and $\overline{CV,V}$ and with hypotenuse $\overline{T3,V3}$, bearing in mind that points V3 and V should be coincident. The sides $\overline{CV,T3}$ and $\overline{T3,V}$ can be measured from the diagram. The height of the viewer can then be measured as $\overline{CV,V}$. The procedure works with any of the $\overline{CV,T}$ distances combined with the matching $\overline{TV}$ distance. Apply this procedure to the triangles in figure 3-25 or figure 3-26, and check the viewer distance used in the construction of the figure.

If part of a space lattice (as shown in plate 1) must be drawn in oblique perspective, the method for constructing a box can be extended to constructing a cube. First, the cube must be oriented as desired in plan and elevation. Then, it should be drawn in perspective, along with its three VPs. Finally, each visible face of the cube in perspective serves as the first quadrilateral for constructing a grid in the corresponding plane, using earlier methods. (Using the mathematical tools discussed in chapter 4 will greatly assist in all stages of this work.)

Wide-angle and Telephoto Views

A variation used in constructing perspective views is wide-angle or telephoto construction. Normally the subject matter is viewed with a 90° angle between VPs, even if other VPs are needed for the view's construction. The angle between VPs can be increased to give a *wide-angle* view or decreased to give a *telephoto* (narrow-angle) view. The angles used here should not be confused with the values used with camera lenses; the principle, however, is the same. A wide-angle view causes the subject matter to occupy less space between the VPs, and the picture appears compressed because more space is crowded into it. The picture is also more distorted and conveys more sense of depth. A telephoto view causes the object to occupy more of the space between the VPs; once constructed, the object appears in the picture in expanded form. The telephoto view gives a "close-up" of the distant object, with less distortion and less apparent depth.

New VPs are found by placing the desired wide or narrow angle at V and drawing lines at that angle to pierce PP at W (wide angle) or T (telephoto). This can be done with an angular view, but if the wide or narrow angle is not symmetrically placed with respect to the normal view, a rotated PP will result. In figure 3-28, angles of view θ_W and θ_T are separately defined to left and right of the line of sight by means of subscripts "L" and "R." Only a view with 90° between VPs can be used to construct the perspective of the cube shown. Therefore, PP must be moved to a new position, PP′, such that the normal pierce points (L and R) on the old PP are aligned with new pierce points (WL and WR or TL and TR) on the new PP′. PP is thus shifted away

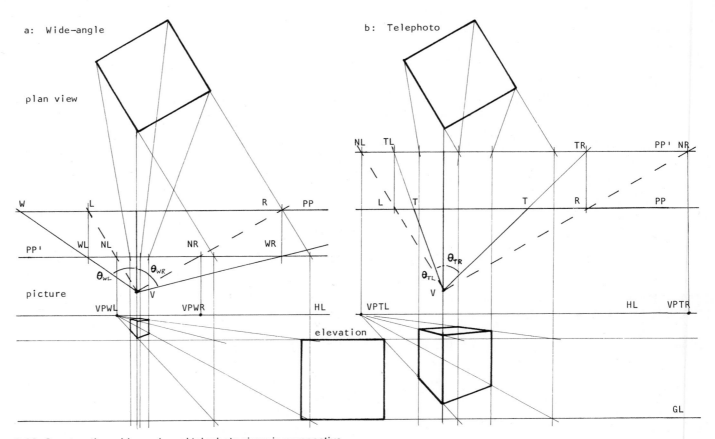

3-28. Constructing wide-angle and telephoto views in perspective

from the object for the wide angle (figure 3-28a) and toward the object for the telephoto view (figure 3-28b). It should be noted that neither V nor the *xy* axes are moved during the procedures.

Correct VPs are found by locating the pierce points for the normal 90° view in the new PP′. These are called NL and NR during the construction and are projected to locate VPWs or VPTs on HL. The necessary but perhaps unexpected effect is that the VPWs to be used for wide-angle construction lie close together so that more picture can be crowded into the frame, and depth becomes exaggerated. Conversely, the VPTs for telephoto construction are pulled far apart so that the object is seen larger and with a flatter field of view. The artist must note the counterintuitive result that a wide-angle view requires VPWs close together and a narrow-angle view requires VPTs far apart!

After PP′ and VPWs or VPTs are obtained (these are seen by the viewer at a normal 90° in plan view), the procedure for plotting points to construct the perspective is the same as that for normal angular perspective. Because PP′ is moved toward the object for a telephoto view, in some cases PP′ might pass through the object. The procedure can still be used, but object points in front of PP′ must be projected back to PP′ for location, and then brought forward for the picture. However, a telephoto view should be used for distant objects and this complication is unlikely to occur. For the wide-angle view, PP′ is in no danger of being brought forward past V. In chapter 6, the mathematical details of wide-angle and telephoto views are supplied, including a proof of the preceding graphic methods and a demonstration of the effect on grid shape. The graphic procedure can also be extended in the same way to oblique perspective. Since angles cannot be mixed, either the wide angle or the narrow angle must be used at both viewer locations. Wide-angle and telephoto views are rarely treated in other sources.[5]

Hidden Lines and Ambiguous Pictures

As was seen in figure 2-14, plotting all points for the perspective of a box produces an ambiguous picture. It is not easy to tell if point B is in front of or behind point H. For many such ambiguous pictures, the brain will "flip-flop" in its attempts to perceive a sensible form, and the picture will seem to shift dramatically from one orientation to another.[6] Points and lines that should be hidden have been suppressed—that is, not plotted or drawn—from the pictures in figures 3-25 and 3-26 to reduce confusion. The elevation in figure 3-26 does show all points, creating a confusing picture. All points are needed for construction, but point-labeling must be careful if error is to be avoided. Mistakenly reversing the two top points would have been easy and would have led the artist to arrive at the wrong di-

rections for VP1 and VP2, giving a totally different and wrong picture.

Q3-13. Exchange points C and B in figure 3-26 and find the new VPs. Note that CV is then wrongly required to be in a different place than V.

Following the guideline that bottom front points be plotted before top rear points allows line segments that should not be hidden to be drawn first. This guideline must be applied in accordance with the artist's determination of which parts of the object are closest to viewer, as shown in plan and elevation. Ambiguity is not as serious a problem in perspective views as it is in orthographic views, however. The perspective usually gives the viewer sufficient depth clues to perceive the figure properly. The artist may show all lines (including hidden ones) during practice construction, either for efficiency or for aid in construction. This type of drawing has been called "wire-frame" construction because the viewer can look through the figure and see edge lines as if they were wires.

Graphic procedures exist for determining what features are hidden by others. Ambiguities in any plan view can be resolved by plotting the corresponding front view. Two points on top of each other in plan appear separated in the front view, with one farther than the other from GP. The object's appearance in front view is a strong clue to its appearance in perspective.

Distant and Inaccessible Regions

If one VP is located off the paper, either more paper must be temporarily added, or one or more other VPs must be relied upon. (Chapter 10 discusses tools that help graphically; calculation of perspective bypasses the problem.) The subject matter may also possess features that allow the use of additional and closer auxiliary VPs—for example, the diagonals of a grid.

Considering the construction of a grid offers a way to solve the problems of inaccuracy that occur when working on pictorially distant regions. In figure 3-29, more grid is wanted in the right region near HL. Lines $\overline{CV,N}$ from CV to successively more distant N-marks on the measuring line GL grow too close together to distinguish. Their intersections with horizontal grid lines such as $\overline{MM}$ grow erratic. The erratically aligned "grid squares" that result are a clue to the partial solution. The eye notices the diagonals of the squares; therefore, if the diagonals are made straight, the perspective will be convincing when the detail is small and distant. In this case, VPR is the vanishing point for all diagonals, including those through the region of interest. All diagonals from VPR extend to the same marks on GL. If these diagonals are constructed, finding the "squares" in the distant region becomes easier. The

intersections of the diagonals with either the horizontal lines or the $\overline{CV,N}$ lines becomes more distinguishable, depending on the region, and the work can be continued.

Beyond these regions, useful procedures available to the artist include the following:

1. In line drawings, do not crowd many lines near HL. The darkening resulting from such lines would be contrary to the lightening effect desirable at the horizon.
2. Shade or blend the features of the subject matter together near HL, lightening the brightness and color saturation (see chapter 9).
3. Watch for features that converge toward VPs and show these standing out slightly from the "haze" near HL.
4. Nearby objects hide parts of the background. Yet features of hidden objects may extend into view. VPs and HL may lie behind objects. Use thin, light construction lines throughout the drawing to make locating partially hidden objects possible or to provide VPs for features on close-up objects.

In the perspective of an orderly pattern such as a grid, additional VPs appear, which may be helpful. These correspond to higher-order alignments of grid unit cells. For example, a set of squares may be seen as related to the neighboring squares that are one square farther back and two squares over. The effect is more obvious if the plane is considered to have vertical poles at each grid intersection. The poles line up in many special directions.

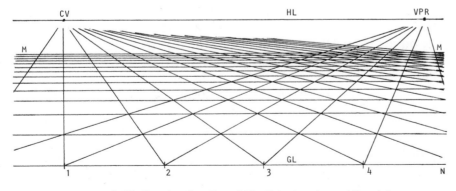

3-29. Constructing the grid in distant regions of the picture

Q3-14. On a grid in plan view, choose an origin and *x* and *y* axes. Mark the points with coordinates, noting that they line up. Find their VPs in perspective. What is special about the VP for coordinates (1,1), (2,2), (3,3), and so forth?

Notes

1. On geometric construction and general drawing practices, see F. E. Giesecke, et al., *Technical Drawing;* F. E. Giesecke, et al., *Engineering Graphics;* A. S. Levens and W. Chalk, *Graphics in Engineering Design;* R. D. Springer, et al., *Basic Graphics;* T. E. French and C. J. Vierck, *Engineering Drawing and Graphic Technology;* or George Beakley, *Introduction to Engineering Graphics.*

2. The shapes of circles, cylinders, and spheres as seen by the eye and on the picture plane are treated in David Yue, *Perspective Drawings by Programmable Calculator* and Robert W. Gill, *Creative Perspective.*

The shapes of spheres and cylinders as photographed with the inherently wide-angle, nondistorting pinhole camera—imitating rectilinear perspective exactly—are shown in M. H. Pirenne, *Vision and the Eye.*

3. Technical drawing methods for ellipses and spheres are given in Giesecke, *Technical Drawing* and *Engineering Graphics;* Levens, *Graphics;* Springer, *Basic Graphics;* French, *Engineering Drawing;* and Gill, *Creative Perspective.*

4. Altering the perspective of circular features is discussed in Gill, *Creative Perspective* and Yue, *Drawings by Calculator.*

5. Wide-angle and telephoto views are discussed briefly in Fred Dubery and John Willats, *Perspective and Other Drawing Systems.*

6. Visual ambiguity is treated in Richard Gregory, "Visual Illusions."

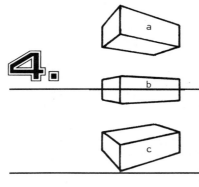

4. **Mathematical Assistance for Perspective**

This chapter presents an intermediate stage in the application of mathematics that allows the perspective view of a grid to be constructed in the picture plane in various ways to solve a variety of artistic problems. Assistance in locating vanishing points for any type of perspective is also given. Laborious graphic construction methods and their accompanying inaccuracy can be avoided for the most part.

Mathematical Terminology

Throughout this and later mathematical discussions, the mathematical symbolism used is as consistent and easy to remember as possible. Conventional symbolism is used where feasible. Most terms and concepts are explained on first use. A suitable alternative introduction to the symbolism and other terms and concepts used here can be

obtained from various elementary mathematics books.[1] Both the discussion here and the references cited are at a level intended to be accessible to any artist. Mathematical results are stated both verbally and in the form of equations. The reader should try to visualize each mathematical description so that it does not remain abstract. General results are given as numbered equations for later reference. Results consisting of several equations may be numbered as a set if the separate equations are never used alone.

Coordinates, their axes, and other "variables" are usually symbolized with lower-case letters from the latter part of the alphabet. In figures, axes are identified with the corresponding upper-case letter. Angles are identified with lower-case Greek letters. Constants and parameters, which are defined as needed, are usually symbolized with lower-case letters from the early part of the alphabet. Points, lines, and other features are identified with upper-case letters in accordance with the usage of chapters 2 and 3. A coordinate plane such as the xy plane is called *the xy* plane if it passes through the origin. A plane parallel to the xy plane is called *an xy* plane. The coordinates of a point are given in the form (x,y,z).

The Perspective of a Grid

The mathematical approach to perspective can begin with a study of the perspective view of a square grid (constructed graphically in chapter 3). Figure 4-1 shows the "normal position" for the grid with respect to picture plane and viewer. The two-dimensional coordinate grid forms the subject matter of the picture; it underlies any other objects to be drawn in perspective. The following constraints hold for the normal position:

1. V stands on the ground plane (GP) that contains the grid.
2. The vision axis (VA)—the line of sight as V looks straight ahead—pierces PP at the center of vision (CV).
3. The x axis of the grid is perpendicular to and beneath VA.
4. The y axis of the grid is parallel to and beneath VA.

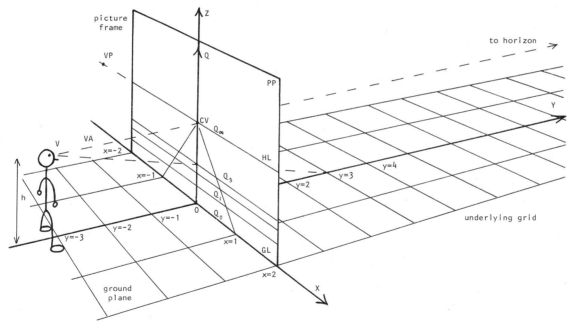

4-1. Perspective of a grid—normal position

5. The *xyz* reference point (O) is at the center of the bottom of the framed picture, in PP.
6. The *z* axis, if needed, is perpendicular to VA and to GP.
7. PP is perpendicular to VA and therefore is parallel to V's face.
8. GP intersects PP to form the ground line (GL) shown in the picture.
9. V sees the horizon line (HL) at eye level in the picture, about 1.5 m above GP and GL.
10. The bottom of the picture touches the ground, so measurements along the *x* axis appear true size at the bottom of the picture along GL.
11. The vanishing points (VPs) for the grid diagonals (if needed) are on HL, each the same distance from the center of vision (CV) as V is from PP.

The viewer looking through PP sees each grid point as a pierce point on PP. Since the viewer is about 1.5 m (5½ ft) tall, considering grid spacings of 1 m in figure 4-1 is convenient. A sample pierce point is shown for the grid point $(x,y) = (0,3)$, and a segment of the line $y = 3$ (parallel to the *x* axis) is displayed as seen on PP. A view of the grid is built on PP in this way, yielding the perspective. The views of lines parallel to the *y* axis can be found either by plotting the perspective of *x* values or by connecting known *x* values on GL to CV with lines. All lines parallel to the *y* axis pass through CV in perspective. The grid squares between $x = -1$ and $x = 1$, up to $y = 3$, are plotted in PP in figure 4-1. No use has been made of VPs here, but they would be necessary if the construction were to be carried out graphically.

In order for the perspective to be explored, locations of views of lines must be designated by a new coordinate system located in PP. The line plotted for grid location $y = n$ (*n* being an integer number of meters) can be called line Q_n in PP. Q is measured along a Q axis, which starts at O at the bottom center of the picture and rises vertically on PP. The sample line $y = 3$ is seen as line Q_3. The actual location of Q_3 on the Q axis is determined mathematically as a later result of this discussion.

For any line Q_n, the spacing between successive lines grows smaller as HL is approached. The spacing between any two adjacent lines can be calculated by subtracting the Q values. The spacing might be thought to decrease by a regular proportion—that is, by a constant ratio. This would require the spacing $(Q_3 - Q_2)$ to be the same fraction of the spacing $(Q_2 - Q_1)$ as $(Q_2 - Q_1)$ is of $(Q_1 - Q_0)$. Since $Q_0 = 0$, another way to present the issue is to postulate:

$$\frac{Q_2 - Q_1}{Q_1} = \frac{Q_3 - Q_2}{Q_2 - Q_1}.$$

As is shown later, no such simple ratio is appropriate for perspective. The first goal, however, is to calculate what does happen.

It should be clear from figure 4-1 that whatever law of spacing holds for Q values also holds for widths of plotted grid "squares." The widths of grid squares in perspective can be measured with a new P axis on PP. P is measured horizontally on PP, as in figure 4-2, with $P = 0$ at bottom center. True sizes occur on the P axis (GL). The P coordinates of grid squares decrease as Q approaches HL.

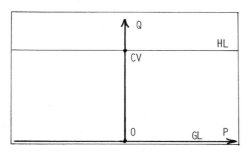

4-2. Picture coordinates

Convergence

The nature of convergence must be discussed further. Consider a number series such as {4, 6, 7, 7.5, 7.75, 7.875, 7.938, 7.969, 7.984, 7.995, . . .}, where ". . ." indicates that the series goes on without an end to the number of terms. The number 8 nevertheless appears to be the limiting value approached by these terms. The view of grid lines shows that their locations (Q coordinates) in figure 4-1 approach a limit called Q_∞, also known as the limit line (HL). In mathematical language, Q_n converges toward Q_∞ as $n \to \infty$. Similarly, the widths (in P coordinates) converge toward zero as CV is approached. Within the given spacing from Q_0 to Q_∞, many different rates of convergence are possible, and many different line spacings can be made to fit. Only some are correct for rectilinear perspective, and they depend on simple parameters such as the location of the viewer. An "incorrect" rate of convergence is explored later in the book.

The following procedure can be useful even to nontechnical artists. For example, if a landscape contains randomly distributed trees or rocks, the typical Q and P locations of the objects must change in the distance at the proper rate or the perspective will appear (and be) wrong. The average number of trees at each Q location must increase properly as HL is approach (figure 4-3). (The height of each tree must also decrease properly, as discussed later when z coordinates are represented as Q locations on PP.) As another example, in a large room viewed in perspective, the height of each furnishing must be in the proper relation to its location.

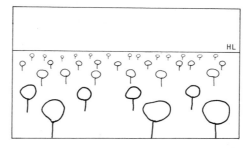

4-3. Proper convergence in a landscape in perspective

Calculating Lines that Converge

The procedure is simplest for the rectilinear grid in normal position. Increased flexibility is obtained by letting the symbol a stand for the grid spacing in place of units of measure such as the meter. The symbol a thus serves as the arbitrary unit of measure, and each grid square measures a by a on the ground plane. The height of the viewer is denoted by h; therefore, the distance in PP from Q_0 to Q_∞ is h, and Q_∞ equals h. An infinite number of units a seen in perspective must fit within distance h. In the picture, the apparent sizes of a decrease at a certain rate, converging toward zero.

Figure 4-4a shows a side view of the viewer looking at the grid through PP. The viewer is at distance d from PP. The viewer looks at the nth square of the grid, which is a distance na from PP. Its pierce point is seen at Q_n on PP. By simple proportion applied to the triangles shown, the height Q_n can be shown to have the same ratio to length na as the viewer's height h has to the distance $(d + na)$. The triangle with Q_n as side and na as base is *similar* to the triangle with h as side and $(d + na)$ as base. "Similar" is a geometric term meaning that the figures have the same shape and proportions.

Since calculation of Q_n is wanted, rearranging terms in the ratio $Q_n/na = h/(d + na)$, using simple algebraic laws, gives the expression:

$$Q_n = nh/(n + d/a) . \qquad (4.1)$$

The mathematically inclined will note in equation 4.1 that as $n \to \infty$, $Q_n \to h$. The meaning of any mathematical relation should be examined by testing its behavior in extreme cases. The expected result here is that looking toward the horizon yields a pierce point $Q_\infty = h$. (The limit was obtained for the equation by observing that as n becomes very large, d/a becomes negligible and can be ignored. Then Q_n simplifies to nh/n, or h. Recall that ∞ cannot be inserted into calculations. The "trick" is that the n values in the numerator and denominator cancel each other before ∞ is approached.)

Q4-1. Try to use equation 4.1 to prove the earlier assertion that the ratio of consecutive grid spacings is not constant. Start with $(Q_{n+1} - Q_n)/(Q_n - Q_{n-1})$ for the general case.

The horizontal spacing between grid lines seen in perspective can also be calculated. In figure 4-4b, a top view shows the grid spacing a located na from PP. In PP it is seen as size ΔP. Again the use of similar triangles shows that the ratio of ΔP to d is the same as the ratio of a to $(d + na)$. (If the triangles, shown as nonright, confuse the reader, the proof may be enlarged to include the distance from VA to the line segments used.) The result for the

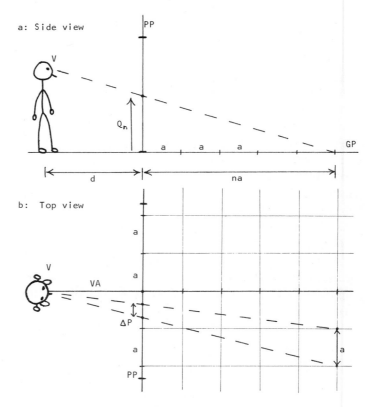

4-4. Locating picture coordinates for a grid

perspective view of the grid spacing is as follows:

$$\Delta P = d/(n + d/a) . \qquad (4.2)$$

For any given grid line $y = na$ in the distance (seen as Q_n in the picture), the regular spacing between grid lines crossing it can be calculated.

Before equations 4.1 and 4.2 can be used, the actual problem to be solved must be identified. If the artist knows where HL should fall and envisions an underlying grid of size a coming to the bottom of the picture, then h and a are known. A distance d must also be chosen (based on considerations covered later). All desired values of Q_n can then be calculated for the grid, using $n = 0$, $n = 1$, $n = 2$, and so on. As a general rule, calculations should be carried out to two more decimal places than can be measured with the ruler, to avoid errors. If the values of h, a, and d are in centimeters, then Q_n is in centimeters, too, and the locations can be marked on the paper. Otherwise, scaling is needed before sizes can be calculated to fit the desired paper. Spacings smaller than 1 mm are too small for hand instruments, so calculation can stop at whatever n yields a remainder $(Q_n - Q_{n-1})$ less than 1 mm.

Q4-2. What viewer distance d is needed to see the top of the first grid square (size $a = 3$) halfway up the picture from GL to HL? What is the expectable width at the top of this square?

A set of calculated grid lines is shown in figure 4-5 in centered form. The spacings in the P direction could be found for any line Q_n or could be drawn from P values marked on GL. The reader can check

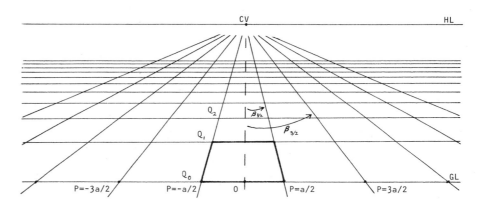

4-5. Calculated perspective for a centered grid ($d = 3a$, $d = 3h/2$)

the work, given that $d = 3a$ and $d = 3h/2$. VPs are not needed to draw this view. The angles shown are discussed later.

The behavior of the perspective view can be studied by examining the shape of the foremost grid square. The actual shape seen is a trapezoid. The term "grid square" can refer either to the real grid on the ground or to the figures seen in perspective, but the term "trapezoid" or "quadrilateral" more clearly refers to what is seen in perspective. The trapezoid at front center was symmetrically placed in figure 4-5, indicating that for this view, the grid was centered about the y axis. The x lines were shifted half a unit, giving P values along the bottom of $\pm a/2$, $\pm 3a/2$, and so on. The result is more pleasing.

The "height" of the front trapezoid is given by $Q_1 = h/(1 + d/a)$, from equation 4.1. The numerical ratio d/a tells much about the appearance of the grid and of any objects shown. If d/a is large, Q_1 is small, and many grid squares of gradually decreasing size occur. A large d/a ratio means that the viewer is far away relative to a. If d/a is small, then the viewer is close or a is big, and the apparent size of the grid squares diminishes rapidly after an initial large one.

In figure 4-5, the center trapezoid (and all others) may appear taller than they appear wide. This appearance can be disproved with a ruler, but the fact that the eye is fooled means that the perspective is faulty. The drawing has been done correctly, but the view is sufficiently extreme here to show distortion. In fact, the ratio d/a is 1 here, indicating that the viewer is rather close to the subject matter. A later section shows how to calculate better arrangements.

The width of the top or bottom of any quadrilateral representing a grid square is determined by lines drawn from P values at the bottom of the picture to CV. By calculating and drawing the shape of the first trapezoid, the artist can quickly find the effect of parameters h, d, and a. Conversely, from a proposed vantage point, the artist can set HL and draw the first trapezoid representing a desired grid square. With h, a, and Q_1 determined in this way, equation 4.1 can be used to calculate the value of parameter d needed to complete the drawing. Equation 4.1 can be rearranged to find any one desired quantity, given the others. For example, the value of n needed to produce a line at a chosen location Q_n can be found.

Equation 4.1 can also be used to subdivide any diagonal line into apparently equal parts in perspective. For the value of h, use the distance from any desired staring point on the line and measure along the line to its VP. The unit size a must be the true size of the first subdivision as it appears when projected to a front view (not in perspective). As an example, consider any axis of the cubic lattice shown in plate 1.

Other sources[2] have claimed that the correct expression for the rate at which spacing diminishes in perspective involves the "cross ratio" (the ratio of the ratios of the spacings of two consecutive sets of grid lines), and that the cross ratio yields a constant value for a given perspective. This is so if the spacings are used in the proper cross ratio, as defined by H. S. M. Coxeter. If equation 4.1 is used with the arbitrarily chosen consecutive squares ($n + 1$),th, n,th, and ($n - 1$) to form the ratio of ratios

$$\frac{(Q_{n+1} - Q_{n-1})/(Q_{n+1} - Q_{n-2})}{(Q_n - Q_{n-1})/(Q_n - Q_{n-2})} =$$

$$\frac{(Q_{n+1} - Q_{n-1})(Q_n - Q_{n-2})}{(Q_{n+1} - Q_{n-2})(Q_n - Q_{n-1})},$$

simple but tedious algebraic work gives the result 4/3(!). Therefore, the cross ratio does not depend on the particular grid squares chosen and is a constant. No other combination of ratios yields a result that does not depend on n (or on h, d, or a).

Equivalence of Graphic and Mathematical Methods—a Proof

For completeness and for further understanding, a simple but formal proof follows, showing that what is drawn by graphic methods gives the same pictorial result as what is calculated with equation 4.1.

Figure 4-6 shows VPR used with a diagonal to locate the horizontal grid lines seen in PP. The grid spacings along the bottom (GL) are connected to CV to complete the construction, giving points Q_1, Q_2, and so on. These points show where to draw the horizontal grid lines parallel to HL. An arbitrary Q_n is shown because the proof must be done for an arbitrary case. VPR is assumed to be distance d from CV, a simple result for parallel perspective that is independently proved in a later section. Distance d is also the distance of V from PP; Q_∞ is the same as h. The diagonal line from CV through Q_n cuts the bottom line at P_n, at distance na from point Q_0.

The proof is accomplished by examining similar triangles. The triangle with vertices CV, VPR, and Q_n has the same interior angles as the triangle with vertices Q_0, Q_n, and P_n. The reason is that two intersecting diagonal lines connecting parallel lines (here, HL and GL) form triangles whose corresponding angles are equal. Angle CV,VPR,Q_n, for example, is equal to $\angle Q_n,Q_0,P_n$. Therefore, the two triangles are similar and have corresponding sides in proportion. The ratio of the altitude to the base for each triangle is also the same. Because the upper triangle is inverted, this ratio can be written as:

$$\frac{\text{alt}}{\text{base}} = \frac{(h - Q_n)}{d} = \frac{Q_n}{na}.$$

Rearranging terms gives $Q_n = (nah)/(na + d)$, equivalent to equation 4.1. The proof is completed.

Calculating Convergent Angles

Parallel lines appear, in perspective, to converge toward a limit line (HL), and all appear to pass through a limit point (VP). In figure 4-5, the angular spacing between the lines shown converges to zero as HL is approached from either side. Sometimes it is most convenient to draw a set of properly converging lines in a region of a picture without going through the entire construction, or without calculating the entire view of a grid. In figure 4-7, the line at angle β_1 is measured from the vertical and constructed for a grid spacing of one unit of a. The line at β_2 arises from spacing $2a$ from the point O, and so forth. The arbitrary line at β_n passes through point P_n at grid location na. VP is any vanishing point and can always have a vertical line constructed through it.

Throughout this book, any angle designated by a Greek letter, such as β or θ, is defined in terms of the sides of a right triangle containing the angle. In figure 4-7, the right triangle defining β_n has vertices

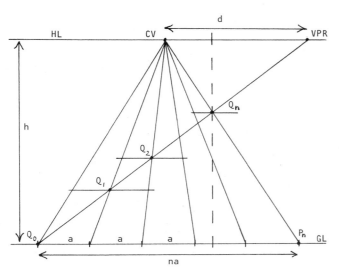

4-6. Proving equivalence of graphic and calculation methods

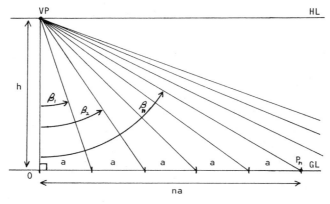

4-7. Convergent angles

at O, P_n, and VP. The sides that define β_n for this application are the sides opposite to and adjacent to the angle; they form a right angle. The ratio of these sides (na/h, in this case) is given the symbolic name "tan β_n." Certain ratios of sides of triangles for a given angle are called "trigonometric" functions of that angle. "Tan" is a symbolic abbreviation for "tangent," the full name of the function (not to be confused with the geometric meaning of the word). The mathematics used here goes no further with trigonometry than to define and explain the functions as they arise and to use them as a shorthand way to discuss the ratios of the sides of right triangles. Tables, calculators, and computer commands can be used to find the numerical relation between a "trig" function (a numerical ratio) and its angle (usually measured in degrees).

Finding β_n involves knowing the values of na and h, calculating their ratio (na/h) to obtain a value for tan β_n, and using a table or calculator to obtain β_n. The relation can be written as follows:

$$\tan \beta_n = (\text{opposite})/(\text{adjacent}) = na/h . \quad (4.3)$$

Angle β_n is usually the desired end result of the calculation. In the procedure for calculating convergent angles, equation 4.3 is used for as many values of n as desired, until the angles are too small to distinguish on a protractor (perhaps a quarter of a degree). The protractor is then used to lay out the angles, putting their vertices at VP and measuring from $\overline{O,VP}$.

In figure 4-5, some angles are indicated for the centered grid. The first angle has an opposite side of $a/2$, not a, and is labeled $\beta_{1/2}$. The next angles are $\beta_{3/2}, \ldots, \beta_{n/2}, \ldots,$ corresponding to grid spacings of $3a/2, \ldots, na/2, \ldots.$ These odd-numbered half values of n can be used in equations 4.1 and 4.3. Alternatively, unit sizes of $a/2$ may be used, and n may be given odd-numbered integral values.

Q4-3. Check the calculations of the angles in figure 4-5 by comparing measured values of β_n with values calculated by equation 4.3. Since angles are independent of the scale of the diagrams, it is sufficient to measure a, h, d, and other sizes with any ruler. Only the ratios appear in calculation, so the effect of the units drops out. ($\beta_{1/2}$ should turn out to be about 14°.)

Calculating the Layout

If a relatively undistorted but large view of an object such as a box or a square is wanted, the guideline is to limit the angular view to about 35°. This angle and the object's width can be used to determine how far away V should be. In figure 4-8, the front face of the box is assumed to touch PP and has width a. A symmetric location is used for estimation purposes, and the viewer sees the object head-on.

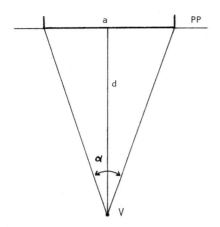

4-8. Maximum angular width for minimal distortion

The box appears to have angular width α as shown. Although an exact computation would require the use of $a/2$ and $\alpha/2$, only a small error is made using the approximation of α given by:

$$\tan \alpha \simeq a/d . \qquad (4.4)$$

The symbol "≃" signifies that the equality established is only approximate. The approximation gives a 3° error for $\alpha \simeq 35°$ and is adequate to roughly 50° ($\tan \alpha/2 = a/2d$ is the equation for exact work at large angles, rarely necessary).

The ratio d/a usefully describes the "character" of the perspective, since it appears in many relations used to calculate perspective. It has the convenient value 3/2 (1.5/1) for $\alpha \simeq 34°$, corresponding to $a/d = 0.666. \ldots$. A simple guideline is that d should be approximately 1.5 times greater than a for relatively undistorted perspective.

Q4-4. Calculate the angular size of the object when $d/a = 1$.

The same approximation can be used to estimate viewer distance d for the best view of an object of a given height. The viewer should be approximately 1.5 times farther away than the object is high. If this makes a thin object appear too far away and too narrow, the object can be shown closer and taller, since distortion is less apparent for tall, thin objects.

The appropriate location of the object's GP with respect to the viewer can also be calculated. If the object is very tall, with a height b much greater than h (expressed in symbols as $b>>h$), the viewer can be on the same GP. The object then lies distance $d = 3b/2$ away from the viewer; PP, however, must be much closer or the picture will be unwieldy in size (figure 4-9). If the picture is chosen to be b'

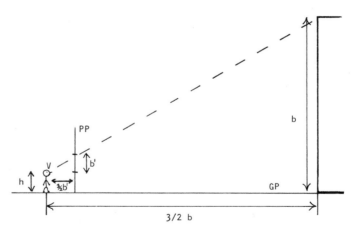

4-9. Tall object

high, then the viewer should stand distance $3b'/2$ from it in order to see it at a suitable angular size.

Suppose that the object is much smaller than the viewer. In this case, the viewing height above the floor (called h') must be distinguished from the height of the viewer's eye above the object's GP (called h). A small object has size $b<<h'$, but h should be about the same size as b to make it appear larger (figure 4-10). If placed far away, the object would appear too small; if set at the viewer's feet, only its top would be visible. It must be raised to eye level and brought close, as in figure 4-10. Its GP lies h below eye level. If the object is placed so that it nearly fills the picture, its picture is b' high and its bottom (GP) is approximately $(h' - h)$ above the floor. The object can also appear larger in the pic-

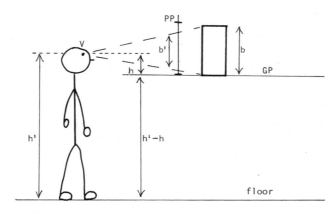

4-10. Small object

ture than it is in reality if it is placed in front of PP before the perspective is constructed, causing magnification. (Another way to achieve magnification is to scale the object size before construction.)

Q4-5. A tall tree is to fill a picture completely. HL is to be in the middle of the 0.8-m-tall picture. How far away from PP must the 1.5-m-tall viewer be? How far above the floor will the bottom of the picture be? Harder: How far from PP and from V is the

first bit of foreground visible in the picture? (Hints: Draw a side view and set up all distances known; assume the ground is level, with the viewer and tree on it, and set up a proportion.)

To show a 30-cm-wide object, d should be about 45 cm. For a parallel perspective, this would establish VPs each 45 cm from CV, making a rather wide picture if VPs are included. To obtain VPs closer together, d can be made smaller and the object scaled down in size. Another solution is to use angular perspective to bring one VP near the center and put the other beyond the frame. Still another solution is to lower the object's GP, giving a large h in the picture and showing the object from above.

If the object were 100 times bigger (30 m wide), the viewer would have to be 100 times farther away to see it with an approximate angular size of 35°. As in the case of the very tall object, the picture must be much closer, in proportion to how much of it is to be filled with the object. An object seen with an approximate width of 35° would fit into a frame about 40° to 50° wide. By means of a different interpretation for a in equation 4.4, the picture width can be found.

Q4-6. Find the picture width for V at a distance of 45 cm, if the angular size of the picture is to appear 40°.

As discussed in chapter 2, the viewer distance d determines the horizontal field of view. The same angular field size occurs vertically, sometimes giving a tall view that is undesirable. The situation is worse if the VPs, which are 90° apart, both appear within the picture frame. The actual viewer is likely to stand farther away than the close location planned, and vertical sizes in the picture may seem too big. Viewer height h also cannot be determined independently.

In summary, for realistic viewing the artist must plan the following:

- Where the actual viewer is to stand or sit
- What the sizes of the picture frame will be
- How high the picture is to hang above the floor
- Where HL is wanted in the picture
- What location the object's GP will have
- What size the principal object in the picture should be

Locating Vanishing Points

For parallel perspective or for symmetric angular perspective with a normal view (no wide-angle or telephoto view), the lines from V to VPL and VPR must form a right angle. Each VP is then seen (in plan view) 45° from the vision axis, as in figure 4-11. Therefore, because of the symmetry of the 45° triangles, the VPs are each distance d from CV, on HL (d always signifies the distance of V from PP). The tan function can be used to find VP locations. In figure 4-11, let θ be 45°, let d be the given adjacent side, and let d_L and d_R be opposite sides for the triangles. Using $\tan \theta = d_L/d$ and $\tan 45° = 1$, the results are:

$$d_L = d(\tan \theta) = d = d_R . \qquad (4.5)$$

By symmetry, the same result d is obtained for left and for right. This result is very useful. It gives the

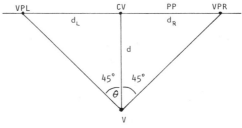

4-11. Symmetrical view for angular or parallel perspective

diagonal VPs for the underlying parallel grid, and it holds true for angular perspective in which the object has been rotated into a symmetric location by 45°.

For an arbitrary angular view, with the object rotated angle θ from PP as in figure 4-12, d_L and d_R are different. VPR is seen, in plan view, at angle θ from the vision axis, and VPL is seen at $90° - \theta$ since the total angle of view must remain 90°. Using

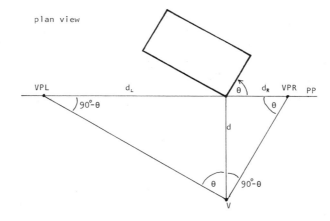

4-12. Angular perspective—asymmetrical view

the tan function with the two triangles shown, the results are as follows:

$$d_R = d \tan \theta$$

$$d_L = d/(\tan \theta) \,. \qquad (4.6)$$

A set of derived relationships, known as trigonometric identities, exist among "trig" functions;[3] from these, facts such as the one used above can be obtained: $\tan (90° - \theta) = 1/(\tan \theta)$.

Q4-7. Consider increasing θ to 90°. Here, $\tan \theta$ approaches ∞, and $1/\tan \theta$ must approach 0. Show that d_R and d_L become consistent with parallel perspective for a box parallel to PP. (Do not become confused with equation 4.5, which gives VPs only for a box with $\theta = 45°$.)

For subject matter lacking right angles but having parallel lines, the VPs should be placed in alignment with the object. A plan view is constructed showing the angular location of each VP with respect to VA. Then the location of each VP on HL can be calculated with the tan function for the appropriate angle. The angles can be measured in plan view or postulated to be whatever the artist wants. A general VP location d_V, for θ_V measured from VA, is given by:

$$d_V = d (\tan \theta_V) \,. \qquad (4.7)$$

If the object has a face tilted up or down, the preceding relations can be used to find the VPs for the resulting tilted plane, provided that the tilt is about the *x* axis only. Figure 4-13 shows, in side view, the grid plane tilted up ϕ from the ground

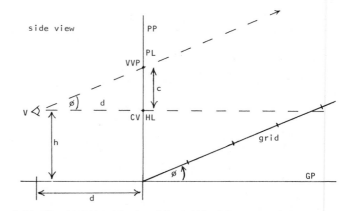

4-13. Tilted grid in side view (HL and PL shown as end views)

plane. (GP does not tilt unless PP is tilted.) The tilted plane carries with it its own horizon line (called a *plane line,* or PL), and PL appears displaced above HL in the picture. In PP, PL appears at distance *c* above HL. The viewer sees the grid slanted at angle ϕ above the horizontal. Distance *c* can be calculated by applying the tangent function to the triangle in figure 4-13:

$$c = d \tan \phi \,. \qquad (4.8)$$

Any VVPs corresponding to any sets of parallel lines in the tilted plane are located on PL, distance *c* above or below HL. Their new locations are above or below the original VPs. Examination of the elevation view for the subject matter immediately shows what angles of tilt apply to what lines, and the VVP for any line can be calculated. If the line tilts below HL, a negative angle is used with equation 4.8. A negative value of *c* is then obtained, which indicates measurement below HL. (The tangent of a negative angle is negative.)

The tangent function aids in the placement of lines aimed at VPs outside the picture frame. In figure 4-14, a line constructed through point P and aimed at VPL—located off the picture at a known distance d_L from CV—is desired. P is at coordinates (P,Q) in the picture. The right triangle with vertices P, VPL, and R is sketched so that the angle γ can be identified. Angle γ is also known as the slope angle for the line $\overline{P,VPL}$. P is distance $(-d_L + P)$ from the left side of the triangle and distance $(h - Q)$ below HL. (Careful attention to algebra shows that d_L must be taken as negative in this case, so $-d_L$ is a positive number.) The slope angle, γ, is then given by:

$$\tan \gamma = (h - Q)/(-d_L + P) . \qquad (4.9)$$

(In analytic geometry, $\tan \gamma$ itself is known as the slope, and strict attention to signs would have established that the slope shown is negative—a matter of no great concern here.)

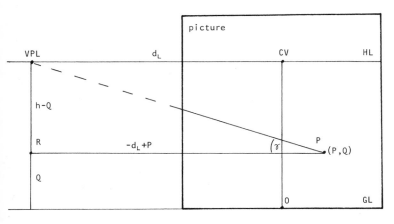

4-14. Constructing a line toward an off-picture vanishing point

Oblique Perspective—Theorems and Calculations

As discussed in chapter 3, an outline box can be rotated with two or three angles to a new orientation, creating three principal VPs. A VP exists for each of the three orthogonal sets of parallel edges forming the sides of a rectangular box. The objective of this section is to calculate the locations of these principal VPs.

Figure 4-15 shows a rectangular box in both plan and elevation views. Not only is the box rotated θ from PP (around the z axis) to form an angular view, it is also tilted upward by ϕ (around the x axis) so that the VPs for the top face are raised distance c above HL. These upper VPs are VP1 and VP2; their location can be found with equation 4.8, as before. In addition, VP3 has been created, for what previously had been the vertical sides of the box. Its location for now is directly below CV, and is given by:

$$f = d/\tan \phi . \qquad (4.10)$$

Distance f is the distance from VP3 to CV. The triangle used to calculate f contains the angle $(90° - \phi)$, hence the use of $1/\tan \phi$.

The horizontal coordinates of VP1 and VP2 are no longer d_L and d_R. The tilt ϕ has changed the apparent sizes of both the rotation angle θ and the 90° corner angle of the box, as seen in plan view. The box sides seem to be spread apart, causing VP1 and VP2 to be spread farther apart, to horizontal positions d_1 and d_2. Angle VP1,V,VP2 is no longer 90°.

For generality, the box is not assumed to be

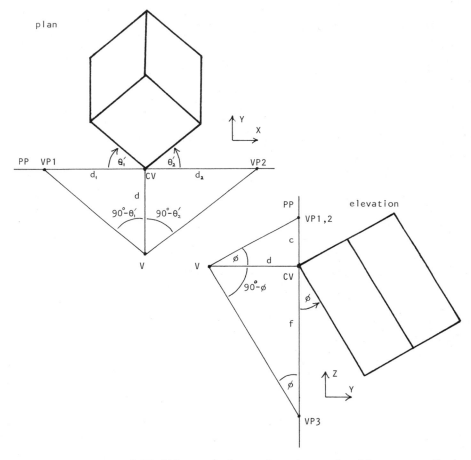

plan

PP VP1

θ'_1 θ'_2

d₁ CV d₂

d

$90°-\theta'_1$ $90°-\theta'_2$

VP2

Y
X

V

PP

VP1,2

c

d

ϕ

$90°-\phi$

CV

ϕ

f

ϕ

V

Z
Y

elevation

VP3

4-15. Object rotated around z and x axes for oblique perspective

onal to the top view. Angle θ is defined by $\tan \theta = b/a$. The untilted triangle, which has sides a and b, is seen as a line segment of length b in side view. When the triangle is tilted upward by ϕ, the projection of side b on PP shrinks to a smaller value b', and θ shrinks to θ'.

Another trigonometric function can be used to calculate the new value θ'. In the side view, where the figure appears as a new right triangle with a side b' and hypotenuse b, the ratio of the side adjacent to ϕ to the hypotenuse is defined as "cos ϕ." "Cos" is an abbreviation for "cosine." Tables and calculators give the numerical relation between ϕ and the cosine. Since $\cos \phi = b'/b$ in figure 4-16, b' can be calculated in terms of ϕ as $b' = b \cos \phi$.

In the top view of figure 4-16, the right triangle containing θ' is shown with a dashed side in its tilted position. Its hypotenuse b and side a remain unchanged, but side b appears to have shrunk to b', and consequently angle θ has shrunk to θ'. The new value of θ' is defined with the tangent function as

rectangular; instead, angles θ'_1 and θ'_2 are defined in figure 4-15 as the directions of the two top edges of the box. Angle θ'_1 can be calculated by considering what happens to the apparent size of an angle as the view of the angle is tilted. In figure 4-16, an arbitrary θ is shown as the angle in a right triangle in "true view" (a top view) and in side view orthog-

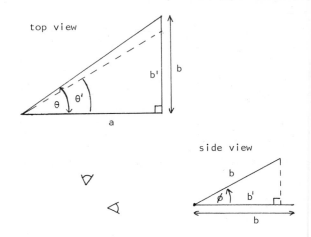

top view

b' b

θ θ'

a

side view

b

ϕ b'

b

4-16. Change in apparent size of an angle due to viewing at a slant

$\tan \theta' = b'/a$. Writing b' in terms of $b \cos \phi$ produces $\tan \theta' = (b \cos \phi)/a$, or:

$$\tan \theta' = \tan \theta \cos \phi . \qquad (4.11)$$

This generally useful result gives the apparent shrinkage of any angle that is viewed tilted, independent of any triangle used to define the angle.

Angles θ'_1 and θ'_2 of figure 4-15 can now be calculated with equation 4.11. Angle θ_1 was the angle between PP and the left box side when the box was untilted, and θ_2 was the angle between PP and the right side. If the top of the box happens to have a 90° corner, then $\theta_2 = (90° - \theta_1)$. Angle θ'_1 is given by $\tan \theta'_1 = \tan \theta_1 \cos \phi$; θ'_2 is found similarly. Distance d_1 can now be calculated from the top view of figure 4-16 because the viewer sees VP1 in the direction $(90° - \theta'_1)$; d_2 can be calculated similarly, using θ'_2. Using the tangent function, the results are:

$$d_1 = d/\tan \theta'_1$$

$$d_2 = d/\tan \theta'_2 . \qquad (4.12)$$

For two-rotation oblique perspective (θ around z and ϕ around x), the coordinates of the three VPs can be calculated by equations 4.8, 4.10, 4.11, and 4.12. The coordinates here and later are always measured horizontally and vertically from CV, in an orthogonal fashion, regardless of any rotations of the object. CV is placed as desired near the center of the planned picture (figure 4-17), and horizontal and vertical are defined by viewer orientation with respect to the picture. The horizontal coordinates of VP1 and VP2 are given by combining equations 4.11 and 4.12. VP3 remains directly below CV. The vertical coordinate c for VP1 and VP2 is given by

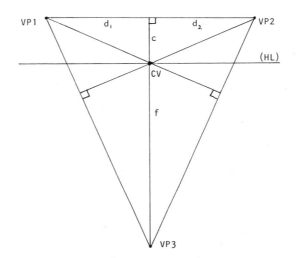

4-17. Locating the three vanishing points for an object rotated around the z and x axes

equation 4.8, and f for VP3 is given by equation 4.10. If the tilt of ϕ around the x axis is opposite to the direction described above, ϕ becomes negative. Then, c becomes negative and is measured below CV; f also becomes negative and is plotted above CV.

In the most general oblique perspective, three rotations occur. In addition to those treated above, a rotation ψ takes place around the y axis, a rotation rarely encountered. All three rotations have been defined as independent of one another. Figure 4-18 shows the object (which already has undergone two rotations) in front view rotated by $-\psi$. The front view appears in the same plane as the picture, but foreshortening and VPs do not occur. The effect of the additional rotation in the other views (plan and elevation) is to distort further the angles that appear in the views (refer to figure 3-26).

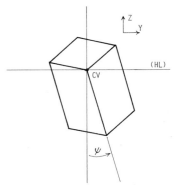

4-18. Front view of object rotated also around the y axis

In this example, ψ is negative because the rotation around the y axis is clockwise when the y axis is viewed from its positive end. A counterclockwise rotation is defined as positive when the viewer is looking along an axis from its positive end. In figure 4-18, ψ appears counterclockwise because the front view shown looks along the y axis from its negative end. The reader must look through the page from the other side to see a rotation angle in figure 4-18 correctly in front view.

The effect of ψ is to rotate the triangle of VPs to the picture orientation shown in figure 4-19. VP1 and VP2 no longer have the same vertical coordinates but new vertical coordinates with respect to CV called k_1 and k_2. Distances d_1 and d_2 are useful in the calculations that follow. All measurements and coordinates on the triangle have been generalized and systematized in their labeling so that each VP is on an equal footing with the others. The horizontal coordinates are called "j," and the vertical ones are called "k." All six coordinates for the three VPs must be newly calculated for three-rotation oblique perspective.

In figure 4-19 the VP triangle has been rotated counterclockwise by ψ. The rotation is around CV, which does not move. Point P is especially useful during the calculations. P is on a line that is distance $(c \cos \psi)$ above CV. The new VP1 can be found with the aid of a "sin" function. This last new trigonometric function "sin" (short for "sine") is defined as the ratio of the side opposite the angle to the hypotenuse of a right triangle. In figure 4-19, line segments o_1 and o_2 are opposite an angle of the same size as ψ in two different places. Therefore, $\sin \psi = o_1/d_1$, and $\sin \psi = o_2/d_2$.

VP1 lies at distance o_1 below P and therefore is distance $(c - o_1)$ above CV. Similarly, VP2 is dis-

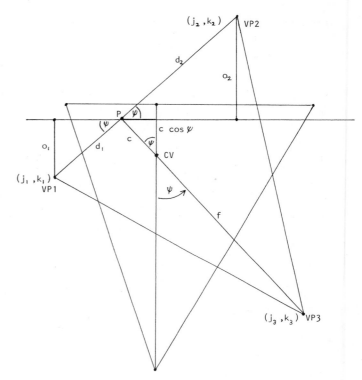

4-19. Locating the three vanishing points for oblique perspective after three independent rotations

tance $(c + o_2)$ above CV. ("Below" and "above" are measured vertically according to the usual convention.) When the cosine function is applied to the location of VP3, $k_3 = f \cos \psi$. After these intermediate calculations are combined, the full set of vertical coordinates for the VPs are:

$$k_1 = c \cos \psi - d_1 \sin \psi$$

$$k_2 = c \cos \psi + d_2 \sin \psi$$

$$k_3 = f \cos \psi .$$

(4.13)

The horizontal coordinates are found by applying the appropriate "trig" functions to the same triangles used for the k coordinates. P is observed to be distance $c \sin \psi$ to the left of the vertical line through CV. The results for the j coordinates are:

$$j_1 = d_1 \cos \psi + c \sin \psi$$

$$j_2 = d_2 \cos \psi - c \sin \psi$$

$$j_3 = f \sin \psi . \qquad (4.14)$$

These coordinates are to be laid out horizontally with respect to CV, as shown in figure 4-19.

Oblique perspective is of such complexity that calculating the locations of the VPs can be substantially easier than drawing the plan, elevation, and front views and constructing the VPs from them. For calculation, the rotation angles must be known. The accuracy of locating VPs is noticeably improved by the mathematical method because many errors tend to accumulate in the graphic method. The actual plotting of object points mathematically is covered in chapter 5.

Q4-8. Use d (measured from figure 3-26) and the rotation angles $\theta = 45°$, $\phi = 30°$, and $\psi = 15°$ (for the same figure) to calculate the location of the VPs (use equations 4.13 and 4.14). Compare the calculated positions with the actual measured positions on paper. The same exercise can be done with figure 3-25.

A cube, box, or lattice in oblique perspective can now be calculated fully and quickly. The orientation angles θ, ϕ, and ψ of the cube are used to find the three VPs and to establish rotated axes. Then each axis is marked off in depth, using equation 4.1

and the front projected view of the cube size a, in the manner discussed earlier. For a box with different sides a, b, and c, each side is so projected and used with its corresponding axis. Viewer distance d can be postulated, or it can be found with the procedure below. It should be clear at this point that three arbitrarily chosen VPs cannot be simply placed on paper to find a perspective of a cube or box that will appear correct. The full method must be followed to avoid a result such as the one shown in figure 2-1c.

If the positions of the three VPs are already known and placed on the picture, the location of CV can be found and the location d of the viewer from PP can be calculated. As shown in figure 4-20, CV is at the orthocenter of the VP triangle. An altitude perpendicular to each side is drawn to the opposite vertex, each passing through CV. For figure 4-20, coordinate locations have been suppressed, and a systematic labeling of measurements has been used so that $f = i_3$ and $c = c_3$. The altitudes divide each side into $d_1 + d_2$, $e_2 + e_3$, and $f_1 + f_3$. The g distances were found graphically to be the distances from the viewer to lines joining VPs in the picture (figure 3-27) and are contained within semicircles joining each pair of VPs on the VP triangle. Mathematically, a line segment so constructed is a geometric mean and has its length given by, for example, $g_3 = \sqrt{d_1 d_2}$ (and similarly for g_1 and g_2).

While it is trigonometrically feasible to calculate the location of CV, given the coordinates or separations of the three VPs, the number of steps required is excessive for the information obtained. The orthocenter of a triangle (such as CV) is surprisingly tedious to calculate from its sides. Two of the interior angles must first be found.

A useful general theorem about the VP triangle

In figure 4-21, a specially selected side view shows V looking at CV in PP, distance d away. Here, g_3 is the distance from V to point S, the end view of the line of sight containing VP1 and VP2. S is distance c_3 from CV. Distance g_3 can be calculated from $\sqrt{d_1 d_2}$. The latter and c_3 can be measured from the VP triangle. By applying the Pythagorean theorem to the right triangle of figure 4-21, d can be calculated:

$$d = \sqrt{g_3^2 - c_3^2} . \tag{4.16}$$

This process could be duplicated for another g with the other measurements shown, constructing an appropriate different side view and producing the same numerical result for d.

Q4-10. Measure the needed values on the VP triangle in figure 3-25 or figure 3-26, and use equation 4.16 to calculate d. Check how closely the calculated d approximates the d used to set up the figure by measuring the distance from CV to PP.

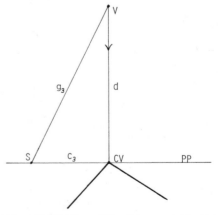

4-21. Calculating the viewer position from vanishing point information

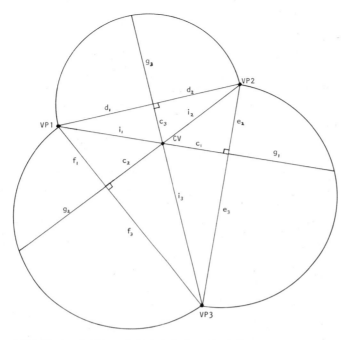

4-20. The vanishing point triangle for calculation

relating d, c, and f (temporarily returning to the use of c and f) can be derived. If CV and two VPs are known (for example, VP1 and VP2), the third (VP3) can be found. The line joining VP1 and VP2 is perpendicular distance $c = c_3$ from CV. The distance f of VP3 from CV can be found if equation 4.10 ($f = d/\tan \phi$) is recalled and $\tan \phi$ is eliminated with equation 4.8 ($\tan \phi = c/d$). The result obtained is:

$$f = d^2/c . \tag{4.15}$$

Q4-9. Measure data from the VP triangle in figure 3-26 and verify equation 4.15. (Results will not be exact because of measuring errors.)

Q4-11. Try to test the equations for the coordinates of VPs by using the limit as the rotations approach zero and seeing if the results proper for angular or parallel perspective are obtained. This involves knowing that $\sin 0 = 0$, $\cos 0 = 1$, and $\tan 0 = 0$. The opposite limits could be checked, too, using $\sin 90° = 1$, $\cos 90° = 0$, and $\tan 90° \rightarrow \infty$. All of these rotations should be visualized.

Special Application—Calculation for Cylindrical Geometry

An example of a simple underlying grid that is not flat, yet still is rectilinear, is one that is rolled onto a cylindrical surface. The ability to calculate convergent spacing is very useful in setting up such a grid. The graphic method for constructing the picture in figure 4-22 is very complex, whereas a few minutes of calculation and compass work produces a fantastic view.

The procedure begins with deciding the distance over which a series of centers of circles is to converge toward the center point. The circles are analogous to curvilinear Q coordinate lines, as if these had been wrapped around the inside of a pipe. The centers of the circles shown are on a straight line, but the procedure could be extended to curved loci (inside a curved length of pipe). The outer circle has center C_0 and radius R_0 and could be in PP. For a more interesting view, the viewer is offset from the cylindrical axis, and CV is placed above the center of the outer circle. The location of CV determines the viewer's apparent height inside the cylinder. CV is a one-point HL in this geometry. For a straight "pipe," C_0 is on a vertical line joining CV to the outer circle.

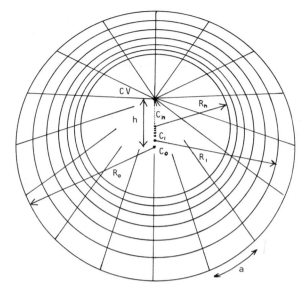

4-22. Cylindrical grid

The distance from C_0 to CV can be called h and must be divided into parts according to the rule for rectilinear perspective (equation 4.1). The center of the nth circle is given by $C_n = nh/(n + r)$, where r is a unitless parameter describing the character of the view. Parameter r describes how the cylindrical grid will look, ignoring the fact that it is curved. A very rapid convergence is given if $r = 1$; $r = 10$, the value used in figure 4-22, gives a leisurely convergence and puts the viewer a substantial distance from PP. In this case, d is ten times larger than the grid size. R_n, which must decrease as C_n increases toward CV, is found by using some multiple of the distance $(h - C_n)$. If CV is one third of the way from C_0 to the outer circle, as shown, then R_n is determined by the reciprocal factor, or three times $(h - C_n)$.

The series of circles is constructed with a compass, using each C_n as a center and using radius R_n for each C_n. The other dimension of the grid, analogous to P coordinates, is shown by the radial straight lines diverging from CV. These lines are determined by dividing the outer circle (or any circle) into an equal number of parts on its circumference (perhaps with a protractor) and connecting CV to the resulting points.

If the perspective is to appear as if a square grid had been wrapped around the cylinder, the arc between two radial lines along the outer circumference (which is shown true size) must be equal to a as used in the ratio $r = d/a$. The spacing between the outer circle and the next one is the foreshortening of a. Since the upper part of the cylinder is seen at a steeper angle than the lower part, the circular grid spacing varies around the circumference. Because the curved plane is "closed" or connected to itself in one dimension (the circumferential dimension), there is a limit on the grid unit size. The arc a must fit around the circumference an integral number of times. Once the size of R_0 is set, the circumference $2\pi R_0$ is set and the choices for a are limited to those that fit a certain number of times around the circumference.

Other Convergent Grids

Using a different way of calculating a grid that converges to HL illustrates what happens when a basic procedure of perspective is altered. The range of possibilities for the artist is expanded.

Many possible kinds of convergent series can be calculated. One of the simplest is the "geometric series" in which each succeeding term is a fixed proportion r less than the preceding term. Parameter r is between 0 and 1. A gradually decreasing series is obtained with r near 1; r near 0 causes a rapid decrease in size from term to term. Figure 4-23 shows a grid for which the spacing between lines decreases by $r = \frac{1}{2}$ at each step into the distance (up the Q axis).

If the spacing a for the underlying square grid is shown true size at the bottom of the picture (on the P axis), the spacing at Q_1 is ar or $a/2$. The spacing $Q_2 - Q_1$ is half of $a/2$ or $a/4$, the next is $a/8$, and so on for higher Q_n. The location of Q_n is found by adding all spacings from the bottom, giving $Q_n = a/2 + a/4 + a/8 + \ldots + a/2^n$. In abstract form, this sum can be written as $Q_n = ar + ar^2 + ar^3 + \ldots + ar^n$. A formula exists for finding the sum $Q_n = -a + a[(r^n - 1)/(r - 1)]$. For perspective, the number of spacings must be infinite (even if they become hard to see!) and must fit into the distance h between GP and HL. For $r<1$ it is permissible to let $n \to \infty$, and the sum becomes $Q_\infty = h = -a - a/(r - 1)$.

In figure 4-23, lines toward CV are constructed with equal spacing from GL and therefore are equally spaced along any line Q_n. A centered grid has been used. The resulting view shows that the diagonals (dashed) do not have normal VPs but instead curve and converge to CV. It is interesting that the eye still sees this bizarre view as a square grid, despite the strange way in which space has been marked out. This example shows the procedure for employing any suitable series (and its infinite sum) to create a new kind of space. Many series exist for which a formula for the sum is available. Many other series exist that do not converge (for example, one whose nth term is proportional to

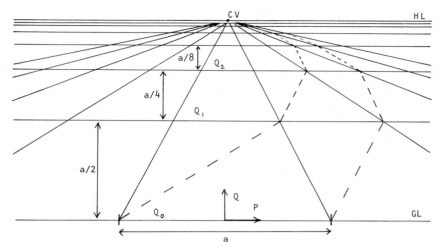

4-23. Nonperspective grid, based on a geometric series

$1/n$). If a nonconverging series is used, there is no proper place for HL and the results become stranger.

Q4-12. Check the calculations for figure 4-23 with a ruler to see that $h = a$ and $r = d/a = \frac{1}{2}$.

Q4-13. Suppose the nth grid spacing is $1/n^2$ times the size of a. The sum of such a series is $\pi^2 a/6$ as $n \to \infty$. Choose values and calculate and construct the grid in PP. Test the diagonals and their VPs to see if this is a "normal" rectilinear perspective of a square grid.

Q4-14. Try to find a grid spacing in which the diagonals are all parallel lines as seen in PP. Try to find a grid spacing in which the diagonals bend outward to left and right. This is very hard to find mathematically (some methods will be shown in chapter 7), but it should be fairly easy graphically. There should be no VPs.

The perspective of a square grid as found with equations 4.1 and 4.2 has line spacings that decrease in proportion to $1/n^2$ as n, the number of the grid line, gets large. Readers who attempt to calculate the exact general grid spacing will get more complex expressions, but the spacing's dependence on n^2 dominates its behavior. This is a fundamental characteristic of rectilinear perspective.

Notes

1. For a general introduction to mathematics, suitable for artists, see Jacobs, *Mathematics* or Frank Land, *The Language of Mathematics*.

2. The cross ratio is not defined clearly in Yue, *Drawings by Calculator*, but it is well defined (and predicts the perspective result) in H. S. M. Coxeter, *Non-Euclidean Geometry*.

3. Trigonometric relations and much more can be found in Richard Burington, *Handbook of Mathematical Tables and Formulas*.

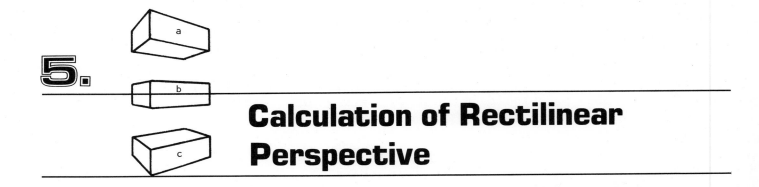

5.

Calculation of Rectilinear Perspective

The relatively simple calculation method given in this chapter may be used to find the perspective view of any object point by point. The method is very general, and no differentiation among types of perspective (such as the three required for graphic presentation) is necessary. Since vanishing points need not be used, the orientation of the object has no effect on the mathematics. Parallel, angular, or oblique perspective is produced—according to the orientation—from the same general calculation method for rectilinear perspective. Nevertheless, mathematical reorientation may be desirable before a perspective is calculated. Some methods for translating or rotating objects are therefore given. All the methods can be done by hand calculation, but some can be done much more efficiently on a calculator or computer.

Either the general mathematical theory that fol-

lows or point-by-point calculation may also be used to discover or prove how certain kinds of subject matter appear in perspective. Some applications and proofs—which substantiate methods and claims made in regard to graphic perspective—are given in this chapter, and some are given in the next chapter.

Coordinate Systems and Notation

The conventions used in this book for the mathematical symbolism of features, axes, variables, and constants are described at the beginning of chapter 4. Some alphabetical symbols must be used for different purposes in different sections and chapters, but the more basic a particular term, the less likely its symbol to be put to other uses.

The normal position already established (see

figure 4-1) can serve as the foundation for the theory and method that follows. The objects of interest are located by means of the *xyz* coordinate system, and the picture is to be viewed in a plane (PP, the *xz* plane) that is perpendicular to the ground plane (the *xy* plane). Object heights are measured with the *z* coordinate. Previously, it was convenient to locate objects in the picture plane by means of the PQ coordinate system, with the Q axis vertical at the center, and the P axis horizontal at the bottom of the picture. A way to calculate P and Q was provided only for locating grid lines a known spacing apart. Now any point in the picture can be found by calculation.

During the discussion of the calculations for setting up a perspective, positions in the picture were frequently more naturally located with respect to the center of vision (CV) on the horizon line (HL). Henceforth, new picture coordinates *p* and *q* will be defined as in figure 5-1. Coordinate *p* is identical to P, which it replaces; *p* still measures positive locations to the right from picture center. Coordinate *q* replaces Q and measures positive locations upward, starting from reference point O at CV. The axes continue to be labeled P and Q, as in figure 5-1, in accordance with the convention for diagrams. While much pictorial subject matter is expected to appear below HL, and thus to have negative *q* coordinates, the advantages of having *q* = 0 at HL generally outweigh this minor inconvenience. When points are being plotted, the artist usually references the ruler to HL; keeping locations accurate with respect to HL keeps small errors from being apparent near HL.

Three-dimensional *xyz* information about an object is combined mathematically to form a two-dimensional picture. The *x* information is compressed along the *p* axis, depending on the depth *y*. The *y* information is compressed along the *q* axis. The *z* information is also compressed along the *q* axis, depending on the depth *y*. The two mathematical expressions for calculating *p* and *q* from *x*, *y*, and *z* explicitly show this reduction of dimensions from three to two, as three coordinates for each object point are combined to create two coordinates to plot in the picture.

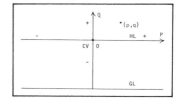

5-1. General picture plane coordinates

Plan and Elevation Data

Calculating perspective requires exact knowledge of certain *x*, *y*, and *z* coordinates of the subject matter. Previously, this information was available in drawn plan and elevation views. If these views are available, the artist need only assign appropriate coordinate axes to them at a suitable scale. A complete elevation or front view to accompany the complete plan view may be necessary. Since the *xyz* system cannot be moved about, the plan and elevation must be arranged on the fixed *xyz* coordinate system in accordance with the desired relation to viewer (V) and picture plane (PP).

Figure 5-2 shows a rectangular box oriented in the most general way possible with respect to PP. As shown in plan and elevation, it has undergone three independent rotations and its front corner is at an arbitrary position. An *xy* grid for the plan view and a *yz* grid for the elevation have been overlaid so that the coordinates for each useful point of the object can be measured.

Sometimes, instead of moving a plan about on a coordinate system, the artist might prefer to calculate the result of moving the object. The simplest

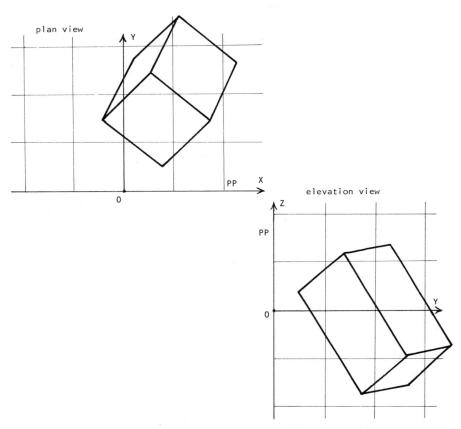

plan view

PP

elevation view

PP

5-2. Using coordinates in plan and elevation views

coordinates to form new coordinates (x',y',z'):

$$(x',y',z') = (x + u, y + v, z + w) . \quad (5.1)$$

For a translation of u just along the x axis, $v = 0$ and $w = 0$ would be used. For a translation in a negative direction, a negative value of u, v, or w would be used. The old coordinates (x,y,z) can be recovered from the new (x',y',z') by what is called the *inverse translation:*

$$(x,y,z) = (x' - u, y' - v, z' - w) . \quad (5.2)$$

Another way to interpret translation of points is to realize that a new coordinate system (x',y',z') is being created when an arbitrary point (x,y,z) is translated. It has an origin O′ located at coordinates $(-u, -v, -w)$. Figure 5-4 shows the translation in the xy plane when z coordinates are ignored. Point P, read at coordinates $(2,3)$ with respect to the x and y axes, would be read at $(2 + u, 3 + v)$ with respect

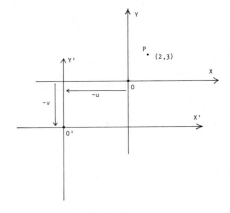

5-4. Translating the coordinate system

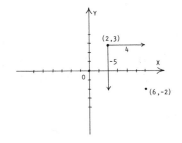

5-3. Translating coordinates

change is a *translation,* wherein the object is slid along one, two, or all three possible axes. These operations may be done one at a time. For example, moving the point $(x,y) = (2,3)$ by $+4$ units along the x axis would make its new location $(6,3)$. Including a translation of -5 units along the y axis would move the point to $(6, -2)$, as in figure 5-3. The general translation involves adding (u,v,w) to the old

to the x' and y' axes, where u and v are positive numbers.

The artist using mathematics, not necessarily on a computer, may occasionally find it necessary to use a coordinate system translation. Rotations applied to object points or to coordinate systems may be used more often. This complex subject is covered later. Another occasionally useful transformation is reversal of an axis (a 180° rotation in disguise). Reversal is done simply by applying a minus sign to the coordinate(s) of interest. Unless two axes are reversed, the resulting coordinate system does not observe the right-hand rule discussed in chapter 1.

If plan and elevation information is not obtained by measuring plan and elevation views, it must be supplied in a more abstract manner. For example, the pyramid shown in figure 1-5 can be supplied simply as a set of numbers, $\{(40,40,0),$ $(40,-40,0),$ $(-40,40,0),$ $(-40,-40,0),$ $(0,0,50)\}$. The perspective transformation can then be used to find a new set of numbers which, when plotted, gives the perspective view. Admittedly, providing sets of numbers for complex objects such as trees or people is very difficult. Usually, the best that can be done in these instances is to establish the coordinates of the outline boxes. Chapter 6 demonstrates that only two sets of numbers are needed to work with a difficult but common feature—the circle. A circle can be completely described by the coordinates of its center and the size of its radius (assuming it is conveniently located in a plane orthogonal to the xyz system). Some other objects are also simple to handle mathematically but complex to construct graphically.

Calculation of Picture Plane Coordinates

Prior to calculation of the picture, the viewing parameters (d and h) must be chosen in accordance with the methods given previously. Simple objects require only a few calculations. The mathematics in chapter 4 can be used to locate vanishing points as an aid to drawing. The picture is then constructed by plotting each point with respect to the pq coordinate system in PP.

In figure 5-5, the viewer is shown in plan and elevation looking at a general object point P with coordinates (x,y,z). V stands at $y = -d$, and V's eye is at height $z = h$. In plan view (figure 5-5a), the x and y coordinates are seen, and the pierce point of a light ray from P to V is shown at the general PP coordinate p. Coordinate p is measured from the center line of the picture as determined by CV. In elevation view (figure 5-5b), the y and z coordinates are seen, and the pierce point of the light ray is shown at general PP coordinate q. Positive q is measured upward from CV. (Since z is below HL for the situation shown, q has a negative value, and a minus sign must be used with q.)

Similar triangles are used to derive expressions for p and q. In the plan view, the triangle with sides d and p is similar to the one with sides $(d + y)$ and x. Therefore, $p/d = x/(d + y)$. Rearranging gives:

$$p = \frac{xd}{y + d}. \qquad (5.3)$$

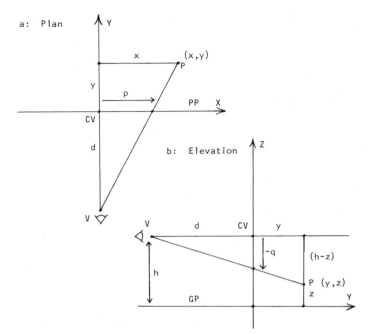

5-5. Calculating picture plane coordinates

In the elevation view, the triangle with sides d and $-q$ is similar to the one with sides $(d + y)$ and $(h - z)$. Therefore, $-q/d = (h - z)/(y + d)$. Rearranging gives:

$$q = \frac{(z - h)d}{y + d} . \tag{5.4}$$

These simple equations are the basis for much of the rest of this book. A surprising degree of complexity can result from attempts to apply them to other theoretical matters, but numerical calculations often remain easy. One simplification is also possible. For grids or other subject matter confined to the xy plane, $z = 0$ and equation 5.4 simplifies to $q = -hd/(y + d)$. As expected, q appears negative, since the values of h, d, and y are usually positive.

As a first example, the perspective of the angular view of the rectangle shown in figure 5-6 can be calculated. In the plan and elevation views, the coordinates are shown for the axes available in each view. The front edge of the rectangle is in PP and touches the origin O. The back edge in plan view has coordinates $(x,y) = (1,1)$, corresponding to a 45° rotation from PP. The z coordinates are not conveniently shown in plan but appear in elevation, where x coordinates are suppressed. Quantities d and h, called "parameters" because they are adjustable but fixed for one view, are assigned the values $d = 3$ and $h = 2$.

Perspective transformations can be calculated conveniently by forming a table of values for each of the four points of the rectangle:

Point	x	y	z	p	q
bottom front	0	0	0	0	-2
bottom rear	0	0	1	0	-1
top front	1	1	0	0.75	-1.5
top rear	1	1	1	0.75	-0.75

The picture is plotted in figure 5-6. As might be expected from the object's structure and orientation, the result is equivalent to angular perspective. A VPR is indicated and should be at $d \tan 45° = 3$.

Q5-1. Examine every operation performed to obtain figure 5-6, interpreting every plotted point. For example, where is GL, and does the bottom front point show GL correctly? Does the calculated VPR agree with where the bottom and top edges of the rectangle aim? What is the apparent length of the

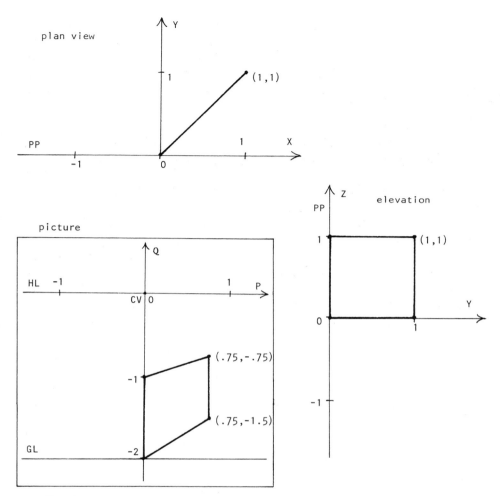

5-6. Calculating the perspective of a square

rear edge, and could it be predicted from the front edge (which appears true size)?

Q5-2. Choose another value of h, such as $h = 0.5$, and replot the picture. Compare the results with what is expected.

Q5-3. For practice with an object whose surfaces have a different orientation, apply equations 5.3 and 5.4 to the pyramid in figure 1-5. Calculate the perspective for suitable values of d and h (try 100 for both), and plot on paper in pq coordinates.

Q5-4. Check whether equation 5.4 is analogous to equation 4.1 for a grid in the xy plane. Note that $y = na$. Find a coordinate transformation to change q to Q, noting that the origin of Q is at $q = -h$.

Test your coordinate transformation at points $q = 0$ and $q = -h$.

General Properties of the Perspective Transformation

For more familiarization, the behavior of the perspective equations should be examined in some extreme cases. As x becomes large, p also becomes large, falling outside the picture frame. As y becomes large, both p and q approach zero. For q near zero, the picture point is near HL; for p near zero, it is near CV, as must happen with all points that have large y coordinates. As z becomes large, q becomes large, in either a positive or negative direction depending on the sign of z.

For $(x,y,z) = (0,0,0)$, equations 5.3 and 5.4 give $(p,q) = (0, -h)$. This is the point at bottom center of the picture, at the origin of the xyz system. (Because h is measured downward from HL, it is negative.) For $x = 0$, equation 5.3 gives $p = 0$, regardless of the values of y and z. For $y = 0$, all points are in PP and therefore are seen at their true locations. The case $z = 0$ has been discussed in the previous section.

The effect of the picture parameters d and h can also be examined. For very large values of d, the effect of adding y to d in the denominators of equations 5.3 and 5.4 becomes negligible and all ds cancel. The values of p and q, and therefore the sizes of objects in perspective, are no longer affected by viewer distance. An infinite d converts perspective into a parallel projection. (Of course, an observer must move closer to the picture to see it; standing a large distance away makes the picture appear very small.) For intermediate values of d

comparable in magnitude to y or to object size, the magnitude of d has a major effect on the character of the perspective. It has already been shown that d affects the locations of VPs, which in turn affect the perspective. For $d = 0$, V is at PP and the size of the picture becomes zero.

For large values of h, q values become large and negative, in accordance with the positions of V and HL far above GP. If the picture is made tall to contain CV, the object points appear near the bottom of the picture. For values of h near zero, HL is near GL; q coordinates lie near zero (near HL) and, therefore, near the picture bottom. An exception occurs if z is large; then object points appear far above HL.

Occasionally, the inverse perspective transformation is needed. Several forms can be used, depending on which variable (x, y, or z) is held constant so that the other two may be considered in a plane. If all three variables remain unfixed, no inverse transformation is possible. The equations for p and q cannot be combined to yield equations for x, y, and z, just as the two dimensions of the picture cannot somehow be converted into three dimensions.

For z fixed in an xy plane ($z = c$) some algebraic work yields the results:

$$x = p(c - h)/q ; \qquad (5.5)$$

$$y = -d + d(c - h)/q . \qquad (5.6)$$

It should be noticed that the left sides contain only the variables wanted after the inverse transformation—x and y. The right sides contain only the quantities p and q, which are to be eliminated by the transformation. If the artist already happens to have the mathematical description of what is to be in the picture, these equations can be used to find what the picture looks like in an xy plane (the plan view). The special case $z = 0$ gives the results for the commonly used xy plane.

Another inverse transformation can be found in the case when $y = b$. This transformation assumes that the subject matter is to be examined in an xz plane. In the case $y = 0$, the plane is identical with PP and therefore very useful. When $y = 0$ is used in equations 5.3 and 5.4, the simple results for x and z are found, after rearrangement, to be:

$$x = p$$
$$z = q + h .$$
(5.7)

The latter equation gives a translational transformation between q and z in PP that is used later.

In the case $x = a,$ specifying a yz plane that can be seen only from the side, equations 5.3 and 5.4 give:

$$z = (qa/p) + h$$
$$y = (ad/p) - d .$$
(5.8)

Inverse transformations are useful in chapter 6 for deriving perspective views of some specific objects.

Calculating the Edges of the Work

In setting up a picture for perspective by calculation, the artist does not want to waste time calculating p and q coordinates that fall outside the picture frame. As larger values of x and y are used, some

fall inside the picture and some outside. In the extreme distance, some very large values of x still plot inside the picture. The viewer looking through the picture frame sees the universe bounded by lines that pierce PP at P_L and P_R, as in figure 5-7 (a plan view). The sample point (x,y) at the right boundary is the last point to the right that V can see inside the picture frame.

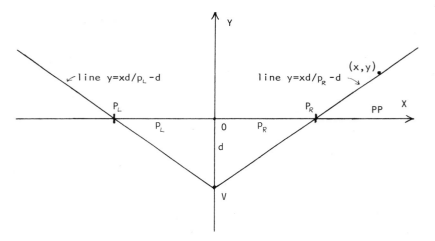

5-7. Boundary lines for calculating a picture

The general mathematical theory of straight lines is helpful for solving this and later problems. The equation from analytic geometry that describes a straight line in the xy plane is:

$$y = (\text{slope})x + (y \text{ intercept}) = mx + b .$$
(5.9)

The parameter m is the slope of the line, and b is where the line intercepts the y axis. The slope is given by the change in y divided by the change in x between any two points on the line (figure 5-8). Pa-

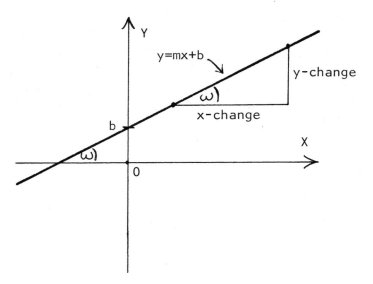

5-8. Equation for a straight line

rameter m also equals the tangent of the slope angle, ω, measured from the x axis to the line.

In figure 5-7 a boundary line intercepts the y axis at $y = -d$. Between points V and P_R, the y change is d and the x change is p_R. The equation for the slope is $m = d/p_R$. The equation for the boundary line is $y = (d/p_R)x - d$. It may be more convenient to find what x values do not plot outside the picture. The boundary line equation can be rearranged to give:

$$x_{max} = (y + d)p_R/d .\qquad(5.10)$$

For a given ''depth'' y and right picture boundary p_R, the largest value of x, called x_{max}, that will plot into the picture is given by equation 5.10. The left boundary is found by the same process, except that

its slope d/p_L is negative because p_L is negative. A similar process could be used to find the maximum values of z that will plot into the top and bottom of the picture frame.

Rotated Coordinate Systems and Views

The mathematical method of rotating views is helpful in performing complex work such as the calculation of oblique perspective. The rotations are applied to two dimensions at a time. For example, to get the tilted block used in figures 3-25 and 4-15, a first rotation of 45° was done around the z axis (in the xy plane) and then a second rotation of 30° was done around the x axis (in the yz plane). A third rotation of 15° around the y axis (in the xz plane) produces the orientation of the block shown in figure 3-26.

In figure 5-9, an object is first shown parallel to the xy axes in plan view. A coordinate system $(x'y')$ containing the object is rotated counterclockwise with angle θ to obtain the object's coordinates in rotated form. For calculating perspective, all coordinates must be measured in the usual xyz system. Therefore, the x' and y' coordinates of the rotated object must be transformed back to the xy system. The simplest procedure is to specify the (x',y') coordinates for each necessary point of the object, and then calculate each (x,y). The rotational transformation that produces unprimed coordinates from primed ones is:

$$x = x' \cos \theta - y' \sin \theta$$
$$y = x' \sin \theta + y' \cos \theta .\qquad(5.11)$$

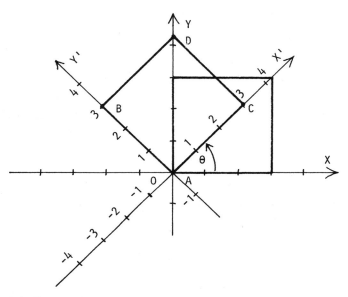

5-9. First rotational transformation—$\angle\theta$ about the z azis (plan view)

It must be emphasized that x and y should be interpreted as the coordinates of an object that happens to be in a rotated position.

Because it is occasionally needed, the inverse transformation is also given here, though it does not come up for some time:

$$x' = x \cos\theta + y \sin\theta$$
$$y' = -x \sin\theta + y \cos\theta . \qquad (5.12)$$

The rectangular box can still be used as an example. Its top is square with edges of 3 units, and its sides are 5 units long. Its (x',y') coordinates in top view are indicated in figure 5-9. For a counterclockwise rotation of $\theta = 45°$ around z, its (x,y) coordinates are shown in the following table.

Corner A: $x_A = 0 \cos 45 - 0 \sin 45 = 0$ $\qquad$ $y_A = 0 \sin 45 + 0 \cos 45 = 0$

Corner B: $x_B = 0 \cos 45 - 3 \sin 45 = -2.1$ $\qquad$ $y_B = 0 \sin 45 + 3 \cos 45 = 2.1$

Corner C: $x_C = 3 \cos 45 - 0 \sin 45 = 2.1$ $\qquad$ $y_C = 3 \sin 45 + 0 \cos 45 = 2.1$

Corner D: $x_D = 3 \cos 45 - 3 \sin 45 = 0$ $\qquad$ $y_D = 3 \sin 45 + 3 \cos 45 = 4.2$

For simplicity, only one-decimal-place accuracy is shown, but this low accuracy is not recommended for final work. The z coordinates for the top points are set at zero, putting the top face in GP. The z coordinates for the bottom points are all $z = -5$. The (x,y) coordinates of the bottom points E, F, G, and H are the same respectively as for A, B, C, and D, at this stage.

Next, a counterclockwise rotation of $\phi = 30°$ around the x axis is applied. The starting position is the θ-rotated box already calculated. Its coordinates are shown with respect to the $y'z'$ axes already rotated in figure 5-10 (elevation view). The viewer height is set to be the same as GP (the xy plane). The primed coordinates must be transformed to unprimed ones, in order for points in the xyz system, usable for a perspective transformation, to appear. A set of equations similar to equation 5.11 is used, except that y' is replaced with z' and x' with y'. This sequential change is known as an orderly "permutation" of the coordinates to generate a proper new equation. The new set is:

$$y = y' \cos\phi - z' \sin\phi$$
$$z = y' \sin\phi + z' \cos\phi . \qquad (5.13)$$

The previously calculated x coordinates are unchanged. The eight corners, after two rotations, are shown in the following table.

$x_A = 0$	$y_A = 0\cos 30 - 0\sin 30 = 0$	$z_A = 0\sin 30 + 0\cos 30 = 0$
$x_B = 2.1$	$y_B = 2.1\cos 30 - 0\sin 30 = 1.8$	$z_B = 2.1\sin 30 + 0\cos 30 = 1.1$
$x_C = 2.1$	$y_C = 2.1\cos 30 - 0\sin 30 = 1.8$	$z_C = 2.1\sin 30 + 0\cos 30 = 1.1$
$x_D = 0$	$y_D = 4.2\cos 30 - 0\sin 30 = 3.6$	$z_D = 4.2\sin 30 + 0\cos 30 = 2.1$
$x_E = 0$	$y_E = 0\cos 30 - (-5)\sin 30 = 2.5$	$z_E = 0\sin 30 + (-5)\cos 30 = -4.3$
$x_F = -2.1$	$y_F = 2.1\cos 30 - (-5)\sin 30 = 4.3$	$z_F = 2.1\sin 30 + (-5)\cos 30 = -3.3$
$x_G = 2.1$	$y_G = 2.1\cos 30 - (-5)\sin 30 = 4.3$	$z_G = 2.1\sin 30 + (-5)\cos 30 = -3.3$
$x_H = 0$	$y_H = 4.2\cos 30 - (-5)\sin 30 = 6.1$	$z_H = 4.2\sin 30 + (-5)\cos 30 = -2.2$

Q5-5. Apply the perspective transformation to these results and plot them. The correct result resembles figure 3-25, except that the scale is different and point A is not aligned with CV. With the sizes used above, $d = 7$ is compatible. The h should be zero because the xy plane (GP) passes through CV.

The third (and least-used) rotation can be illustrated by rotating the preceding object by $\psi = 15°$ counterclockwise around the y axis (figure 5-11—a front view). The counterclockwise rotation is determined as the viewer looks along the y axis from its positive end—the end with the arrow. This end is positive by definition. It appears reversed because in front view the y axis is seen from its negative end. Further permutation gives the primed-to-unprimed rotation as:

$$z = z' \cos \psi - x' \sin \psi$$
$$x = z' \sin \psi + x' \cos \psi. \qquad (5.14)$$

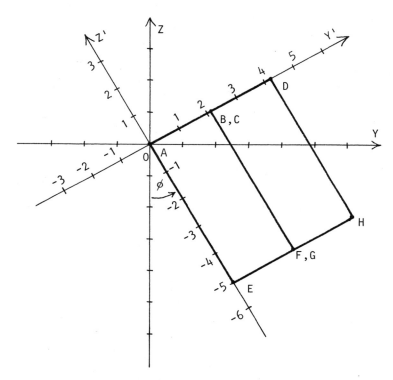

5-10. Second rotational transformation—∡φ about the *x* axis (elevation view)

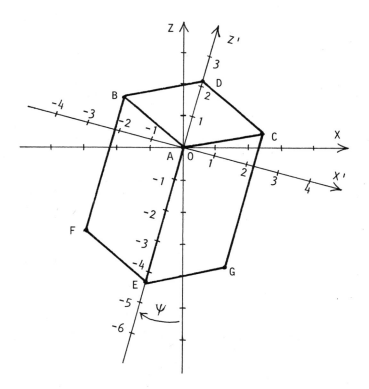

5-11. Third rotational transformation—∡ψ about the *y* axis (front view)

The y coordinates already found are not changed further by this rotation. The transformation shown in equation 5.14 is used to find the (x,y,z) coordinates of the object from its rotated position, with the results shown in the following table.

$x_A = 0 \sin 15 + 0 \cos 15 = 0$ $y_A = 0$ $z_A = 0 \cos 15 - 0 \sin 15 = 0$

$x_B = 1.1 \sin 15 + (-2.1) \cos 15 = -1.7$ $y_B = 1.8$ $z_B = 1.1 \cos 15 - (-2.1) \sin 15 = 1.6$

$x_C = 1.1 \sin 15 + 2.1 \cos 15 = 2.3$ $y_C = 1.8$ $z_C = 1.1 \cos 15 - 2.1 \sin 15 = 0.5$

$x_D = 2.1 \sin 15 + 0 \cos 15 = 0.5$ $y_D = 3.6$ $z_D = 2.1 \cos 15 - 0 \sin 15 = 2.0$

$x_E = -4.3 \sin 15 + 0 \cos 15 = -1.1$ $y_E = 2.5$ $z_E = -4.3 \cos 15 - 0 \sin 15 = -4.2$

$x_F = -3.3 \sin 15 + (-2.1) \cos 15 = -2.9$ $y_F = 4.3$ $z_F = -3.3 \cos 15 - (-2.1) \sin 15 = -2.6$

$x_G = -3.3 \sin 15 + 2.1 \cos 15 = 1.2$ $y_G = 4.3$ $z_G = -3.3 \cos 15 - 2.1 \sin 15 = -3.7$

$x_H = -2.2 \sin 15 + 0 \cos 15 = -0.6$ $y_H = 6.1$ $z_H = -2.2 \cos 15 - 0 \sin 15 = -2.1$

Q5-6. Calculate the perspective for these values, and plot them to find a view similar to figure 3-26— except that the tilt is the other way (figure 3-26 was for $\psi = -15°$) and the scale is different. The calculations for p and q are considerably faster than the calculations for rotations! Extend the sides of the object to locate the three VPs and see how these compare with the ones in figure 3-26. More precision in calculation and plotting is needed to get consistent locations for the VPs.

A computer program provided in the appendix allows calculation of the xyz coordinates and the PP coordinates for a rectangular box (or square or cube) in any orientation. It can be used to verify the preceding example.

Limit Points, Vanishing Points, and Oblique Perspective

That the three-rotation calculated perspective of a rectangular box plots to give an oblique perspective matching that produced by the graphic method constitutes a further proof of the equivalence of the general mathematical method to the graphic method. More work can now be done with the basic equations to offer practice in using slopes, limits, and the equations of lines.

Further confirmation of earlier results for oblique perspective can be obtained by directly using equations 5.3 and 5.4 to locate vanishing points. VP2 can serve as an example. For the two-rotation oblique perspective in figure 5-12, (p_2, q_2)

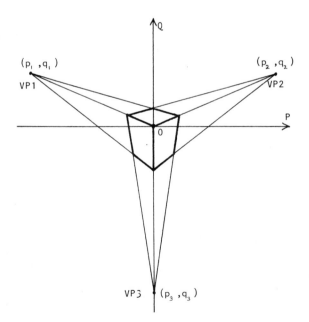

5-12. Calculating the coordinates of vanishing points

are the PP coordinates of VP2. By definition, VP2 is approached when x, y, and z approach infinity. The top and sides of the block shown are not parallel to any coordinate plane, such as the xy plane, and therefore all three coordinates are needed to describe its points. However, within any plane, x, y, and z approach infinity with certain relations to each other, depending on the slope of the plane.

In figure 4-15, which shows the plan and elevation for figure 5-12, the top front right edge of the box in plan view is at θ'_2 with the x axis. Angle θ'_2 is the direction in which V must look to see VP2 in PP. The line from CV in that direction has, by definition, a slope of $\tan \theta'_2$, since CV is at the origin of the xy system. Therefore, the relation of y and x for VP2 is $y/x = \tan \theta'_2$. Similarly, in the elevation view, the line along the same top edge of the block is at ϕ with the y axis. In elevation, where the yz coordinate system is seen, VP2 appears to be in the direction ϕ above CV. Again, the origin of the yz system is at CV. Therefore, the slope of the line gives $z/y = \tan \phi$.

At the limit when x, y, and z are very large, d is negligible, and equations 5.3 and 5.4 become, for the coordinates of VP2:

$$p_2 \rightarrow xd/y = d/\tan \theta'_2 ; \qquad (5.15)$$

$$q_2 \rightarrow zd/y = d \tan \phi . \qquad (5.16)$$

Comparison with equations 4.12 and 4.8, respectively, shows that p_2 may be identified with the earlier quantity d_2, and q_2 may be identified with c (or c_3). These were the coordinates of VP2 for the two-rotation oblique view discussed in chapter 4. Coordinates for VP1 can be found in the same way, except that care must be exercised regarding negative slopes.

Further examination of the elevation view in figure 4-15 allows ready determination of the location of VP3 in figure 5-12. The line along the front edge of the box is in the direction of VP3. This line is at ϕ with the z axis, or angle $(90° - \phi)$ with the y axis. Accordingly, the slope of the line is $-\tan$ $(90° - \phi)$, and z and y are related by $z/y = -\tan$ $(90° - \phi) = -1/\tan \phi$. In the plan view, the same line aims upward and therefore has slope $y/x \rightarrow \infty$. In the limit the results for p_3 and q_3, the VP3 coordinates, are that $p_3 \rightarrow 0$ and $q_3 \rightarrow zd/y = -d/\tan \phi$. The latter result is identical with that from equation 4.10 for f. VP3 must be below the p axis because q_3 is negative.

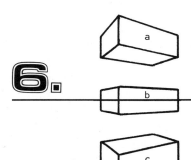

6.

Applications of the Perspective Transformation

Both theoretical and practical applications are given in this chapter for the equations that calculate perspective. Proofs, some lengthy, are included. The reader seeking mainly the results for perspective is encouraged to read the background material accompanying each topic and to note the summary of useful results given at the end of the chapter. The topics parallel those for graphic applications in chapter 3: lines; planes; angles; circles; spheres; grids; and special topics. The general theory for curves and curved surfaces is deferred until chapter 7. Completely general three-dimensional descriptions are given where feasible. Some of the mathematical theory for lines, planes, circles, and spheres is introduced for perspective applications and for general use.

Lines

The perspective transformation produces a non-Euclidean space in the picture plane; the transformation is not "linear." It is fortuitous that the perspective of a straight line is a straight line. A "nonlinear" transformation of coordinates often distorts shapes, changes angles and sizes, and may even bend or eliminate coordinate axes. The rectilinear perspective transformation does all of this (except bending axes); yet straight lines remain straight. The abstract but well-defined mathematical concept of "linearity" is beyond the scope of this book, but the reader's intuition may be aided by the knowledge that translation and rotation are linear transformations.

In this section, the general mathematical description of a straight line is introduced, and then the way equations 5.3 and 5.4 can be used to find the equation for any line in perspective is discussed. Unless stated otherwise, the lines discussed are assumed to be straight and indefinitely long. The equation for a straight line ($y = mx + b$), used earlier, describes the line in only two dimensions. The artist will encounter lines in almost every direction in three-dimensional space. Such a line can be described by the following set of equations from analytic geometry:[1]

$$\frac{x - x_1}{i} = \frac{y - y_1}{j} = \frac{z - z_1}{k} .$$ (6.1)

Here, (x_1, y_1, z_1) is any point specified numerically for the line. Constants $i, j,$ and k are constants that tell the direction of the line. Equation 6.1 actually consists of three separate equations. The left and middle terms are equal, the middle and right terms are equal, and the left and right terms are equal. The equation for the left and middle terms, for example, has the same form as was previously used for straight lines if it is rewritten $y = (j/i)x + [-(j/i)x_1 + y_1]$.

Only two of the three equations in equation 6.1 are independent; the third can easily be derived from the other two. Since a line can be thought of as the intersection of two planes, the two independent equations that describe the line also represent the two planes. (Equations for planes are discussed later.) Each equation defines an orthographic view of the line for the coordinate plane that contains the coordinates used in that equation. For example, the preceding equation describes the projection of the line as seen in an xy plane. Since two orthographic views are sufficient to describe any object, only two of the equations can be independent.

The constants $i, j,$ and k are known as the *direction numbers* for the line. Since only the ratio of one direction number to another matters in equation 6.1, these numbers are not restricted to specific values but can have any values, subject to the restriction that the ratios $i:j$ and $j:k$ are fixed for a particular line. One way to visualize the direction numbers is to think of the line as rising by i along the x direction, while rising by j along the y direction, while rising by k along the z direction. Each of the numbers $i, j,$ and k can be either positive or negative; a line can rise by i along the x direction while falling by j along the y direction. The situation is best visualized by holding three pencils for the axes and orienting a fourth pencil until it meets the stated requirements. Direction numbers may be fractions or integers.

As an example, the line $\overline{L}$ with equations $(x - 4)/1 = (y - 5)/2 = (z - 6)/3$ is shown in figure 6-1 in oblique view (not to be confused with oblique perspective). The projection of the line onto the xy plane (where $z = 0$) gives a line (called a "trace") in the xy plane, whose equation is found from the left and middle terms to be $y = 2x - 3$ (after rearranging). Projection to the yz plane (where $x = 0$) gives a line described by $(y - 5)/2 = (z - 6)/3$ or $z = 3y/2 - 3/2$. The projection (not shown) to the xz plane would give the line described by the first and last terms, since $y = 0$. The result is $z = 3x - 6$. The projection of the line onto the xz plane (which is identical to the picture plane) should not be confused with the perspective view of the line that also appears there. The perspective must take into account the "depth" y of various parts of the line; the perspective of the line lies closer to CV and has less slant than the orthographic view of it in the xz plane.

The direction numbers of the example line are $i = 1$, $j = 2$, and $k = 3$. They may also be written 1:2:3. The line recedes from the $+z$ axis at the greatest rate—three times the rate it recedes from the x axis. A point moving along the line recedes from the y axis by two units for every unit it moves along the x axis. Since only the ratios matter, the direction numbers could be written as 2:4:6 or 5:10:15, but it is preferable to use the simplest numbers that preserve the ratios. The direction numbers must not be confused with slopes. Slopes are calculated from them. For example, in the yz plane the projected line has slope $3/2 = 1.5$, calculated from the ratio k/j.

Q6-1. Check the calculations of each view of the line for figure 6-1, plot the intercept for each view, and examine each slope.

Q6-2. Plot all three orthographic views of the line for figure 6-1 (noting that neither orthographic nor perspective is shown), and check their consistency.

Q6-3. Noting that the line for figure 6-1 passes through the point (4,5,6), calculate another point it passes through. Then use the perspective transformation to calculate the perspective, plot it, and compare it with the xz plane projection. (Plotting two points is sufficient to determine a line.)

Q6-4. What direction numbers describe a line in the xz plane? (For this question, only the direction numbers that equal zero can be found explicitly; find them.) Differently phrased, the question is: in the

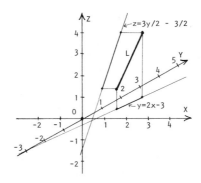

6-1. A straight line in three dimensions, with two projected traces (oblique view)

xz plane what direction number(s) should be zero, signifying that the line has no change in that direction?

Q6-5. Where is the line with direction numbers 0:0:1? Write its equation. (Note: a zero in a denominator renders that term useless.)

After the perspective transformation is done, a single equation relating p and q is desired, with x, y, and z eliminated. It should be of the form $[q =$ (slope) $p + (q$ intercept)] for a straight line. The process of substituting for x, y, and z in equation 6.1, using equations 5.3 and 5.4, and then solving for q as a function of p is quite tedious for such an apparently simple problem. The inverse transformation (equations 5.5 and 5.6) cannot be used because the problem is not restricted to $z = 0$. A shorter procedure is to observe in figure 6-2 that any line $\overline{PL}$ in the picture can be described in terms of its q intercept, q_0, and its slope, m'. The angle of slope is δ. If one point (p_1, q_1) is known, the slope can be found by using $m' = \tan \delta = (q_1 - q_0)/p_1$.

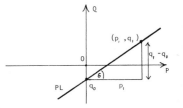

6-2. A straight line in picture coordinates

The general equation of the line has the form:

$$q = m'p + q_0 = \frac{p(q_1 - q_0) + q_0}{p_1}. \quad (6.2)$$

Since (p_1, q_1) is on the line, it can be transformed from another point known to be on the line, (x_1, y_1, z_1), using equations 5.3 and 5.4. The q intercept occurs when $p = x = 0$ (unless $y \rightarrow \infty$). Some point $(0, y_0, z_0)$ exists on the line which transforms (by equation 5.4) to the q intercept to give $q_0 = (z_0 - h)d/(y_0 + d)$. The y_0 and z_0 can be calculated from the two equations for the general line that involves x, noting that $x = 0$. The left and middle terms of equation 6.1 give $y = (-jx_1/i) + y_1 = y_0$. The left and right terms give $z = (-kx_1/i) + z_1 = z_0$. The q intercept becomes:

$$q_0 = \frac{[(-kx_1/i) + z_1 - h]d}{(-jx_1/i) + y_1 + d}. \quad (6.3)$$

The q intercept is zero if the line is parallel to the y axis, regardless of other values. The slope m' becomes:

$$m' = \tan \delta = \frac{q_1 - q_0}{p_1} =$$

$$\frac{-j(z_1 - h)/i + k(y_1 + d)/i}{(-jx_1/i) + y_1 + d}. \quad (6.4)$$

The equation for calculating the perspective of any line is rather complex if obtained by using equations 6.3 and 6.4 to find the values needed in equation 6.2. Calculation is simplified somewhat because the denominators for the slope and intercept are the same. Beyond that, however, no significant algebraic simplification can be achieved. The work of calculation almost obscures these equations' ability to convert six numbers (three direction numbers and a point with three coordinates) into a perspective view determined by the values of d and h. The artist is likely to find it faster to calculate the perspective of two points on the line directly, assuming two points are known. (One point must be known; the second could be found with equation 6.1.)

When equations 6.3 and 6.4 are used, the results may be taken directly to the picture. The q intercept is plotted; then, the slope m' is converted to δ by means of $\tan \delta = m'$; next, the angle is laid out with a protractor, measuring from a line parallel to the p axis (see figure 6-2).

Q6-6. Use equations 6.2, 6.3, and 6.4 to calculate the perspective of the line for figure 6-1 directly. Compare with the results of **Q6-3.**

Another terminology commonly used to describe line directions is shown in figure 6-3. A line $\overline{L}$, skewed in space with respect to an xyz system, has angles λ, μ, and ν with the x, y, and z axes,

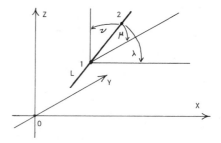

6-3. Direction cosines for a stright line

respectively. (The Greek letters λ, μ, and ν designate angles corresponding to the direction numbers.) Generally, none of these direction angles is measured in a plane parallel to a coordinate plane. The projection of a segment of the line onto each axis can be calculated with the cosine of the corresponding angle. The projections are shown in figure 6-4 for a line in the same direction but through the origin. The right angles of the projection triangles are also shown. A projecting line from P to an axis forms a right angle with that axis. The numbers cos λ, cos μ, and cos ν are called the *direction cosines* of the line. Their ratios are the same as the ratios of

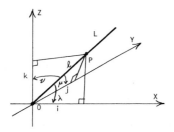

6-4. Direction numbers for a straight line

the direction numbers: cos λ:cos μ:cos ν = $i:j:k$. If needed, a direction number can be calculated by:

$$i = \cos λ$$

$$j = \cos μ$$

$$k = \cos ν . \qquad (6.5)$$

The resulting i, j, and k are shown in figure 6-4. However, a direction cosine cannot be calculated directly from a direction number. For example, i is usually greater than 1, and the cosine of an angle

is always less than or equal to 1. The additional constraint on the direction cosines is that $\cos^2 λ + \cos^2 μ + \cos^2 ν = 1$. As a result, cos λ, for example, can be found from $\cos λ = i/\sqrt{i^2 + j^2 + k^2}$.

For any line (not necessarily one through the origin), the direction cosines can be calculated by finding the projections of the line onto lines parallel to the axes, as in figure 6-3. If two points (x_1,y_1,z_1) and (x_2,y_2,z_2) define the line, the length l of the line segment between the two points is given by:

$$l = \sqrt{(x_2 - x_1)^2 + (y_2 - y_1)^2 + (z_2 - z_1)^2} . (6.6)$$

The direction cosines can then be found from:

$$\cos λ = (x_2 - x_1)/l$$

$$\cos μ = (y_2 - y_1)/l$$

$$\cos ν = (z_2 - z_1)/l . \qquad (6.7)$$

Q6-7. If the line is in a coordinate plane such as the *xy* plane, what happens to the direction cosines? Which one becomes 0, and what is the geometric and mathematical relation of the other two?

Q6-8. Calculate the direction cosines for the line plotted in figure 6-1.

Formulas giving the perspective transformation for quantities pertaining to lines—such as slopes, direction cosines, and line segment lengths—may be desirable. However, the resulting equations are usually very complex, and shorter procedures can be used for these and other cases. For example, a line segment can be viewed in perspective simply by transforming the coordinates of the two points defining the line segment. A slope cannot be directly transformed because it is measured with respect to a line that might be tilted in perspective. However, the slope of a line through two transformed points in PP can be defined as the transformed slope.

Planes and Lines

"Planes" in this book are flat and of infinite extent, unless stated otherwise. The equation of a plane can be expressed in two different ways:

$$Ax + By + Cz + D = 0 ; \qquad (6.8)$$

$$x/a + y/b + z/c = 1 . \qquad (6.9)$$

A little algebraic manipulation shows that these forms are equivalent if:

$$a = -D/A$$
$$b = -D/B$$
$$c = -D/C . \qquad (6.10)$$

The constants A, B, C, and D are called the "coefficients" in the equation. An infinite plane cannot be drawn and has no features. An octant of a plane —a portion delimited by coordinate axes—is shown in figure 6-5. The edges where the plane cuts through the coordinate planes form a triangular shape. The plane intercepts the axes at a, b, and c. The plane cuts PP (the xz plane) to form a line with slope $-c/a$ and intercept $z = c$, as shown in figure 6-5.

Q6-9. Show that the q intercept for the intersection of the plane and PP in figure 6-5 is $c - h$.

Unless intersections exist, it is meaningless to attempt the perspective transformation of a plane. The result would be spread throughout the picture and show no features. An artificial feature that can be assigned to a plane is its *normal*—a line perpendicular to the plane at some point. Working with the normal is useful in perspective.

Some special cases of planes and their equations are useful. Referring to figure 6-1 for a line and its projected views (traces), certain planes containing the line are normal (perpendicular) to the coordinate planes. (A plane can be normal to another plane since it can be thought of as being composed of normal lines.) As an example, the line $\overline{L}$ lies in a plane normal to the xy plane. Coordinate z can have any value in this plane, and the equation $(x - x_1)/i = (y - y_1)/j$ from equation 6.1 describes the plane. Each of the other equations for the line also describes a plane containing the line.

The coordinate planes can be described as $x = 0$ for the yz plane, $y = 0$ for the xz plane, and $z = 0$ for the xy plane. The $z = 0$ plane, for example, can have the equation $Ax + By = D$. This is an alternative form of an equation describing *any* line that can be in the plane, since D can have any value. An xy plane with the equation $z = c$, where c is any constant, is a plane parallel to *the xy* plane. Any point P in the $z = c$ plane is a normal distance c from the xy plane (figure 6-6).

Regardless of the tilt of the plane, D = 0 only if the plane goes through the origin. Then the intercepts are $a = b = c = 0$, and the plane does not intercept the axes anywhere else. Equations 6.9 and 6.10 are meaningless when D = 0. Figure 6-5 shows a case where D is not zero. The values of A, B, C, and D are not unique for a given plane. Although A, B, C, and D can be changed by any multiplier, the

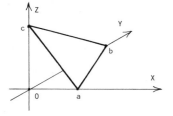

6-5. A plane—one octant intercepting coordinate axes

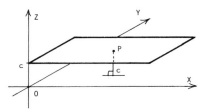

6-6. Portion of an *xy* plane

intercepts *a*, *b*, and *c* remain unchanged. Changing D does not change the plane. D can be calculated from D = *abc*.

A simple and useful result from analytic geometry is that the line normal to a plane has the direction numbers $1/a:1/b:1/c$ = A:B:C, in terms of either set of constants for the plane. The normal line has direction cosines given by:

$$\cos \lambda = \frac{A}{\sqrt{A^2 + B^2 + C^2}}$$

$$\cos \mu = \frac{B}{\sqrt{A^2 + B^2 + C^2}}$$

$$\cos \nu = \frac{C}{\sqrt{A^2 + B^2 + C^2}}. \qquad (6.11)$$

Conversely, if the normal to a plane is known, the equation for the plane can be found. Figure 6-7 shows a normal $\overline{N}$ to a portion of a plane; the normal can pass through the plane anywhere. Usually it is made to pass through some given point P (x_1, y_1, z_1), which then becomes the point used in the equations for the normal line. It makes no difference on which side of the plane the normal is considered; the normal is simply a line that passes through the plane.

The plane defining the top of the block in figure 5-11 can serve as an example. Directly finding the equation of the plane appears difficult. However, the normal is a line that could pass through any known point—for example, point A at CV—and its direction is known from the rotations used to turn and tilt the block. Originally, the normal was parallel to the *z* axis and had direction numbers 0:0:1. From the *z* axis, the direction of the line was changed by −30° from the *z* axis in the *yz* plane, giving direction numbers or cosines 0:cos (90° + 30°):cos (−30°) = 0:−0.5:0.866. (Within one plane the direction angles add to 90°; if −30° is used for one, then 90° − (−30°) must be used for the other.) Next, the direction was changed by 15° in the *xz* plane, giving cos (90° − 15°):−0.5:0.866 cos (15°) = 0.259:−0.5:0.837. (Changing an existing direction cosine is done by multiplication.) To specify the plane, A, B, and C must be in the same ratio. Since the plane passes through the origin, D = 0 is used. Since simple whole numbers are not possible in this example, the plane may be written as $0.259x − 0.5y + 0.837z = 0$.

Q6-10. Refer to the coordinates calculated for any of the points B, C, or D for the top of the block in figure 5-11, and check that the coordinates fit the equation of the plane to the accuracy available.

Q6-11. Noting that the bottom of the same block is described by a plane parallel to the top, and using the same direction of normal, write the equation for the plane. D is not zero, but a value can be found by substituting the coordinates for any bottom point.

The figure 5-11 example can now be resumed, with the equation of the top plane given. At this

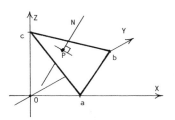

6-7. Finding the normal to a plane

stage, a normal such as the one that goes through point H $(-0.6, 6.1, -2.1)$—the back bottom point—can be found. As before, the direction numbers of the normal must be $0.259 : -0.5 : 0.837$. The equations of the line are $[x - (-0.6)/0.259] = (y - 6.1)/-0.5 = [z - (-2.1)]/0.837$.

Occasionally, the artist may find it useful to calculate the distance n from a given point to a plane whose equation is given. The distance (understood to be the perpendicular distance) is given by:

$$n = \frac{Ax_1 + By_1 + Cz_1 + D}{\sqrt{A^2 + B^2 + C^2}}. \qquad (6.12)$$

The point has coordinates (x_1, y_1, z_1), and the plane has the usual coefficients A, B, C, and D.

Angles and Planes

The procedure for identifying the angle between two planes is to find the normal to each plane that passes through a common chosen point (point P in figure 6-8). The angle η is defined as either the angle between the normals $\overline{N}$ and $\overline{N}'$ or the angle between two lines that meet the intersection at right angles as shown. This angle between two planes is also called the "dihedral" angle. The angle between two lines can then be found by the formula from analytic geometry:

$$\cos \eta = \cos \lambda_1 \cos \lambda_2 + \cos \mu_1 \cos \mu_2 + \cos \nu_1 \cos \nu_2. \qquad (6.13)$$

Subscripts 1 and 2 distinguish the direction cosines of the two lines.

If the equations of two planes are known, the

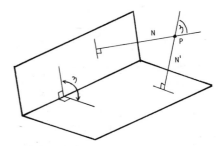

6-8. Angle between two planes

planes' perpendicularity ($\eta = 90°$) can be tested readily. The coefficients from the equations for planes 1 and 2 satisfy the condition $A_1A_2 + B_1B_2 + C_1C_2 = 0$. The case when $\eta = 0$ occurs when the two planes are parallel; this condition is also evidenced when each of the coefficients A_1, B_1, and C_1 is the same multiple of the corresponding coefficients A_2, B_2, and C_2.

The ability to find the angle between a given line and a plane is very useful. The normal $\overline{N}$ to the plane is first calculated or found at the point where the line $\overline{L}$ intersects the plane. In figure 6-9, σ is between $\overline{L}$ and a line $\overline{L}'$ constructed in the plane. Angle σ is given by $\sigma = 90° - \eta$. Angle η can be

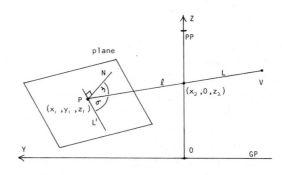

6-9. Viewing a plane at an angle

found using equation 6.13 for the line and the normal. The result ($\cos \eta$) is also equal to $\sin \sigma$.

Often the line of interest is the line $\overline{L}$ from the viewer to a point P in a plane (see figure 6-9). For example, if a circle is to be drawn at a tilt as seen by the viewer, the resulting ellipse can be chosen from a template if the angle of tilt (σ) is known. The equation of the line from V to P can be found if the PP coordinates $(x_2,0,z_2)$—where the line pierces PP—are calculated, using equations 5.3 and 5.4 and the equivalences $x_2 = p_2$ and $z_2 = q_2$ in PP. Because the coordinates of P are (x_1,y_1,z_1), the length l of the line segment can be calculated with equation 6.6. The direction cosines of the line can then be found with equation 6.7. Finally, the normal is found from the equation of the plane, and equation 6.13 is used to find σ, the desired result.

The angle at which a viewer sees a plane varies for different points on the plane. The procedure for finding the angle should be applied to a point central to the feature of interest in the plane. For example, if the feature is a circle, its center should be used. Unless the pierce point of the line from V to P is near CV, the angle as seen in plan or elevation cannot be assumed to be the true angle.

Q6-12. Refer to figure 3-16, and find the angle of tilt at which the viewer sees the middle circle. This requires understanding that the orientation of the circle appears in an elevation view. Assume the proper elevation view and draw it. Try the same procedure with the side circle.

Sometimes an angular size is provided or measured, and the perspective of that angular size is desired. This problem is different from the tilted angle problem of chapter 5, and it is much harder to solve. The completely general case results in an equation too complex to warrant reproducing here. Even the simplest case of an angle located in the xy plane becomes unnecessarily complex. Related quantities, such as slopes or line segment lengths, do not transform simply either. The general procedure is outlined here so that the artist can carry out the specific calculations numerically, step by step.

In figure 6-10a, η is between lines $\overline{L}_{12}$ and $\overline{L}_{13}$, which have point P_1 at (x_1,y_1,z_1) in common. The lines are intersecting but skewed in three dimensions with respect to the coordinating axes. The lines may each have a set of direction numbers or cosines already given, or they may be calculated by knowing another point on each line, P_2 (x_2,y_2,z_2) and P_3 (x_3,y_3,z_3). This amount of information is enough to calculate the perspective of the angle. First the PP equations of the two lines are calculated, using equations 6.2, 6.3, and 6.4 for each line. The resulting perspectives, called $\overline{PL}_{12}$ and $\overline{PL}_{13}$ (shown in figure 6-10b), intersect at (p_1,q_1), transformed from (x_1,y_1,z_1). These lines have slopes m_{12} and m_{13}. A trigonometric identity gives δ between two lines of known slopes as:

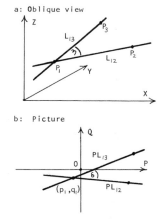

a: Oblique view

b: Picture

6-10. Transforming the angle between two lines to the picture plane

$$\tan \delta = \frac{m_{13} - m_{12}}{1 + m_{13}m_{12}}. \qquad (6.14)$$

Angle δ is measured from line $\overline{PL}_{12}$ to line $\overline{PL}_{13}$ in the picture.

Figure 6-11a offers an example of transformation for an angle in a simple plane. In figure 6-11a (in oblique view), η is in a vertical plane parallel to the yz plane. (If it were in the yz plane, the viewer would see the angle as 180° because V sees the yz

plane in edge view as the q axis.) Since point P_3 at (1,2,1) happens to be directly above point P_2 at (1,2,0) for the coordinates shown, and since η is in a triangle with sides of equal length (1 and 1), η has the value 45°. Line $\overline{L_{12}}$ has direction numbers 0:1:0 because it has no change in x or z. Line $\overline{L_{13}}$ has direction numbers 0:1:1. Direction cosines are not needed.

In order for equations 6.3 and 6.4 to be applied to two lines, their direction numbers must be distinguished by using, for example, i_2 for line $\overline{L_{12}}$ and i_3 for $\overline{L_{13}}$. In equation 6.3 for this example, the value of 0 for i_2 would seem to cause several undefined quantities. The proper procedure is to leave i_2 unspecified but large in denominators. Finite terms added to indefinitely large quantities such as j_2/i_2 are then negligible and "drop out." The slope for $\overline{PL_{12}}$ takes the form

$$m_{12} = \frac{\{[-1\,(0-2)/i_2] + [0\,(1+3)/i_2]\}}{[(-1/i_2) + 1 + 3]},$$

which becomes $m_{12} = -2$ when the zero and small terms are ignored and the i_2 terms are canceled. The intercept for $\overline{PL_{12}}$ is zero because $\overline{L_{12}}$ happens to be parallel to the y axis. The slope for $\overline{PL_{13}}$ has the form

$$m_{13} = \frac{\{[-1\,(0-2)/i_3] + [1\,(1+3)]\}}{[(-1/i_3) + 1 + 3]},$$

which reduces to $m_{13} = -6$. The intercept for $\overline{PL_{13}}$ has the form

$$\frac{\{[(-1/i_3) + 0 - 2]3\}}{[(-1/i_3) + 1 + 3]},$$

which reduces, after negligible terms are ignored and i_3 terms are canceled, to $m_3 = 3$.

The two lines are plotted in the picture in figure 6-11b, using only intercepts and slopes. Plotting a slope is done either by computing the q change for a chosen p change or by calculating the slope angle and using a protractor. Negative slopes are measured from the p axis on the left of the vertical. The perspective of $\overline{L_{12}}$ does not extend above HL.

Angle δ between $\overline{PL_{12}}$ and $\overline{PL_{13}}$ can also be found by applying equation 6.14 to the slopes: tan $\delta = [(-6) - (-2)]/[1 + (-6)(-2)] = -4/13$, or $\delta = -17.1°$.

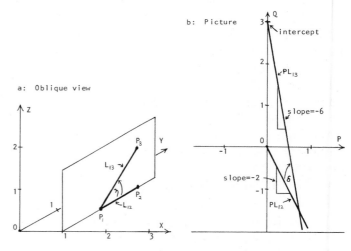

6-11. Example of the perspective transformation of the angle between two lines

Q6-13. Measure δ in figure 6-11b and compare with 17.1°.

Q6-14. Calculate and plot (p_1,q_1) on figure 6-11b from P_1. Observe whether it is at the intersection of lines $\overline{PL_{12}}$ and $\overline{PL_{13}}$, as expected. Measure the slopes for the lines between (p_1, q_1) and the two intercepts.

An alternative (and shorter) procedure for finding the perspective view of an angle is to define and plot three points for the two intersecting lines that define the angle, as shown in figure 6-10b. The angle is then shown between the two intersecting lines in the perspective view. However, if a computer program is to be used to compute angles in perspective, the procedure must include one of the preceding equations that defines the desired angle. The same remark applies to any of the other perspective calculations in this chapter.

The last application involving angles is to remind the reader of the power of the perspective transformation for finding VPs in difficult cases. Any line segment at any angle in plan, elevation, or picture has a VP, whether or not any other lines share that VP. Equations 5.3 and 5.4 can be used to plot two points to find the line segment in the picture, provided the coordinates for the two points are available in plan and elevation. Furthermore, the line segment's VP can be calculated and plotted, using the same equations. Careful track must be kept of signs in complex cases. The method can be extended to plot any irregular polygon, working segment by segment. If any regularity exists in the arrangement of features in the plan, elevation, or picture, VPs can be found for aligning these features.

In figure 6-12, for example, the plan and elevation of a line segment (direction $i{:}j{:}k$) are shown. The line has slope $\tan \phi = k/j$, in yz coordinates. Therefore, in the direction of the line, as z and y

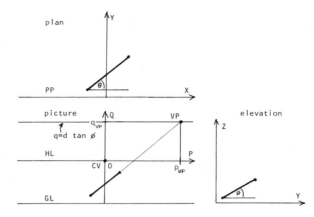

6-12. Finding the vanishing point for any line segment

become very large they approach the ratio $z/y = \tan \phi = k/j$. As seen in chapter 5, the calculation of the q coordinate for large values of z and y is $q_{VP} = d \tan \phi$. This gives the location q_{VP} of the VP above (or below) HL. The p coordinate can be found in a similar way using the slope of the line in plan view. For slope $\tan \theta = j/i$, in xy coordinates, the result for p is $p_{VP} = d/(\tan \theta)$ as y and x become very large. Alternatively, the line segment can be plotted in the picture and extended to the horizontal line $q = d \tan \phi$ to find the VP, as shown.

Circles and Ellipses

One method of finding the perspective of a circle is to calculate and plot it point by point. There exists a relatively simple equation for a circle which can be used for this process. The form in (x,y) coordinates for a circle in an xy plane is:

$$(x - x_0)^2 + (y - y_0)^2 = r^2 . \qquad (6.15)$$

The center is at (x_0, y_0), and the radius is r. The minus signs are used for a center located at positive coordinates. (Coordinates written in the form "x minus a number" represent a translation of coordinates to give a center not at the origin.) The perspective of the circle is an ellipse. All the remarks in chapter 3 on the properties and the drawing of ellipses hold true here. In particular, the center of the circle, if plotted, turns out not to be the center of the ellipse. Unless a large number of points are plotted, the ellipse may still be a challenge to draw carefully. Additional mathematical aid is given later in this section.

The equation for a circle in a plane parallel to the yz plane or the xz plane is obtained by making appropriate substitutions of those coordinates in equation 6.15. The equation for a circle in a plane not parallel to the coordinate planes must be found with rotations. Its form is too cumbersome to use in hand calculation. The hybrid graphic-mathematical approach would be to draw the circle in simple form, rotate it as wanted in plan and elevation, measure points on it, and calculate the perspective.

The first step in finding the perspective of a circle (or of any other curve that may be expressed mathematically) is to assume values of the x coordinate. Then equation 6.15 is used to compute the corresponding y coordinates on the circle, changing it to the form $y = \pm\sqrt{r^2 - (x - x_0)^2} + y_0$. A table such as the following should be created.

x	y	z	p	q

Values are filled in, calculated, and plotted. Point z is set equal to zero or to whatever value describes the xy plane the circle is in. If the circle is in the yz plane, x is set equal to the constant for that plane. At least eight regularly located points should be calculated for a small circle, and sixteen or more for a large one. In the circle's case, substantial symmetry can be exploited. For each positive and negative value of $(x - x_0)$ there is a positive and negative value for y on the circle. The actual number of calculations for y is halved. Experience is needed for judging what x coordinates to start with and how to interpret the results. A computer can be programmed to systematically fill out the table once x_0, y_0, r, d, and h are supplied. A sample program is given in the appendix which will calculate perspective coordinates for a circle in any specified orientation.

Q6-15. Start practice with a centered circle with $(x_0, y_0) = (0,0)$. Then attempt a circle such as $(x - 5)^2 + (y + 6)^2 = 9$, plotting it in perspective.

A complex mathematical analysis using the perspective transformation is presented in full below for the problem of locating and defining a circle in perspective. The power of the results obtained makes this application well worth the effort. The mathematical success in solving the problem also constitutes proof that the shape of a circle in perspective is an ellipse and not some other, similar curve.

The problem is succinctly stated as follows: given the coordinates of the center of a circle in plan or elevation and given its radius, what are the coordinates of the center of the ellipse that must be drawn to represent the circle in perspective, and what are its axes? The viewing parameters h and d must be included in the analysis, and the analysis must account for the fact that the center of the ellipse is different from the center of the circle. The method to be derived includes the specification of the eccentricity (tilt angle) and the orientation of the ellipse so that the correct ellipse for drawing may be selected from a set of templates.

The derivation is carried out first for a circle with radius r in an xy plane, as shown in figure 3-16. The plane is $z = c$. The equation for such a circle, centered at (x_0, y_0), is equation 6.15. The inverse perspective transformation equations 5.5 and 5.6 are used to convert the xy language to pq language. The fact that $z = c$ for all points is incorporated. The substitution into equation 6.15 gives:

$$[(c - h)p/q - x_0]^2 + [(c - h)d/q - d - y_0]^2 = r^2 .$$

After the binomial terms are squared, r^2 is moved to the left, and the whole equation is multiplied by q^2 to eliminate denominators. The various powers of p and q are then collected in an orderly fashion to give:

$$p^2[(c - h)^2] + pq[2x_0 (c - h)] +$$
$$q^2[x_0^2 + d^2 + y_0^2 + 2y_0d - r^2] +$$
$$q[(c - h) (-2d^2 - 2dy_0)] + d^2(c - h)^2 = 0 .$$

The appearance of the pq term is an indication that, when plotted, the ellipse will appear rotated; that is, its major axis will be at an angle with HL—an expected occurrence for an off-center circle position. Figure 6-13a shows the ellipse in PP.

It is algebraically convenient to redefine the constant terms appearing in brackets in the equation above so as to show the normal form of a rotated ellipse. Throughout this discussion, so many constants must be used that they cannot be kept distinct from other uses of the same symbols in other sections and chapters. The standard ellipse coefficients appear in the equation:

$$p^2A + pqB + q^2C + pD + qE + F = 0 . \quad (6.16)$$

D is already known to be zero for an xy circle because no p terms were present. The following equations can be used to calculate these coefficients from the original parameters:

$$\begin{aligned}
A &= (c - h)^2 \\
B &= 2x_0(c - h) \\
C &= x_0^2 + d^2 + y_0^2 + 2y_0d - r^2 \\
D &= 0 \\
E &= (c - h) (-2d^2 - 2y_0d) \\
F &= d^2(c - h)^2 . \quad (6.17)
\end{aligned}$$

The next step is to find the angle δ that is needed to rotate the ellipse into "normal" position so that its equation can be analyzed for its position and axes. A recognizable equation for an ellipse must have the form:

$$(p - p_0)^2/a^2 + (q - q_0)^2/b^2 = 1 . \quad (6.18)$$

The coordinates of the center of the ellipse, (p_0, q_0), must not be confused with a perspective transformation of the center of the circle (x_0, y_0). Constants a and b are the lengths of the semimajor and semiminor axes, respectively. To rotate the ellipse to this form, the rotational transformation (equation

Plate 1. A three-dimensional lattice in oblique perspective.

Plate 2. Sierpinski Sponge.
Approximating a fractal object
in oblique perspective.

Plate 3. Hexagonal Grid.
A rectilinear perspective
with vanishing points 60° apart.

Plate 4. Airy Function. A projected grid in telephoto perspective.

Plate 5. Hyperbolic Paraboloid. A projected grid in rectilinear perspective.

Plate 6. Symmetric Pattern of
Logarithmic Spirals.
A limit point without perspective.

Plate 7. Quarter Cylinder.
A curvilinear grid in rectilinear
perspective.

Plate 8. Sinusoidal Surface.
A curvilinear grid in perspective,
with varying reflection angle.

Plate 9. Cylindrical Perspective.

Plate 10. A Catenary and Its Shadow.
A photographic perspective.

5.11) is used in pq language. The expressions for p and q in terms of p' and q' are:

$$p = p' \cos \delta - q' \sin \delta$$

$$q = p' \sin \delta + q' \cos \delta . \qquad (6.19)$$

Figure 6-13b shows the primed coordinates aligned with the axes of the ellipse. When the two parts of equation 6-19 are substituted into equation 6.16 and the p' and q' terms are collected together, the result is:

$$p'^2[A \cos^2 \delta + B \sin \delta \cos \delta + C \sin^2 \delta] +$$
$$p'q'[-2A \cos \delta \sin \delta + B \cos^2 \delta - B \sin^2 \delta +$$
$$2C \sin \delta \cos \delta] + q'^2[A \sin^2 \delta - B \sin \delta \cos \delta +$$
$$C \cos^2 \delta] + p'[E \sin \delta] + q'[E \cos \delta] + F = 0 .$$

Some value of δ exists for which the coefficient in brackets for the $p'q'$ term is zero. Use of trigonometric identities gives:

$$\tan 2\delta = B/(A - C) . \qquad (6.20)$$

This expression gives the angle the major axis of the ellipse is rotated from the horizontal. The equivalencies in equation 6-17 must be used to calculate δ. Angle δ can be positive or negative; a counterclockwise rotation is positive. Figure 6-13b shows a negative δ.

Proceeding further, more simplification is obtained by defining the constants k and l in terms of the constants in equation 6-17 and in terms of δ:

$$k^2 = A \cos^2 \delta + B \sin \delta \cos \delta + C \sin^2 \delta$$

$$l^2 = A \sin^2 \delta - B \sin \delta \cos \delta + C \cos^2 \delta . \quad (6.21)$$

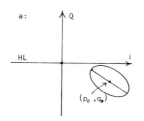

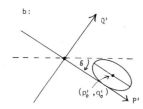

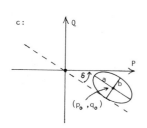

6-13. Calculating the perspective of a circle—an ellipse in the picture plane

The ellipse equation in rotated coordinates then has the form $p'^2k^2 + p'E \sin \delta + q'^2l^2 + q'E \cos \delta + F = 0$.

This equation can be brought into normal form by completing the squares in p' and q' to reveal the center coordinates. To complete the squares it is necessary to use:

$$p'_0 = -E (\sin \delta)/2k^2$$

$$q'_0 = -E (\cos \delta)/2l^2 . \qquad (6.22)$$

The result for the ellipse equation is $(p' - p'_0)^2/l^2 + (q' - q'_0)^2/k^2 = -F/k^2l^2 + p'^2_0/l^2 + q'^2_0/k^2$. The semimajor and semiminor axes are therefore given by:

$$a^2 = -F/k^2 + p'^2_0 + q'^2_0l^2/k^2 ; \qquad (6.23a)$$

$$b^2 = -F/l^2 + p'^2_0k^2/l^2 + q'^2_0 . \qquad (6.23b)$$

For convenience, these expressions are left in squared form until numerical calculations are completed; then roots can be taken to obtain the axes.

The center (p'_0, q'_0) of the ellipse happens to be expressed in rotated coordinates. The coordinates can be returned to normal picture plane coordinates by an inverse rotation to give:

$$p_0 = p'_0 \cos \delta - q'_0 \sin \delta$$

$$q_0 = p'_0 \sin \delta + q'_0 \cos \delta . \qquad (6.24)$$

Figure 6-13c shows (p_0, q_0) located with respect to pq axes, and the semimajor and semiminor axes a and b.

An *xy* circle in perspective has now been completely described mathematically. The calculations are somewhat laborious, but once they are mastered, the time required to locate and draw an ellipse with template is often substantially less than the time required for the graphic method. A summary of the procedure for application of the preceding equations is given at the end of this chapter. The computer artist can use the program for plotting a circle in perspective (see the appendix) for applications or to verify numerically the preceding derivation.

Q6-16. Make appropriate measurements in figure 3-16 for the circles and values of *d* and *h*. Calculate the parameters for the corresponding ellipses, draw the ellipses, and compare them with the ellipses in the figure.

The eccentricity and the foci of the ellipse can be calculated if necessary. Eccentricity *e* is given by:

$$e = \sqrt{1 - b^2/a^2} \,. \qquad (6.25)$$

The eccentricity is related to the angle of tilt σ at which the plane of a circle is viewed, by the relation:

$$e = \cos \sigma \,. \qquad (6.26)$$

Ellipse templates usually specify the shape of an ellipse in terms of this tilt angle. Both foci are located a distance $\sqrt{(a^2 - b^2)}$ from the center of the ellipse, along the major axis. The ratio of major axis to minor axis can be found from $a/b = 1/\sqrt{1 - e^2}$.

If the circle is located in a plane parallel to the *yz* plane, with center at (x_0, y_0, z_0), the plane has the equation $x = x_0$. A similar analysis could be done, and similar expressions for the location and shape of the ellipse could be obtained. If the circle is in an *xz* plane, it is seen as a circle in perspective. Its appearance in plan and elevation is an edge view—a line. There is no dependence of the circle on *y* coordinates, so its shape is not distorted to an ellipse. Methods given earlier for plotting the location of its center and one point on its circumference are sufficient to find and draw such a circle in perspective.

Some consideration of the case of the generally oriented circle will be given. As will be discussed in detail in the next chapter, a curve such as a circle with a general orientation in three dimensions must be described mathematically as the intersection of two surfaces. In this case, an indefinitely long cylinder of radius *r* (the radius of the circle) cut perpendicularly by a plane defines the general circle. The general case is solvable in principle, as guaranteed by the result in projective geometry that the perspective view of any circle must be an ellipse, but the details are so complex as to be impractical for the artist. Some simpler approaches will be outlined.

To aid the artist in keeping track of how the circle is to be oriented, the same rotation angles (θ, ϕ, and ψ) that were used for the rectangular box will be employed. Again, all rotations will be referred to a coordinate system aligned with the basic *xyz* system, to prevent the ambiguity of applying rotations to rotations. Figure 6-14a shows (in oblique view) the unrotated circle in an arbitrary location on an xy plane (the plane $z = z_0$). Its center is at (x_0, y_0, z_0) so that its equation (from equation 6.15) is $(x - x_0)^2 + (y - y_0)^2 = r^2$. Its center is taken as the location of an auxiliary primed coordinate system $(x'y'z')$, so that the circle has the simple equation $x'^2 + y'^2 = r^2$ in that system. This approach prevents the circle as a whole from being swung around the x axis, as, for example, when a rotation is done. The artist is interested only in re-orienting the circle with respect to its own center. Later, the circle is returned to the xyz system so that the perspective for a viewer in that system can be obtained.

Rotations of the circle around the z' axis, using angle θ, are superfluous, as no change is made in the circle. Let it be assumed that two other independent rotations might be wanted, ψ around the y' axis, and/or ϕ around the x' axis. These rotations around primed axes are equivalent to rotations around unprimed (xyz) axes if displacements of the circle center can be ignored or allowed for. It is better to ask the reader to visualize the rotations mentally rather than to attempt to provide the complex diagrams that would result.

Rotating ψ around the y axis is a reorientation likely to be needed by the artist. Figure 6-14b shows the circle in a plane tilted at angle ψ with respect to the xy plane. If ψ has the value 90°, the circle is rotated into a yz plane (the plane $x = x_0$). Rotation by ψ around a y axis (this can be any axis parallel to the y axis but not parallel to any other axis) gives the same reorientation in the xyz system as it does in the picture (pq system). However, the circle (an ellipse in the picture) will be displaced by the rotation unless it is done about the center of the ellipse in the picture plane.

Assuming that the circle in an xy plane has been drawn in perspective as an ellipse (as in figure 6-13a), the rotation ψ can now be applied to rotate this ellipse to represent a circle rotated by ψ. If a template is used to draw the ellipse, then the template need merely be rotated about the ellipse's center by angle ψ. If other means are used to draw the ellipse, it can then be copied from its original position as follows. First, temporarily rotate the pq axes through ψ about an axis through the ellipse center (p_0, q_0) to a new position, as shown in figure 6-14c. The ellipse assumes its new position. Next, restore the pq axes by rotating them back through angle ψ about the same axis, as shown in figure 6-14d. The ellipse has its new correct position with respect to the original pq axes.

If a circle is to be tilted by angle ϕ around the x axis, this is equivalent to a rotation of the picture plane around the q axis. However, the angle is not the same, and a complex displacement of the circle relative to PP occurs also, resulting in an incorrect new view of the circle. Figure 6-14e shows that the rotation of the circle does result in an increase (or decrease) in the size of the ellipse in the picture. The only size change occurs in the q direction—the width in the p direction is unchanged. The original height of the ellipse is $\Delta q = q_2 - q_1$. It is readily calculated from the radius and center of the circle to be:

$$\Delta q = \frac{-2rd(z_0 - h)}{y_0^2 + 2y_0 d + d^2 - r^2}. \qquad (6.27)$$

The circle is originally in the "flat" position, as shown in figure 6-14a, and in edge view, as shown in figure 6-14f. When it is rotated by ϕ around its

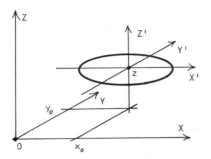

a: Unrotated circle, oblique view

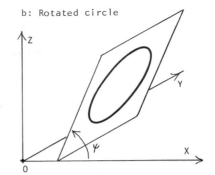

b: Rotated circle

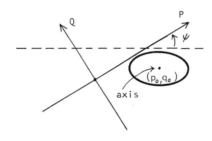

c: Rotated picture plane
   (and ellipse)

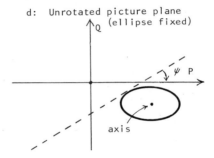

d: Unrotated picture plane
   (ellipse fixed)

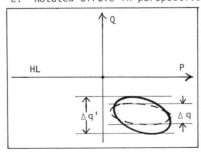

e: Rotated circle in perspective

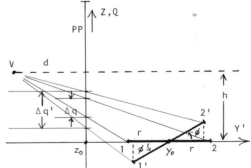

f: Rotated circle, side view

6-14. Calculating the perspective of an arbitrarily oriented circle

117

center (around its x' axis) to position $1'2'$, figure 6-14f shows it to have a new height of $\Delta q'$ in the picture plane. This is readily calculated with the perspective transformation to give the following equation:

$$\Delta q' = d \, \frac{2r \sin \phi \, (y_0 + d) - 2r \cos \phi \, (z_0 - h)}{y_0^2 + 2y_0 d + d^2 - r^2 \cos^2 \phi} \, .$$

$$(6.28)$$

It should be noted that equation 6.28 reduces to equation 6.27 when ϕ is zero. Neither equation is limited to circles; both can be applied to any object which is symmetrical about its x' axis, having size $2r$.

Another way to carry out rotations of a circle for its perspective is to work numerically. First, calculate a table of points (x, y, z_0) describing the circle in its original plane, as before. Then, these points should be calculated in the primed system, using the translation:

$$x' = x - x_0$$

$$y' = y - y_0$$

$$z' = z - z_0 \, .$$

$$(6.29)$$

Next, the points should be relabeled as double-primed, representing a circle about to be rotated back to the $x'y'z'$ system. The transformation that rotates it by ϕ about the x' axis is structured after equation 5.13, as follows:

$$y' = y'' \cos \phi - z'' \sin \phi$$

$$z' = y'' \sin \phi + z'' \cos \phi$$

$$x' = x'' \, .$$

$$(6.30)$$

If another rotation by ψ is needed, the resulting points are again relabeled as double-primed to represent a circle about to be rotated back to the $x'y'z'$ system. The transformation that rotates the circle by ψ about the y' axis is structured after equation 5.14, as follows:

$$z' = z'' \cos \psi - x'' \sin \psi$$

$$x' = z'' \sin \psi + x'' \cos \psi$$

$$y' = y'' \, .$$

$$(6.31)$$

After the rotations are completed, the table of points is translated back to the xyz system by using the reverse of the transformation in equation 6.29:

$$x = x' + x_0$$

$$y = y' + y_0$$

$$z = z' + z_0 \, .$$

Finally, the perspective is calculated point-by-point, using the perspective transformation in equations 5.3 and 5.4. The (p, q) coordinates are plotted to form the picture of the rotated circle. A BASIC program that carries out these steps, printing a table of points for plotting the ellipse in the picture, is provided in the appendix.

An artist with computer assistance can write simple programs to expedite the use of any of the preceding equations, including those for calculating an ellipse. For the special case of the circle in an xy plane, the coordinates of the circle center and the size of its radius can be input to the program and the center coordinates, orientation, size, and shape of the ellipse will be printed as output. The process of obtaining circles in perspective can be made very efficient.

Spheres

The mathematics for treating spheres in perspective is substantially more complex than for circles. Some discussion, a simple proof, and some simple derivations are given for relatively easy cases.

The outline of a sphere is an ellipse in the picture plane. The proof is simply that a cone of light comes from the circular edge of the sphere and converges on the viewer. Regardless of the location of the viewer or sphere, the cone intersects the picture plane as an ellipse. (More discussion on the curves formed when a plane intersects a cone is provided in chapter 7.)

The general equation for a sphere is as follows:

$$(x - x_0)^2 + (y - y_0)^2 + (z - z_0)^2 = r^2 . \quad (6.32)$$

Points calculated with this equation can be plotted in perspective. A table should be made, listing in an orderly fashion calculations of x, y, z, p, and q. The result of the plotting is a number of points filling the region the sphere would occupy if it were solid. A computer program for the perspective of a sphere is provided in the appendix. It can be used to verify numerically the following arguments. It, too, provides points as if the sphere were solid. Programs to suppress points hidden by the "front" of the sphere and showing just its outline are much more complex (see chapter 10).

Aside from the brightness pattern of its surface, all that is wanted is the outline of the sphere. It is difficult for the mathematical artist to guess which values of x, y, and z to use to obtain the outline. Only if the sphere is centered on the vision axis is its outline the circle of points obtained when the sphere is cut by a plane parallel to PP. For other cases, some guidance can be given, but the instances when an accurate ellipsoidal "sphere" is needed in a drawing are too rare to justify an extensive and complex mathematical treatment.

The outline of a sphere in perspective is generally not a circle. It would be useless to find the center (x_0, y_0, z_0) of the sphere in PP, since this would not give the center of the ellipse representing the sphere. When the sphere is so near the vision axis that CV will fall inside its outline in the picture, it is a safe approximation to draw a circle to represent the sphere (as in figure 3-20). The center of that circle is at the center of the ellipse obtained from a horizontal slice of the sphere. The ellipse can be calculated.

A proof that the perspective of a sphere is not circular was seen when the perspective of an off-axis sphere was constructed in chapter 3 (figure 3-21). An elliptical outline was obtained in the picture.

Mathematically, one approach is to choose an off-axis view and check for any distortion of the sphere. The sphere is placed to the side of the x axis, as shown in figure 6-15 in plan view, and it is located below HL, as shown in the elevation. The center of the sphere is located behind PP at $(x_0, y_0, 0)$ in GP. Because V is height h above GP, the sphere is seen at a slant. (Here, as elsewhere, V is obligated to look straight ahead at CV on HL. To lower V's line of sight to look directly at the center of the sphere would indeed cause its outline to be circular, since PP is understood to be normal to the vision

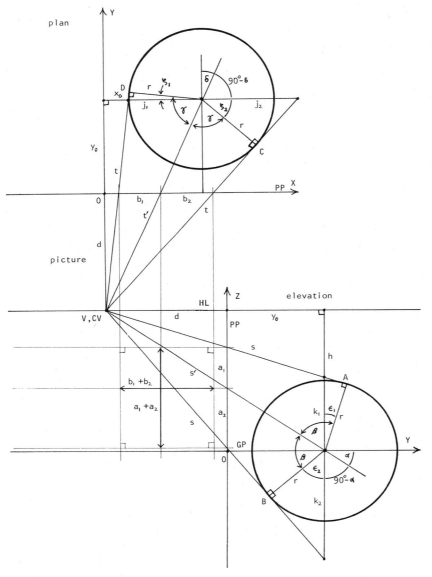

6-15. Calculating the rectangular outline for the perspective of a sphere viewed asymmetrically

axis.) V never sees the off-axis sphere as an object of diameter $2r$ but always as something smaller.

The proof begins with the temporary assumption that a circle is seen in PP. It would have the equation $(q - q_0)^2 + (p - p_0)^2 = R^2$, where R is the radius of the circle. Equations 5.3 and 5.4 are substituted into this equation, and the resulting equation contains only powers and products of x, y, and z. When the numerous terms are analyzed, no way can be found to obtain the simple equation of a sphere with center at some $(x_0, y_0, 0)$. (An exception occurs if $(p_0, q_0) = (0,0)$; then a sphere can be found with its center at $(0, y_0, h)$, putting it on the vision axis.) In general, since the circle is not the perspective transformation of a sphere, a sphere cannot be transformed to a circle in perspective. This brief proof should be sufficient.

Figure 6-15 can be used to derive some mathematical assistance for constructing the perspective of a sphere. The only aid that can be obtained while restricting the mathematics to a level compatible with its expected usefulness involves calculating the width and height of the outline of a sphere in PP. This is done here using the plan and elevation views of figure 6-15. If the sphere were viewed asymmetrically in only one respect (a simpler situation than used for figures 3-21 and 6-15), then direct calculation of major and minor axes would be possible.

As constructed in chapter 3 for figure 3-21, lines of sight from V touch the sphere at points A and B in the elevation view and at points C and D in the plan. These points are not necessarily at the "edge" of the sphere as seen by V, although they appear to be so in orthographic views. The limits of the outline of the sphere are located in PP by projection from the pierce points in both views of PP as shown, forming a rectangle. The elliptical outline is enclosed by the rectangle, with points A, B, C, and D somewhere on its perimeter. Locating A, B, C, and D explicitly in the picture would not help because they are not tangent points for V. The major axis of the ellipse is aimed toward CV and bisects the rectangle.

The height of the rectangle can be found with the aid of the elevation view of figure 6-15 after substantial trigonometry. In that view, the lines of sight each have length s (by symmetry), and the distance from V to the center of the sphere is s'. These quantities can be calculated from the triangles shown, giving:

$$s'^2 = h^2 + (y_0 + d)^2$$
$$s^2 = s'^2 - r^2 . \qquad (6.33)$$

The vertical line through the center is cut into pieces $k_1 + k_2$. The viewer looking through PP sees $k_1 + k_2$ projected to size $a_1 + a_2$ in PP. Segments k_1 and k_2 can be found if angles ϵ_1 and ϵ_2 can be found. The relations are: $r = k_1 \cos \epsilon_1$ and $r = k_2 \cos \epsilon_2$. Angle α between HL and the line of length s' can be found from $\tan \alpha = h/(d + y_0)$. Angle β can be found from $\cos \beta = r/s'$. Then ϵ_1 is given by $\epsilon_1 = -90° + \alpha + \beta$, and ϵ_2 is given by $\epsilon_2 = 90° + \alpha - \beta$. The ambitious reader can assemble all these ingredients to find that:

$$a_1 + a_2 = \frac{2drs'}{(y_0 + d)^2 - r^2} =$$
$$\frac{2dr\sqrt{h^2 + (y_0 + d)^2 - r^2}}{(y_0 + d)^2 - r^2} . \qquad (6.34)$$

This equation can be used when the sphere is not at $z = 0$, provided that h is used as the vertical distance from z_0 to HL.

An identical procedure is used with the aid of the plan view to find the width of the rectangle. Instead of h, x_0 is used. The lines of sight have length t, and the line through the center has length t'. The length $j_1 + j_2$ is projected to PP to find $b_1 + b_2$. The same reasoning is used with angles δ (not to be confused with earlier uses of δ), γ, and ζ. These have the same uses as α, β, and ϵ, respectively. The result is:

$$b_1 + b_2 = \frac{2drt'}{(y_0 + d)^2 - r^2} =$$
$$\frac{2dr\sqrt{x_0^2 + (y_0 + d)^2 - r^2}}{(y_0 + d)^2 - r^2} . \qquad (6.35)$$

If the sphere is centered at $x_0 = 0$, equation 6.35 gives the minor axis ($2b$) of the ellipse in the picture, and equation 6.34 necessarily gives the major axis ($2a$), oriented vertically. If the sphere is being viewed symmetrically, centered on the vision axis, then either equation gives the diameter ($2R$) of the circle seen in the picture.

Q6-17. Make appropriate measurements on figure 6-15, and calculate and check the rectangle shown in the picture.

Grids and Topography

Practice using the perspective transformation for grids is very helpful for laying out a picture and for understanding some later topics. The discussion starts with flat square grids. Extension of the dis-

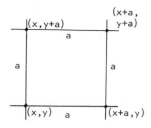

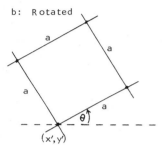

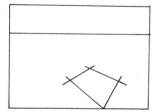

6-16. Calculating the perspective of any square grid

cussion to curved surfaces is presented as topography and in chapters 7 and 8.

In the most general case, four sets of (x,y,z) coordinates must be available for one unit square of the grid. These twelve numbers include information on the orientation of the grid. If the coordinates of just one point in the grid are known, and the rotation angles (θ, ϕ, and/or ψ) used to orient it are known, the unit square and the complete grid can be calculated. First, the four corners of the unit square are calculated by adding the unit size a to the coordinates of the starting point P, as in figure 6-16a. Then the rotational transformations, if any, are applied to these four points (figure 6-16b). Finally, the perspective is calculated and plotted (figure 6-16c).

Graphic construction could be used to complete the grid, since the unit square indicates the VPs. However, for more accuracy, many more points of the grid can be calculated in (x,y,z) coordinates, transformed to perspective, and plotted. This is best done on a systematic basis at the first stage. Grid coordinates are calculated as in chapter 4 by means of relations such as $x_n = na$ and $y_m = ma$. The general counters n and m can be carried through the rotational and perspective transformations, so that formulas for p_n and q_m are obtained. These coordinates are then evaluated and plotted for all desired integer values of n and m.

The procedure can be extended to three-dimensional lattices. A unit cube is to be repeated throughout the space wanted. The z coordinate takes on values $z_n = na$. Then rotations are done for each point and the perspective calculated. Plotting can be confusing unless the points are preorganized into "planes." If use is made of the three VPs, this method can be much faster than the tra-

ditional one of building and photographing a model. The computer program in the appendix for calculating a rectangular box can be extended to calculate a grid or lattice.

A practical question is: how many squares does a grid have to have to show a strong sense of depth in perspective? In contrast to pictures of strongly converging grids, an actual tile floor hardly shows convergence within a large room. This misleading effect is partly due to the observer's viewing height above the floor. The effect is improved by placing the viewer's head near the floor. Another contributing factor is that, in looking down at a tile floor, the viewer sees much foreground that would not appear in the equivalent picture viewed straight ahead. A photograph of a long straight railroad track[2] illustrates how many railroad ties (about 100) must be shown before the ones near VP appear vanishingly small. Equations 4.1 and 4.2 can be used to design desired effects as shown in the question that follows. For planes other than the xy plane, equivalent forms of these equations can be found.

Q6-18. Compute the distance to which a floor must be tiled in order for the most distant tiles to appear half the size of the tiles (a) 1 m away, and (b) 10 m away. Use typical tiles $a \simeq 0.3$ m square, and assume (unnecessarily) a PP with viewer distance $d = 1$ m and viewer height $h = 1$ m. Count tiles with $n = 0$ at PP. Try first with equation 4.2; then see that equation 4.1 also solves it. In real situations, viewers tend to compare the most distant tiles with others rather far off, hence case (b).

A topography is a map of a three-dimensional surface such that the underlying xy grid is preserved. Heights or altitudes (z) are shown by means of contours placed on the xy grid. Topographic maps usually show contours at intervals of 10 ft in height and are referenced to three-dimensional reference points called "benchmarks." An *xy* grid does not conform to the spherical earth's surface on a large scale, so large-scale topographic maps must have some distortion in the arrangement of the *xy* grid. (This can be witnessed in a practical way by tracing the section boundary roads in some Great Plains states. East-west roads are straight, but north-south roads occasionally jog to preserve equal areas of land as east-west coordinates shrink toward the north pole.)

Topographic plots are useful on a medium scale for architecture, and are easy to plot in perspective. The *z* coordinate (altitude or height) for the land surface is read from a map at regularly spaced *x* and *y* grid coordinates. Equation 5.4 is used to calculate the perspective coordinate *q* for each altitude. The *xy* grid is constructed in the perspective. Each *q* value is then measured upward from the corresponding grid point in the picture to locate the surface point. If the plot is to make sense, some regular way of depicting the surface must be used. Either the contours can form a series of levels or "strata" in perspective (figure 6-17a), giving a "laminated look," or the altitude at each regular grid point should be plotted and connected to form a deformed grid (figure 6-17b). The former inherently shows finer detail than the latter. A third possibility is to calculate (or guess) the illumination of the topography and show it by means of shading (a subject for chapter 9).

Wide-angle and Telephoto Views

The calculation of a wide-angle or telephoto perspective can help solve some difficult problems. For

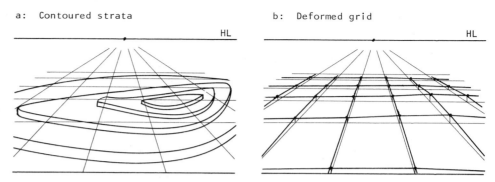

a: Contoured strata   b: Deformed grid

6-17. Topography in perspective

example, the peak surrounded by rings depicted topographically in plate 4 would appear too far away in a regular perspective view to preserve the dramatic effect of the peak while keeping at least one ring in the foreground. A telephoto view has the effect of compressing distance (in the *y* direction), bringing all features "closer" without losing the foreground.

The general procedure is to apply a magnification factor M to *y* in the perspective transformation (equations 5.3 and 5.4). M is greater than 1 for telephoto views and less than 1 for wide-angle. The value of *y* is divided by M. The effect is to reduce the denominator, making the picture appear bigger for telephoto, or to increase the denominator, making the picture coordinates smaller for wide-angle views. The effect on both equations is as follows:

$$p = xd/(y/\text{M} + d) ; \qquad (6.36)$$

$$q = (z - h)d/(y/\text{M} + d) . \qquad (6.37)$$

These equations give telephoto or wide-angle effects, depending on the value of M chosen.

Figure 6-18 shows what the magnification does

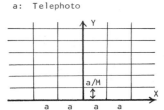

a: Telephoto

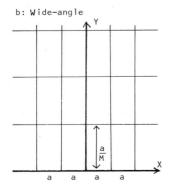

b: Wide-angle

6-18. Grid modified for telephoto and wide-angle views (plan view)

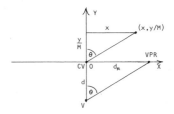

6-19. Calculating a vanishing point for a wide-angle or telephoto view

to the underlying xy grid with squares of unit size a. In figure 6-18a (telephoto), M is greater than 1 and the grid spacing along the y axis is reduced from a to a/M, a smaller value. In figure 6-18b (wide-angle), M is less than 1 and the grid spacing along the y axis is increased from a to a/M, a larger value. While the artist may arrange other ways to calculate and use wide-angle and telephoto views, the single parameter M should be used as described to keep new equations at a minimum. Chapter 3 presents other discussion of wide-angle and telephoto views. Equations 6.36 and 6.37 make clear that the expansion or compression of the view is applied uniformly to both the x and the z coordinates, a desirable effect.

The calculation of VPs for wide-angle and telephoto views is easy. Figure 6-19 shows in plan view a general case with a grid point $(x, y/M)$ and a viewer who can see VPR in direction θ from CV. A line through the origin O (at CV) and through point $(x, y/M)$ aimed toward VPR must also be at θ with the y axis. Since $\tan \theta = x/(y/M) = xM/y$, the tangent of any viewing angle is simply multiplied by M. The calculation of the position of VPR is given by $d_R = d \tan \theta$. After magnification is applied to the coordinates, the VP is moved outward (or inward) along the x axis by the factor M. For telephoto views, the VPs are farther apart to make the picture bigger; for wide-angle views, they are closer together to bring more subject into the picture region. This change in the VPs may seem contrary to the notion of "narrow" and "wide" angles. The picture designer who already has a wide angle of view θ_w in mind cannot lay out this angle directly but instead must compute the reduction M from $M = 1/\tan \theta_w$. M is then used with equations 6.36 and 6.37.

Q6-19. What Ms should be used for 20°, 90°, and 120° fields of view for a box? (Do not confuse θ with the total angular field.)

General Remarks on Transformations for Graphics

The mathematical methods given in chapters 5 and 6 for translating and rotating an object point by point are general transformations useful for graphics done by hand, by calculator, or by computer. A more complete list of transformations would also include scaling, mirroring, deleting, duplicating, and distorting. Only deleting and duplicating cannot be done by straightforward algebraic or numerical calculation; they are better handled by paper methods or by computer. For the others, the calculation methods used in most computer programs are different from those presented here. Further details are given in chapter 10.

The general technical theory of graphics can be found in any good reference on computer graphics, but no available book seems to cover both the graphics and the mathematics of lines, surfaces, and other features.[3] For reference purposes, the full list of graphic transformations is given here with a brief discussion or review. For each transformation, an "inverse transformation" is possible unless otherwise stated.

Translating is done one dimension at a time, even though the method is presented for all three dimensions in equation 5.1. The inverse is given by equation 5.2.

Rotating with one, two, or three angles is done in one plane at a time, using the methods given in equations 5.11, 5.13, and 5.14. Equation 5.12 and its permutations give the inverse rotation. The order in which rotations are done is critical. For example, a different position is reached if rotation by ϕ is done before rather than after rotation by θ.

Scaling can be done mathematically by multiplying the coordinate system by a scale factor s. The point (x,y,z) then becomes (sx,sy,sz). The scaled point's location is farther from the origin if s is greater than 1 and closer to the origin if s is less than 1. The inverse scaling is done with the factor $1/s$. Factor s can be different for each dimension.

Mirroring is done by changing the sign of half of a coordinate axis. For example, the yz plane becomes a mirror if the $(-x)$ axis is changed to a $(+x)$ axis, causing positive x to be measured in both directions from origin O. Values of negative x would not be used in this situation. Points plotted to the left of the yz plane are said to be "antisymmetric" to those plotted to the right. The symmetry is the same as if a mirror were used to locate points, plotting on the left what is seen in the mirror reflected from the right. A mirror transformation is also called a "parity" transformation. It is incorrect to say that a mirror exchanges left and right or that it exchanges top and bottom. A mirror changes the sign of the coordinate axis that is normal to the mirror. The inverse of mirroring is to use the mirror again, putting things back the way they were originally.[4]

Deleting is the removal of points or of collections of points (objects). It cannot be done selectively with ordinary mathematical calculation; it requires intervention by the artist or by a computer program. There is no inverse here because points once lost cannot be regained.

Duplicating consists of copying an established point or feature at a different position. Obviously, a translation must be applied, and rotation is also possible. The mathematical description of pictorial subject matter requires an underlying coordinate system that cannot be moved piecemeal. Therefore, human or programmed intervention is required for duplicating. Duplication can be done in an orderly way, taking advantage of the possible symmetries of the plane or of three-dimensional space to create complex symmetric patterns.[5] A grid is the symmetric duplication of a unit square, using translations equal to the unit size. The inverse of duplication would be deletion.

Distorting is an operation done to the whole underlying grid, or to the coordinates for a selected object. Undesirable connotations of the term are not intended; distortion is used to produce orderly changes in shape, often for the better. For example, one dimension of the grid may be stretched relative to another to obtain a wide-angle or telephoto view. In chapter 8, as part of an attempt to lessen the distortion inherent in rectilinear perspective, coordinate systems are proposed that are distortions of the xyz grid—counterdistortions to remove distortion! The inverse transformation to undo a distortion does not always exist, or it may be extremely complicated.

The discussion here concludes with a few general remarks about the perspective transformation. The graphic operations listed above are usually carried out before the perspective transformation is done. The effects of the other transformations are carried into the picture in changed or distorted form. The perspective transformation itself is a "distorting" transformation. The only features it does not distort are lines and planes.

Rectilinear perspective has been called "linear," perhaps because it preserves straight lines. But the transformation is definitely nonlinear in the mathematical sense. It does not preserve rotations, translations, or scaling, since it does not preserve angles or sizes. The quantities and features that are invariant under the perspective transformation are discussed, in a fashion too abstract for the artist, by mathematicians interested in projective geometry.[6] Perspective creates a two-dimensional nonEuclidean space.

When equations 5.3 and 5.4 (the transformation) are reexamined, they each can be seen to possess the same "singularity." A singularity occurs any time a way exists for the denominator of a mathematical expression to become zero, resulting in an infinite value for the expression as a whole. When y happens to take the value $(-d)$, the singularity occurs, and neither p nor q can be calculated. This unfortunate event occurs at the position of the viewer. This one point cannot be calculated in perspective, but no artist would care to anyway because the entire projection passes through the point $(x, y, z) = (0, -d, h)$.

The transformation is essentially symmetric with regard to x and z. If the translation h that was applied to z coordinates is ignored, then p and q have the same form whether x or z is used. This corresponds to the fact that scenes in the world should show the same perspective whether viewed sideways or normally. Only the y dependence of the perspective transformation causes the reduction in size characteristic of perspective, and this occurs because y appears in the denominators. Further properties of the perspective transformation are left for the mathematically inclined reader to explore.

To calculate perspective when V looks straight up toward the zenith, the artist must either reorient the xyz system with the y axis up, or form a new version of equations 5.3 and 5.4, using z for "depth."

Summary of Perspective by Calculation

This summary gives in concise form the procedural steps and equations previously discussed and derived in chapters 4, 5, and 6 that allow the calculation of certain points and features in perspective. For other mathematical support, the reader should see the background given in the chapters, the graphics summary above, and the references cited.

The first step in preparing to calculate perspective is deciding upon viewer distance d from PP and viewer height h above GP. Subject matter is placed in relation to PP and GP (assistance can be found in chapters 1, 2, and 4). Subject matter must be described in terms of (x, y, z) coordinates measured according to the xyz system in normal position (figure 4-1). Plan and elevation views can be translated and/or rotated graphically or mathematically to achieve final desired positions of objects for measurement or calculation of coordinates.

The coordinates of any object point in the picture are calculated with the perspective transformation:

$$p = \frac{xd}{y + d}; \qquad (5.3)$$

$$q = \frac{(z - h)d}{y + d}. \qquad (5.4)$$

Coordinates p and q are measured from the p and q axes as defined in figure 5-1. It is most convenient to form a table of calculations.

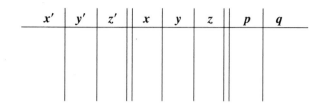

x'	y'	z'	x	y	z	p	q

The primed coordinates are for object points identified before rotation and/or translation is used to bring the coordinates to normal position.

If grid-line spacing is wanted, the following modifications of chapter 4 equations, rewritten for pq coordinates, can be used:

$$q_n = -hd/(na + d) ; \qquad (4.1')$$

$$\Delta p_n = ad/(na + d) . \qquad (4.2')$$

These give the location of the nth grid line in depth and the spacing of grid lines converging to CV, as measured on the line q_n.

Points of the subject matter that fall outside picture boundaries need not be calculated. For example, the largest x coordinate that appears in a picture with the frame at $p = p_R$ is:

$$x_{max} = (y + d)p_R/d . \qquad (5.10)$$

If wanted, the VP for any line at any angle can be calculated using equations 5.3 and 5.4 in the limit for large values of $x, y,$ or z. For example, if the line is at θ with respect to the x axis in plan and at ϕ with respect to the y axis in elevation (a two-rotation case in which θ is transformed to θ'), the following general forms of equations 5.15 and 5.16 can be used:

$$p_{VP} = d/\tan \theta' ; \qquad (5.15')$$

$$q_{VP} = d \tan \phi . \qquad (5.16')$$

If no tilt ϕ exists, then θ can be used by itself for the one-rotation case.

Given the direction numbers $i{:}j{:}k$ and a point (x_1, y_1, z_1) on any line, or given the line's equation (equation 6.1), the equation of the line in perspective can be found from the general form:

$$q = m'p + q_0 \qquad (6.2)$$

with the slope m' for the line at δ from the p axis given by:

$$m' = \tan \delta = \frac{-j(z_1 - h)/i + k(y_1 + d)/i}{(-jx_1/i) + y_1 + d} , \qquad (6.4)$$

and the q intercept given by:

$$q_0 = \frac{[(-kx_1/i) + z_1 - h]d}{(-jx_1/i) + y_1 + d} . \qquad (6.3)$$

If the line is parallel to the y axis, $q_0 = 0$.

A circle, as shown in equation 6.15, in an xy plane ($z = c$) with center (x_0, y_0) and radius r will be seen in PP as an ellipse tilted by angle δ from the p axis. Angle δ is given by:

$$\tan 2\delta = B/(A - C) . \qquad (6.20)$$

Coefficients A through F are given by:

$$A = (c - h)^2$$
$$B = 2x_0(c - h)$$
$$C = x_0^2 + d^2 + y_0^2 + 2y_0d - r^2$$
$$D = 0$$
$$E = (c - h)(-2d^2 - 2y_0d)$$
$$F = d^2(c - h)^2 . \qquad (6.17)$$

The semimajor and semiminor axes are given by:

$$a^2 = -F/k^2 + p'_0{}^2 + q_0'{}^2 l^2/k^2 \qquad (6.23a)$$

$$b^2 = -F/l^2 + p'_0{}^2 k^2/l^2 + q'_0{}^2 , \qquad (6.23b)$$

where rotated center coordinates p'_0 and q'_0 are given by:

$$p'_0 = -E (\sin \delta)/2k^2$$

$$q'_0 = -E (\cos \delta)/2l^2 \qquad (6.22)$$

and k^2 and l^2 by:

$$k^2 = A \cos^2 \delta + B \sin \delta \cos \delta + C \sin^2 \delta \qquad (6.21a)$$

$$l^2 = A \sin^2 \delta - B \sin \delta \cos \delta + C \cos^2 \delta . \qquad (6.21b)$$

The location of the center of the ellipse is found from p'_0 and q'_0 by:

$$p_0 = p'_0 \cos \delta - q'_0 \sin \delta$$

$$q_0 = p'_0 \sin \delta + q'_0 \cos \delta . \qquad (6.24)$$

A circle in a plane viewed at σ in the xyz system is seen in the picture as an ellipse of eccentricity:

$$\rho = \cos \sigma . \qquad (6.26)$$

A sphere offset from both the yz plane and GP (equation 6.32), with center at (x_0, y_0, z_0) and radius r, is seen in PP as an ellipse with major axis aimed at CV and bounded by a normally oriented rectangle of height:

$$a_1 + a_2 = \frac{2dr\sqrt{h^2 + (y_0 + d)^2 - r^2}}{(y_0 + d)^2 - r^2} , \qquad (6.34)$$

and width:

$$b_1 + b_2 = \frac{2dr\sqrt{x_0^2 + (y_0 + d)^2 - r^2}}{(y_0 + d)^2 - r^2} . \qquad (6.35)$$

These sizes do not give the minor or major axis unless the sphere is centered about the yz plane or HL. When z_0 is not zero, h must be the vertical distance from the center to HL.

A telephoto (or wide-angle) view is obtained using a magnification or reduction factor M applied to y coordinates, modifying the perspective transformation to:

$$p = xd/(y/M + d) ; \qquad (6.36)$$

$$q = (z - h)d/(y/M + d) . \qquad (6.37)$$

Notes

1. The mathematics of lines and planes can be found in such analytic geometry/calculus books as George Thomas, Jr., *Calculus and Analytic Geometry;* Angus Taylor, *Calculus with Analytic Geometry;* and Edwin Purcell, *Calculus with Analytic Geometry.*

The same information, with accompanying graphics text, appears in Springer, *Basic Graphics.*

2. This illustration is nicely discussed in Gregory, "Visual Illusions."

3. For general mathematical descriptions of graphics, see Springer, *Basic Graphics* and David Rogers and J. Adams, *Mathematical Elements for Computer Graphics*.

4. On the mathematics and physics of mirroring, parity, and right/left, at a nontechnical level, see Martin Gardner, *The Ambidextrous Universe*.

5. On symmetry in space, see Weyl, *Symmetry;* Holden, *Shapes, Space, and Symmetry;* Gardner, *Ambidextrous Universe;* and Harold Coxeter, *Introduction to Geometry*.

6. Projective geometry and other topics are covered at a non-elementary level in Coxeter, *Introduction to Geometry* and Coxeter, *Non-Euclidean Geometry*.

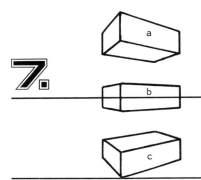

7.

Mathematical Curves and Surfaces

The power of the perspective transformation can be more fully exploited by hand or computer calculation if the artist has an elementary working knowledge of available mathematical functions and operations. Lists and descriptions of the simpler curves and surfaces are provided in this chapter, together with explanations of relevant mathematical terminology and operations. Knowledge of the mathematical background given previously is assumed. Some applications of the concepts to perspective are discussed; all of the concepts are helpful in working with irregular curves and surfaces. Alternative coordinate systems are introduced. A thorough understanding of this subject matter constitutes a good preparation for learning and using calculus. While not required in this book, calculus is a highly recommended mathematical tool for advanced graphics, with or without the computer.

Mathematical Functions

The perspective transformation for most curves is difficult if not impossible to find analytically, but the descriptions in *xyz* space are very useful. The mathematical analysis is given in algebraic symbols, as before, for general results that are not restricted numerically. The reader may refer to any college algebra or analytic geometry text for more detail.[1] The material given here is only a summary of the essential terminology and the resources available to the artist.

A mathematical *function* of one, two, or three variables is a carefully defined procedure stating that a certain value can be obtained by calculation if certain operations are done on the variable(s). The general notation is to write a function in the form $f(x,y,z)$, where f denotes the set of operations.

The f could be thought of as a little computer program, accepting certain values for the variables as input and producing an output. Actual functions of interest have an output called the "dependent" variable. This variable is dependent on the values of the input or "independent" variables.

The simplest function is the straight-line function: $y = mx + b$. Here, y is the dependent variable that results from using the function $f(x)$; the function has the explicit form $f(x) = mx + b$. In the case of the equation seen earlier for the circle ($x^2 + y^2 = r^2$), the variables are "mixed together" by the function. But f has no *explicit* form unless one of the variables is pulled out by rearrangement to yield, for example, $x = \pm\sqrt{r^2 - y^2}$—the explicit form of $x = f(y)$. The circle equation was the *implicit* form. The r can be thought of as a constant or as an adjustable parameter.

When the explicit form of the function is defined as $y = f(x)$, then the inverse function which calculates x from y is written with the notation $x = f^{-1}(y)$. To get the actual form of f^{-1} could be a hard problem in algebraic calculation.

The symbols used for the variables here follow the usual guidelines: lower-case letters near the end of the alphabet for variables and lower-case letters near the beginning for constants and parameters. Temporarily, x, y, and z appear as any variables, not just as variable coordinates, although the principal application of the functions discussed here is to coordinates. Upper-case letters near the end of the alphabet are used to label coordinate axes on diagrams or to label features. Other coordinate systems can be used with the same functions. The function $y = f(x)$, for example, is a "generic" function, not limited to specific interpretations of x and y. Either x or y could be an angle, so the use of Greek letters for angles is temporarily discontinued at this point.

For graphic purposes, the central interest is in calculating locations in space. Hence calculating a function must yield a coordinate from some combination of one, two, or three coordinates. To obtain a curve in a plane or in space, at least two different coordinates must be related by the function. The function with one variable, $x = c$, describes a plane, but one that has no useful features.

Units of measurement of both sides of an equation like $y = f(x)$ are the same. Regardless of the units of x, the operations done to x as part of the function f must introduce appropriate adding and multiplying constants in appropriate units so as to achieve the desired units for y. For graphics, the coordinates must be measured in degrees or in metric or other units. All constants in graphics are measured in the same units (or degrees). The result of calculating with f is to produce a value in compatible units.

Properties of Curves

Calculating a table of values for a function and plotting them on paper with two coordinate axes and a square grid produces a *graph*. The visual form of a function can be found by graphing it. Graphs of functions in three dimensions can also be represented on paper with three axes or in space with a model. The graph of a function is a curved line (a "curve") or a surface in two or three dimensions. Since a curve obtained from a function is necessarily very well-defined, it cannot be called irregular. Nevertheless, many of the following terms describing the behavior of curves can be applied to irregular curves for which no explicit mathematical description exists. Having the terminology at hand may aid the artist in working with any curves. The examples are in two dimensions, for planar curves, but the concepts can all be extended to three dimensions. Some of the terms are not new, but all are collected here as a complete summary.

Many useful terms exist for describing the behavior of the slopes of curves. Figure 7-1a shows lines with zero slope, with constant positive and negative slopes, and with infinite slope graphed in *xy* coordinates with *y* as dependent variable. When *y* increases as the result of a decrease in *x* (which is another way to say that *x* is increasing in the negative direction), the slope of the line or curve is negative. A positive but decreasing slope is shown in figure 7-1b.

An *asymptote* is a line (usually straight) that a curve approaches as the variables become large (see figure 7-1b). It should not be confused with the "limit line" discussed in chapter 1. Since perspective often involves the behavior of curves or functions as infinity is approached, the asymptotic behavior of curves is important. The horizon line (HL) is the asymptote in the picture plane (PP) for any curve in an *xy* plane. For curves in tilted planes, the asymptote is the plane line in the picture.

A line that curves has a property called *curvature* which can be defined mathematically and calculated. The calculation requires calculus, but the curvature itself simply expresses the fact that any curve may be approximated on a small scale with circular arcs. Figure 7-1c shows the arc of radius R from center C approximating the curve near point P. The *tangent* line $\overline{T}$ at P (not to be confused with the "trig" function of the same name) is perpendicular to the radius line. The slope of the radius line $\overline{CP}$ can be found as the negative reciprocal of the slope of the tangent line.

A little farther along the curve in figure 7-1c, an *inflection* point I occurs where the center of curvature recedes toward infinity and the curve is momentarily straight. The tangent $\overline{T''}$ at I crosses the curve. Past I, at point P', the radius R' is centered at C' on the other side of the curve. The tangent line, which had been positive and decreasing in slope in this illustration, now begins to increase in slope, as seen for $\overline{T'}$. The tangent need not have zero slope at an inflection. Since it would be useless to calculate the radii of curvature for a curve prior to transforming it to perspective, the mathematical treatment is not attempted here.

A curve has variable slope. The arbitrary curve in figure 7-1d varies between minimum and maxi-

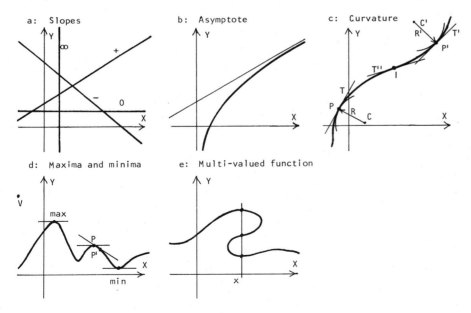

7-1. General properties of curves

mum values of y over the range of x shown (only two are labeled). Identifying *maxima* and *minima* for curves or surfaces is useful for perspective because the viewer usually cannot see into the dips but instead sees mostly the peaks. A curve has zero slope at maxima and minima, which indicates a way to find these points. They should be located in perspective, since the viewer looking through PP sees different maxima and minima, depending on the line of sight. When figure 7-1d is considered as an elevation view, V sees the top of a peak at P', whereas the mathematical maximum is at P.

When a curve doubles back on itself, as in figure 7-1e, it is called *multivalued*. Here, for a certain value of x, the curve shows three different values of y. The ambiguity can make mathematical treatment difficult. The circle is an earlier example of a function with two values of y for every value of x (except at $x = \pm r$).

Curves in Two Dimensions

The most common functions relating two variables fall in several groupings: power laws, algebraic functions, trigonometric functions, exponentials, and other more advanced functions. All these basic or "elementary" functions are "planar" curves; that is, they can be drawn in a plane. In almost all cases, "inverse" functions exist. All can be calculated numerically on the better-endowed pocket calculators and personal computers. The constants usually can be positive or negative; the effect of their signs must be explored with each individual function. Wherever a constant multiplies a variable, a negative constant has the effect of reversing the axis for that variable.

Power-law functions are ranked by the largest power (exponent) appearing in the function. Using x as the independent variable and y as the resulting dependent variable, simple examples are: $y = cx^0 = c$ (a constant), $y = cx^1 = cx$, $y = cx^2$, $y = cx^3$, and so on. The general form is $y = cx^n$. The multiplying constant c has the effect of expanding or contracting the scale of y, depending on whether c is greater than or less than 1. The first-power function $y = cx$ is the expression for a straight line (with intercept 0 and slope c). The second-power function is graphed as a *parabola*, with the open part placed symmetrically along the y axis and the *vertex* (the sharpest bend) at the origin. Except for occasional use of "cubic" for $n = 3$ and "quartic" for $n = 4$, no standard names exist for higher powers, but they create progressively more interesting curves.

More general forms of the power functions are obtained by adding lower powers and constants to each. Adding a to $y = cx^n$ has the effect of translating the curve a distance a along the y axis in the positive direction. Often the inclusion of scaling and translational constants does not make the function algebraically more difficult to work with. The general equation for a parabola is better written as:

$$y = ax^2 + bx + c, \qquad (7.1)$$

where the inclusion of the first-power term has the effect of sliding the vertex in the x direction. Completing the square to obtain the form $(x - x_0)^2$ locates the x coordinate of the vertex. An example of a parabola, $y = 2x^2 - 1$, is graphed in figure 7-2.

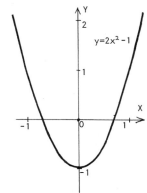

7-2. Graph of a parabola

Q7-1. Plot the graph of $y = x^3 + x^2$ to discover a double bend in the curve. Use values of x from -2 to $+2$, plotting with increments of 0.5 or smaller.

The perspective transformation for any power function can be found. For simplicity, the power function can be taken to represent a curve in the xy plane. Some other curve is seen in perspective. For the general case $y = cx^n$, equations 5.5 and 5.6 can be substituted (with $z = 0$) to obtain p as a rather complicated power function of q. When $n = 2$, a simple parabola $y = cx^2$ in the xy plane is transformed to $q^2 + qh + ch^2p^2/d = 0$, an ellipse, when the square is completed and rewritten in the form $(q + h/2)^2 (h^2/4) + p^2/\sqrt{d/4c} = 1$. The semimajor axis must be $h/2$, the semiminor axis (width) must be $d/4c$, and the center must be at $(0, -h/2)$. A parabola along the y axis must appear to close upon itself at HL in the picture. Figure 7-3 shows that the perspective is indeed an ellipse with a major axis along the q axis equal to h. This is an example of the possible treatment of the few functions that have simple and interpretable perspectives that can be calculated.

A special group of the second-power functions are the *conics,* the curves that can result when a cone is cut by a plane. Figure 7-4 shows (in cross section) the four distinct ways in which the xy plane can pass through a cone. The cone must be thought of as indefinitely long. Because lower powers than the second can appear in the equations of the conic curves, they are more properly called ''second degree'' equations, implying that the highest power they can possess is two. Every conic has one or two foci.

These curves are the same as those produced by a more fundamental definition of conics. That definition requires only two dimensions to express and involves special conditions on the distance between a point on the conic curve and a fixed line called the ''directrix.'' The ratio of the distance to the point from the focus, and to the distance from the directrix, is a constant—the eccentricity e. This approach does not aid the artist except in constructing conics with pins and string.

In figure 7-4a, a cut straight across a cone with the xy plane produces a circle (eccentricity $e = 0$; one focus at the center). It has the equation $x^2 + y^2 = r^2$, a second-degree function. A cut through the cone at a slant (figure 7-4b) produces an ellipse ($0 < e < 1$; two foci), with an equation of similar form but having more constants: $x^2/a^2 + y^2/b^2 = 1$. A cut through the cone parallel to its side (figure 7-4c) produces a parabola ($e = 1$; one focus), just discussed. The shape of a parabola fits some arches and describes the cables of suspension bridges; the latter example is discussed at the end of this section.

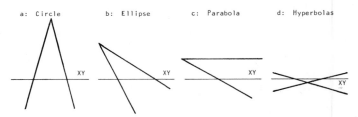

a: Circle   b: Ellipse   c: Parabola   d: Hyperbolas

7-4. Conics formed by the intersection of the xy plane with a cone (in cross section)

A cut at a steeper angle passes through both cones (if a second cone is placed with its apex touching the apex of the first, as in figure 7-4d). The resulting pair of *hyperbolas* ($e > 1$; one focus for each) have the equation:

$$x^2/a^2 - y^2/b^2 = 1 . \qquad (7.2)$$

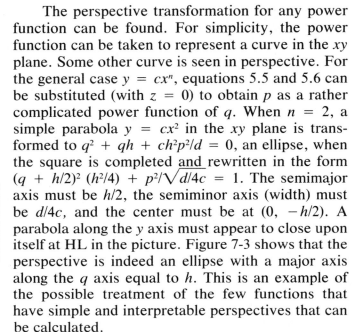

7-3. Perspective of a parabola—an ellipse

This equation resembles that for an ellipse, but with a crucial subtraction included. The two cuts produce two curves, which would be graphed in a symmetric fashion if all possible positive and negative values of x and y that fit the equation were plotted. These particular hyperbolas open outward toward the positive and negative sides of the x axis, and they are centered about O.

When the asymptotes of conics are considered, the "legs" or "sides" of the parabola in figure 7-2 do not approach any straight line but continue to curve out indefinitely, with the curve growing more gradual as x (and therefore y) becomes very large. The sides of a hyperbola asymptotically approach straight lines of a certain slope that pass through the origin. Both hyperbolas expressed by equation 7.2 approach the straight lines $y = +bx/a$ and $y = -bx/a$. This can be verified if the equation is examined for its form when x and y approach ∞.

The simplest *reciprocal* power function, $y = ax^{-1} = a/x$, is an alternative expression for a pair of hyperbolas; but this set opens outward diagonally and approaches the x and y axes asymptotically. The equation can also be written as $xy = a$. A general graph for it is shown in figure 7-5. The more complex algebraic reciprocal functions, $y = a/(x + b)$ or $y = ax/(x + b)$, have almost the same form as the perspective "function." The former function expresses how grid lines are spaced in perspective. Still more complex functions, such as $y = ax^2/(b + cx^2)$, come in great variety and often cannot be simplified. The mathematical artist will occasionally encounter one in solving some graphic problem and must study it carefully.

The *trigonometric* functions can be used to express "waviness" in lines or surfaces. The function

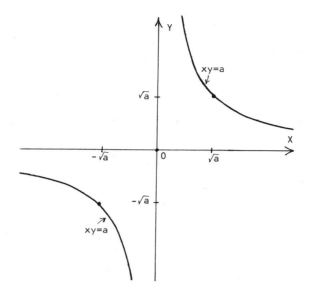

7-5. Graph of a hyperbola

$y = a \sin bx$ varies smoothly between $y = +a$ and $y = -a$ as the function is graphed along the x axis (figure 7-6). Variable a is called the *amplitude*. There are several forms for the variable on which the "trig" function acts. If x is in meters, the con-

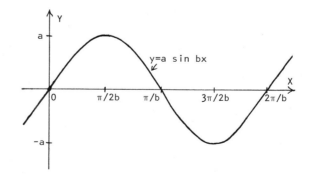

7-6. Graph of a sine function

stant b must be in units such that the variable or "argument" within the function has units of radians or degrees. The wave repeats at intervals of $2\pi/b$ or $360°/b$ in x; that is, after x has varied by an amount equal to $2\pi/b$, the function returns to the same values. The function $y = a \cos bx$ acts the same, except that $\cos x$ has positive peaks at $x = -2\pi/b$, $x = 0$, $x = +2\pi/b$, and so on, while $\sin bx$ has positive peaks at $x = -3\pi/2b$, $x = \pi/2b$, $x = 5\pi/2b$, and so on. Both sine and cosine have the same shape, which is called "sinusoidal."

The function $y = a \tan bx$ acts quite differently: as x varies from $-\pi/2b$ to $+\pi/2b$, y goes from $-\infty$ to $+\infty$, passing through 0 at $x = 0$. The function $\tan bx$ asymptotically approaches the lines $x = +\pi/2b$ and $x = -\pi/2b$—lines parallel to the y axis with infinite slope. Trigonometric functions, while originally defined for use with angles, are not limited to angles for their independent variables. Inverse trigonometric functions, for example $y = a \sin^{-1}(bx)$, also exist and must not be confused with reciprocal functions. The perspective transformations of trigonometric functions and their inverses cannot be calculated algebraically, only numerically.

Q7-2. If you have a trigonometric calculator, you may benefit from practice in graphing some "trig" functions. Graph $y = 2 \cos x$ and $y = 3 \tan 2\pi x$, and compare the functional behavior in each case with the above description. Use a range of x large enough to get at least two complete "cycles" or repetitions. Note the effect of using x in radians and degrees.

The *exponential* functions may be as useful as the power functions. The usual form is $y = ae^{bx}$, but other constants may be used in place of the special number $e = 2.7182. \ldots$ A general graph is shown in figure 7-7. The special property of any exponential function, whether e or some other constant is used, is that for each increment *added* to the independent variable x the value of y is *multiplied* by some number. Certain increments of x cause doublings of y, certain larger increments cause y to grow by factors of 10, and so on. The

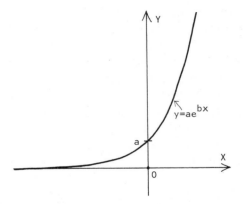

7-7. Graph of an exponential function

exponential is the most rapidly growing elementary function. Small increases in x can lead to very large increases in y. The exponential asymptotically approaches the x axis as $x \to -\infty$, but has no asymptotic limit for positive x. An especially useful form of the exponential is written $y = a (1 - e^{-bx})$. This function approaches the limit a for large values of positive x and is unbounded for values of negative x.

The *logarithmic* function, the inverse of the exponential, is called the "ln" function if it undoes the effect of the e function, and "log" if it undoes the work of 10^x. The logarithmic function is the slowest-growing elementary function when x is greater than 1, hardly growing faster than a constant function (which never changes). Large increases in x lead to very leisurely increases in y. Logarithmic functions are not defined for negative x. They become negative and change very rapidly for $0<x<1$. The perspective transformation of exponential and logarithmic functions does not work out algebraically. Other intractable functions include the "hyperbolic" sines and cosines ($y = a\ \sinh bx$ and $y = a\ \cosh bx$), which are combinations of exponential functions and have inverses.

An interesting application of exponential functions is their use for drawing a "catenary"—the function describing the shape of a heavy hanging cable or of some arches. The name comes from the Latin for "chain." The function is:

$$z = a\ \cosh (y/a) = (a/2)\ (e^{y/a} + e^{-y/a}) . \quad (7.3)$$

As shown in figure 7-8, the "cosh" function has its minimum at $y = 0$ and rises indefinitely from there, without asymptotes. The artist might encounter substantial difficulty in drawing a catenary in elevation view (not to mention the difficulty of obtaining the perspective), when trying to show a dramatic picture of a hanging chain, rope, wire, or cable (see plate 10). With this function at hand, values of y may be selected over the desired span of the cable, values of z may be calculated, and values of p and q may be calculated and plotted. The variables in this case were chosen so that z represents height as usual and y represents depth. Variable a is the height of the lowest part of the cable above $y = 0$. The engineering artist would calculate a from

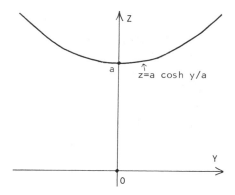

7-8. Graph of a hyperbolic cosine or "cosh" function

the tension in the cable and its weight per unit length.

The catenary should not be confused with the shape of the cables in a suspension bridge. A bridge suspended from cables loads the cables in such a way that their shape becomes parabolic ($z = cy^2$). The artist wishing to draw a hanging cable or a suspension bridge using the appropriate function may want to rotate the coordinate system for an angular view. The position of the dip or vertex can be translated to some more distant value of y than $y = 0$. The height a of the dip can be adjusted by raising or lowering the y axis. Half the length of the span determines a. The inverse for the catenary, $y = a\ \cosh^{-1} z/a = \ln [(z/a) + \sqrt{(z/a)^2 - 1}]$ (obtained from tables), or for the parabola, $y = \pm\sqrt{z/c}$, may be needed to find the constant to set the size. Tables and some calculators can be used to evaluate these functions. The angle at which a cable hangs from a pole or tower is determined by the values chosen for a and the span, but whether the angle is (or appears) correct is an engineering matter.

Working with the catenary or with the parabola

illustrates the process of adjusting the constants and parameters in a function to fit its shape to the desired use. Any function can have an additive (or subtractive) constant that allows the function to be translated in the direction represented by the dependent variable. It can also be translated in the direction of the independent variable, by means of a constant added to that variable. Multiplicative constants can increase or decrease the effect of the independent variable. Any given function has the same characteristic shape, regardless of the scale. In fact, the behavior of each function is so distinctive that precise analysis of even a tiny piece of it can identify the function. But seeming adjustments in the shape can be achieved, within limits, by the choice of constants and of scale. For example, the exponential appears to bend very sharply when a large value of b in e^{bx} is chosen.

Many more advanced functions may occasionally be of artistic use. Standard mathematical tables should be consulted. The probability function $z = ae^{-by^2}$ makes a hump when plotted. Curves called "cycloids" are obtained by tracing a point on a circle as it rolls along a line. These and the several kinds of spirals are more easily handled in a coordinate system to be introduced later—polar coordinates.

The reader may wish to explore the theory of meandering rivers, a frequent landscape subject. The curves of a river are more squared-off than the gentle curves of the "sine wave" discussed earlier. Only nature or mathematics can create such a form correctly. The artist must observe nature very carefully to render the perspective properly or must study how to calculate it. A good introduction to this surprisingly extensive subject at an elementary mathematical level is available.[2]

Of architectural interest is a curve called the "superellipse."[3] Using an equation of the form $(x/a)^n + (y/b)^n = 1$, architects in Sweden have been able to solve practical and aesthetic design problems in situations where an ellipse curves too sharply. The superellipse has more of an oval shape, with blunter "ends." An ideal shape uses $n \simeq 2.5$.

Irregular Curves and Space Curves

Irregular curves can be approximated mathematically over short spans. The simplest approximation uses a straight line and is called the "linear" approximation. It is not very serviceable for perspective purposes. The equation of the straight line that approximates a curve at a given point is simply the equation of the line tangent to the curve at that point. Either the work must be done graphically, with measurements made, or the slope of the curve and the coordinates of the point must be provided. (The slope of a curve is defined as the slope of the tangent at a particular point. The term "tangent" is used here in the graphic rather than in the trigonometric sense.)

The next approximation uses a second-power function, a portion of a parabola. Three points on the curve must be known. Then the three coefficients of the general equation for the parabola (equation 7.1) can be found. The theory for solving the three simultaneous equations that result can be found in any algebra or calculus text. It is not covered here because the potential applications in noncomputer graphics are limited.

A curve is a line, straight or not. A nonstraight line traced through three-dimensional space is a difficult shape for the mathematical artist to deal with. While such "space curves" are seen every day in urban and natural settings, few can be expressed mathematically. One of the best known is the "helix," for which equations do exist. Sometimes point-by-point information about the curve, stated in the form of a series of coordinates or as measurements on plan and elevation views, is available. In addition, the equations for two-dimensional curves that lie in planes can be used, regardless of how the plane is tilted. Translations and rotations can be used to transform the equation of the curve, together with its plane, to any position desired. Two different curves can be joined smoothly at one point; for instance, a straight line that blends into a curve.

Any space curve lies at the intersection of two surfaces. Sometimes the mathematical description of the surfaces is known, and therefore the curve can be described. The planes that determine a straight line have been discussed in chapter 6. Any circle is the intersection of a plane and a circular cylinder. Such curved surfaces are covered in the next section. In general, two equations are needed to define a space curve, one for each surface.

A more advanced procedure called "parametric representation" can be used to trace mathematically the points along a space curve, using a single parameter aided by a set of the usual two-variable functions. For example, the set of functions $\{x = a \cos t, y = bt^2, z = a \sin t\}$ describes a helix with the x axis as its axis and with an expanding coil spacing. Increasing the value of t has the effect of tracing a point along the helix. Most of this subject is beyond the scope of this book, although the reader already has been given the essential tools for mastering it.

Q7-3. First study $\{x = a \cos t, z = a \sin t\}$ to see that it describes a circle in an xz plane as t steadily increases. How much must t change before the circle is retraced? Then study how the inclusion of $y = bt$ produces a helix in space with constant coil spacing. Finally, study the expanding helix discussed above.

Surfaces in Three Dimensions

What an observer usually sees in a landscape, a room, or an abstract design are surfaces. These are often curved in three dimensions, and some of the more regular and symmetric ones can be expressed with extensions of the mathematical functions already discussed. The surfaces can be thought of as thin sheets or hollow shells, or as surfaces of solid objects. One group of surfaces consists of those formed by revolution; another group (cylinders) consists of surfaces formed by translation. A function of two or three coordinate variables is needed to describe a surface. Moving about on a surface involves two independent degrees of freedom. A three-variable equation has two degrees of freedom because, once two variables are determined, the equation makes calculation of the third possible. A solid consists of points with three degrees of freedom. Its points can be encountered anywhere inside the solid.

The surface of a sphere can be expressed with an equation (equation 6.32, an implicit function of three variables), or it can be described by rotating a circle about any axis that goes through its center. In the same way, each of the other conics can be used to generate a curved surface. An ellipse rotated around its major (or minor) axis produces an "ellipsoid'' with three orthogonal axes, two that are equal and one that is not. A hyperbola can be rotated around either of its symmetry axes to produce one or two ''hyperboloids.'' A parabola can be rotated around its central axis to produce a ''paraboloid.'' Any surface of revolution can also be made by translating a circle of variable size along a symmetry axis.

Each revolved conic can be described with a surface equation that is a little more complex than that for a sphere. For example, an ellipsoid that has three different axes (a, b, and c) is described by the equation: $x^2/a^2 + y^2/b^2 + z^2/c^2 = 1$. The conics can be combined, in a sense, to produce other surfaces. An object that has an elliptical cross section in any xy plane and a parabolic cross section in any plane through the z axis is the ''elliptic paraboloid'' expressed with the equation $x^2/a^2 + y^2/b^2 = cz$. The ''hyperbolic paraboloid'' has the equation $x^2/a^2 - y^2/b^2 = cz$. Also known as the ''saddle surface,'' it is shown in perspective in plate 5, where the viewer seems to be sitting high on the saddle. (The behavior of the grid on a curved surface is discussed later.) The double cone itself, consisting of circles around the z axis, can be described by the second-degree equation $x^2/a^2 + y^2/b^2 - z^2/c^2 = 0$. When the equation for the surface is available, it can be plotted in perspective by the methods given for a sphere or for topography in chapter 6.

Q7-4. Examine one at a time the simpler functions formed when the preceding equations are tested with $x = 0$, $y = 0$, or $z = 0$. Familiar curves in those planes should appear, justifying the names of the surfaces.

As mentioned in chapter 3, revolved surfaces can be made by revolving almost any two-dimensional object—for example, a rectangle—about any line whatsoever. If the axis passes through the object, a closed-curved surface is obtained. If the axis is outside the object, the curved surface includes a hole. The doubly circular ''torus'' (shaped like a doughnut) can be made by revolving a circle around an exterior axis as shown in figure 7-9. Most surfaces created by revolution do not have equations describing them. They are partly described by the circles that result from the process of revolution, and these can be used to draw the plan and elevation. Then slices and/or the outline box method can be used to draw the perspective.

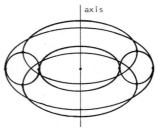

7-9. Torus made by revolving a circle around an axis

Another way to obtain and describe surfaces is to translate a planar curve along any direction not in the plane (but usually perpendicular to it). For example, the circle in an xy plane translated along the z axis produces a right circular cylinder. The general name of these surfaces is ''cylinders.'' If the equation for a planar curve is stated without a specification for the third coordinate, a surface is automatically understood to be generated mathematically and graphically in space. A sine curve when translated produces a wavy wall. For an xy curve, z can have any value; the surface must have its "ends" expressed in terms of values for z in order for it to be seen.

Interesting surfaces for the artist are available from relatively simple functions. The number of variations is immense, and occasionally new ones are invented. Some surfaces use trigonometric functions, such as the Airy Function of plate 4: $z = a \sin^2 b(x^2 + y^2)/b(x^2 + y^2)$. They will be easier to do in terms of polar coordinates (in the next section). Some are combinations of power functions and exponentials. Two different mathematical surfaces can be joined smoothly at a curve of intersection, as in a hemispherical cap joined to a truncated cone. While it may seem that a computer-driven plotter is mandatory for such diagrams, at the most a computer or calculator is needed to calculate coordinates in the quantity needed for hand plotting. A computer graphics system (see chapter 10) is mandatory, however, for creating the new irregular but organized fractal surfaces that look "natural."

Polar Coordinates and Functions

A different and potentially useful orthogonal coordinate system is based on radii from an origin and on angular positions. Polar coordinates are used in a plane analogous to the xy plane. In figure 7-10, point P can be located by coordinates (x,y) or by (r, θ) with respect to the same origin, Coordinate r is measured radially outward in length units and is never negative. Angle θ is measured counterclockwise from the $+x$ axis; values of θ in degrees and radians are shown at the axis at the beginning of each quadrant. The $+y$ axis, for example, is in the direction $\theta = 90°$ or $\pi/2$ radians. The coordinates are orthogonal in the sense that, for a small region near a point, small changes in the coordinate r are in a direction at right angles to small changes in θ. Polar coordinates are best suited for a curve or function that has some degree of radial symmetry or is obtained by rotation. The equation for a circle with center O is very simple: $r = c$, a constant; there is no θ dependence. Any curve can be expressed in polar coordinates.

The conversion from one set to the other is made by means of mathematics already familiar. To change any function from (x,y) coordinates to (r, θ) coordinates, the transformation uses:

$$x = r \cos \theta$$

$$y = r \sin \theta . \tag{7.4}$$

To change a function of r and θ to a function of x and y, the transformation is:

$$r = \sqrt{x^2 + y^2}$$

$$\theta = \tan^{-1} (y/x) . \tag{7.5}$$

The above expression for θ is another way to write the usual form $\tan \theta = y/x$.

Since the xy system is natural for rectilinear perspective, the polar system should be used only when it is a better match to a particular function. Chapter 8 explores other perspectives more compatible with polar and other curved coordinates. For present purposes, if a function is described in polar coordinates, they must be converted to rectilinear coordinates before the perspective is calculated. Since the algebra can become excessively complex, the conversion is normally done numerically.

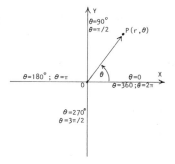

7-10. Polar coordinates superimposed on the rectilinear xy system

Numerous polar functions may be added to the list of elementary functions. Their names are often as beautiful as their shapes: cycloid, cardioid (so named because of its heart shape), limacon, cissoid, conchoid, involute, spirals, lemniscate, and rose. The cycloids are obtained when circles are rolled on planes or around other circles. The involute is a spiral traced by the end of a string unrolled from a cylinder. The lemniscate has the shape of a two-petaled flower, and the rose has as many petals as desired. The spirals are subdivided into Archimedean, hyperbolic, reciprocal, and logarithmic types. The last group is discussed in an example of the general procedure; the artist is left to explore the others independently. Their shapes can be intriguing. The functions are described in any book on analytic geometry and in mathematical tables.

Despite its name, the "logarithmic spiral" has the equation $r = ae^{b\theta}$, which is an exponential equation. It can be rewritten as $\theta = (1/b) \ln (r/a)$, a less obvious form. The multivalued behavior of θ is illustrated with this function. Normally, θ is thought of as ranging from $0°$ to $360°$ or from $-180°$ to $+180°$. With the spirals, though, θ is useful over an indefinitely large range. When θ passes through a multiple of $360°$, it returns to the same direction on a polar graph (figure 7-11), but for this function, r has increased and new points are plotted. Extremely large negative values of θ give points so near the center as to be indistinguishable from it. The spiral continues outward more and more rapidly as θ takes on increasingly large positive values. Parameter b adjusts the rate at which θ affects r in the function.

Q7-5. Where is the point on the spiral at which $\theta = 0$?

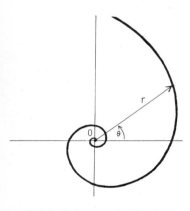

7-11. Polar graph of a logarithmic spiral function

The convenience of polar coordinates is best appreciated if the reader attempts to express the "log spiral" in xy language. The result is formidably complex to plot as a graph, and y cannot be written as a function of x. The algebra is not solvable. Graphing $r = ae^{b\theta}$ is simple, once suitable numerical sizes for a and b are chosen. Since the expression in the exponent must be unitless, b must be in units of reciprocal degrees or radians.

Since rectilinear perspective must be done with rectilinear coordinates, it makes no difference where the polar origin is located. It can be centered at the viewer or at $(x,y) = (0,0)$ or at any other point. The procedure for obtaining the perspective of the "log spiral" or any other polar function is as follows:

1. Decide upon the polar center and adjust the constants to fit the desired layout. Trial calculation and sketches may be needed. The center must be the origin of an $x'y'z'$ system if not at O.

2. Plan the perspective layout as usual, determining the sizes of d and h. It is always wise to sketch plan and elevation views.

3. Translate or rotate from $x'y'z'$ to xyz if necessary.

4. Form a table of calculations thus:

r	θ	x'	y'	z'	x	y	z	p	q

5. For selected values of θ, preferably equal

subdivisions of 360°, calculate the values of r over the range needed. Angle θ should be tested over more than 360° if the function has several revolutions. Values of r less than 1 mm will not be useful; values of r greater than the size of the picture are not needed.

6. Calculate x and y using equation 7.4.
7. Calculate p and q and plot the picture.

If a polar function is to be used in a plane other than the xy plane, equation 7.4 can be modified as needed to obtain the rectilinear coordinates for the function. Rotating polar graphs in xy coordinates should never be necessary. The modification is much more easily accomplished by adding a suitable constant angle to the θ variable. A computer program is provided in the appendix that will calculate the perspective for a "log spiral" or any other polar function substituted in the program.

If the artist does not want a perspective but does want to create a planar design with one of the polar functions, a useful graphic shortcut exists. The procedure is to calculate the table of r and θ values and plot the function as a graph on cardboard, using enough points to obtain smoothness when the curve is drawn. A template of the function is made by cutting out the curve. This method is especially useful when the same curve with the same constants is to be used repeatedly in a regular and symmetrical manner (see plate 6). Plate 6 happens to give the illusion of distance, as if it were a perspective, but no perspective theory was used in its construction. The illusion may be attributed to the use of functions with unusual asymptotic behavior. The log spirals converge toward the center as a limit point.

Spherical and Cylindrical Coordinates

The three-dimensional counterpart to polar coordinates is the spherical coordinate system. Again it is best suited for functions with some radial or rotational symmetry. The simplest surface that can be expressed in spherical coordinates is the surface of a sphere. Then the radial distance is a constant, and no angular dependence is necessary. Otherwise, to preserve three independent dimensions, two angles are needed to locate points. The notation for the three coordinates is (ρ, θ, ϕ). The Greek letter ρ (a length, not an angle) is measured radially outward from the origin in any direction, as determined by the angles, and is never negative. The most common convention for the angles assigns the same meaning to θ as is used for the polar angle. Figure 7-12 shows (in oblique view) a point located with spherical coordinates, superimposed on an xyz system. Angle θ is measured by considering the projection of the point and its radial line onto the xy plane, giving polar coordinates. Angle ϕ is measured from the $+z$ axis to the radial line for the point. Spherical coordinates are orthogonal in that, for a small region around a point, a small change in one of the coordinates is at right angles to small changes in either of the others.

Conversions are possible between the two systems and are needed if a rectilinear perspective is to be calculated. The conversion from spherical to rectilinear is:

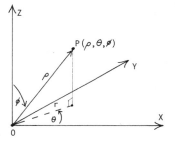

7-12. Spherical coordinates shown on the rectilinear xyz system (oblique view)

$$x = \rho \sin \phi \cos \theta$$

$$y = \rho \sin \phi \sin \theta$$

$$z = \rho \cos \phi . \qquad (7.6)$$

Plotting the perspective involves following the same steps presented earlier for working with polar coordinates.

Most functions expressed in spherical coordinates are complex to interpret. Many beautiful ones are available, but they are likely to be of interest only to the dedicated experimental artist. The most familiar functions (the spherical harmonics) have been found valuable for modern descriptions of the atom, for electromagnetic radiation, for the shape of the earth, and for a wide variety of other physical theories. Of course, the mathematical form is abstract and consequently may be found useful for almost any purpose. The more common spherical functions (besides the sphere) have lobes in space, like two or more eggs centered about an axis. The reader should consult an atomic physics text if interested in pursuing the mathematics further.

Spherical coordinates have been presented here in case the artist can find a use for them. Any subject matter having a center and radial or rotational symmetry might lend itself to these coordinates, simplifying the process of getting the perspective. Chapter 9 shows another form of spherical coordinates centered on the viewer that describe the position of the sun in the sky and, therefore, the illumination it gives.

Cylindrical coordinates, though probably less useful for application, are helpful theoretically. In figure 7-13 (an oblique view), an arbitrary point is located by means of its height z above the xy plane and by means of r and θ for the point's projection onto the xy plane. The coordinates are written in the order (r, θ, z). They can be useful for analyzing cylindrical surfaces that involve rotational symmetry in xy planes and translation symmetry in the z

direction. They can be reoriented if needed, replacing z with x or y. The conversion to xyz coordinates involves procedures already discussed.

There is almost no limit to the ways in which basic functions (power, trigonometric, exponential, and so on) can be combined by addition and multiplication to form new, previously unexplored functions. Some are most conveniently formed in rectilinear coordinates; others are simpler or more natural to form in spherical coordinates. The behavior of the functions should be visualized individually at the outset. Then their effects on each other should be visualized. Polar or spherical coordinates become involved if angles are used as variables in any of the functions, and if r or ρ is used instead of x, y, and z.

Normals and Gradients

The normal for a plane was readily defined and calculated. The normal to a curved line, if ever needed, is simply a line perpendicular to the line tangent to the curve at a given point. The normal to a curved surface is the normal to the plane that is tangent to the surface at a given point. This normal is useful in chapter 9 in the discussion of which way light reflects from a curved surface. It also helps specify the angle at which the viewer sees a surface. For a surface expressed in equation form, the methods of calculus are needed to find the normal. Graphically, the normal can be found by obtaining a view in which the tangent plane is seen edge-on.

The slope of a curved surface is everywhere changing. While a plane has one slope, defined by the direction of its normal, a curved surface has continually varying slope, with the variation occur-

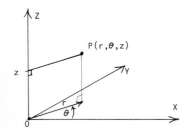

7-13. Cylindrical coordinates shown on the rectilinear *xyz* system (oblique view)

ring in two independent directions. Slopes can be found numerically from topographic contour lines. The slope is then the change in altitude divided by the corresponding change in distance along GP. This should be done on a small scale for accuracy when the surface has much variation. The slope at any given place is also called the "dip" or "grade." Dip is expressed as an angle measured from the ground plane to a line tangent to the surface. Since tangent lines can be drawn in almost any direction at a given point, the one that must be used for slope or dip is defined to be perpendicular to the horizontal tangent line to the surface at the point of interest (called the "strike"). Hence the needed line is the one with greatest slope. The grade is expressed as a percentage calculated by dividing the vertical "rise" by the horizontal "run" for a line matching the slope. It is specified in a particular direction called the "bearing." At any point on a complex surface, the slope or grade is different in different directions unless this condition is specified.

The mathematical concept that expresses both the amount of the slope and its direction is the *gradient*. At any point on a curved surface, the direction of steepest slope is the direction of the gradient. It is also the direction in which the contour lines bunch together the most on a topographic surface. A line in that direction is perpendicular to the contour lines. Vector calculus is needed to obtain the gradient analytically from the surface function. Based on the fact that a topographic map is a way to show a three-dimensional map of a function $z = f(x,y)$, the magnitude and direction of a gradient can be found numerically in a simple manner. The function f gives the value of z, the altitude of the surface above each point in the xy plane. The gradient ob-

tained is two-dimensional in form and lies in the xy plane, yet it will specify the slope of a surface near a point.

In figure 7-14a, on a topographic map in plan view, measurements are made in two dimensions of the number of contour lines that cross x and y line segments of a chosen unit length Δx and Δy. These measurements are made in the vicinity of point P where the gradient is sought. For accuracy the measurements should be made on a small scale where the contours are as nearly uniform as possible. Each contour line represents so many units of altitude. The change in altitude over the distance Δx in the x direction is the number of contours multiplied by the contour interval and is designated as Δf_x. In the y direction, Δf_y is obtained similarly. The ratio $\Delta f_x/\Delta x$ is known as the "component" of the gradient in the x direction, and similarly for $\Delta f_y/\Delta y$. These components are shown at a suitable scale in figure 7-14b for the measurements made on figure 7-14a. The direction ω (measured from the x axis) and the magnitude Δf of the gradient are given by:

$$\tan \omega = \frac{\Delta f_x/\Delta x}{\Delta f_y/\Delta y}$$

$$\Delta f = \sqrt{(\Delta x)^2 + (\Delta y)^2} . \qquad (7.7)$$

The magnitude and direction can also be found graphically in figure 7-14b by completing the rectangle formed by the two components. The magnitude is the length of the diagonal shown in the rectangle, measured with the same scale as is used for the components. (A scale of 1:2 was used here, and Δx and Δy each had length 1.) The direction is given by angle ω. The line segment within the rectangle, in

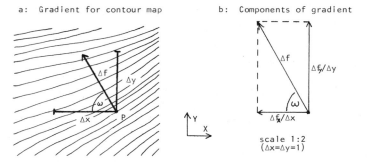

a: Gradient for contour map   b: Components of gradient

scale 1:2
($\Delta x = \Delta y = 1$)

7-14. Finding the steepest slope on a topographic surface—the gradient

the direction shown, represents the gradient. When its length is multiplied by the scale factor (2, here), it gives directly the number of contours crossed in its direction.

The resulting gradient is shown superimposed on figure 7-14a in the correct direction and represents the steepest slope for the contours near point P. The gradient is aligned perpendicularly to the average direction of the contour lines, as it should be. The gradient shown in figure 7-14a cannot be obtained from the line segments Δx and Δy independent of the steps enumerated above. The gradient is sometimes abbreviated "grad." This discussion has not only presented the calculation of a special concept of slope but has also provided a brief introduction to vector analysis by means of components.

Some other generally descriptive terms for the slopes of surfaces may be useful. Examination of a topographic map is likely to reveal "saddle points" between two hilltops. At these points the slope increases in one direction and decreases in the orthogonal direction. They are points of ambiguity in the slope. The hyperbolic paraboloid (plate 5) illustrates

a saddle point. Other interesting features are the maxima or peaks (where the slope must approach zero in all directions), the longitudinal valleys or troughs (where the slope is zero in one direction and increasing in the other), and the minima or depressions (where the slope approaches zero in all directions). The contours at peaks and in depressions must become circular.

Distorted Grids, Curved Spaces, and Anamorphic Art

When the underlying grid is transposed to an overlying curved surface, the grid can either remain as nearly square as possible or be distorted. In the former case, the grid is replotted on the curved surface, and the curved grid is likely to be out of step with the underlying grid. In the latter case, the grid is projected to the surface so that it is stretched to fit the curves of the surface.

Figure 7-15a shows the "curvilinear" method where the grid is replotted on the curved surface, seen in edge view. A grid that had 1-cm spacings flat now has 1-cm spacings on the curved surface. If the surface were unrolled and flattened, the curvilinear grid would be found to be the same size as the underlying grid. The curvilinear grid appears distorted only because the viewer does not realize that it is laid out as if by tape measure over the hills and valleys of the surface. Plate 7 shows a curvilinear grid on the inside of part of a cylinder, in perspective. Unexpectedly complex patterns may occur. Plate 8 shows a curvilinear grid on a sinusoidal surface, in perspective.

Figure 7-15b shows (in edge view) the same grid projected to the same surface. In places where

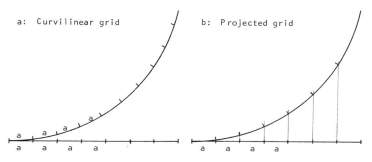

7-15. Two ways of transposing grids to a curved surface

the surface has steep slope, grid spacing is stretched on the surface. Projection can only increase grid sizes, not decrease them. Plates 4 and 5 show a grid projected to the complex curved surface. The artist can choose which method to use if a grid is needed. Whether or not the grid is shown, its pattern determines the location of other objects on the surface.

Q7-6. Which grid method should be used to get proper locations of uniformly spaced trees on a curved surface?

Mathematically, curvilinear grids are much more difficult to work with than projected ones, but they can be more satisfying and more natural. Topographic maps use projected grids; the methods of locating points on surfaces with them have been covered. Their perspective is easy to calculate. Curvilinear grids may require the calculation of "arc length" with calculus. Arc length is simply the distance measured along a curve or surface if a flexible tape measure is used. The ruler should conform to the surface, even over the sharpest peaks. The work of obtaining the grid and plotting the perspective

can all be done graphically or can be aided mathematically.

For figure 7-15a, the work is easy because uniform spacing on a cylindrical surface can be laid out by subdividing the circular arc into equal angles. Arc length *s* along a circular arc is given by the equation that defines an angle (figure 7-16). The useful form is:

$$s = R\theta \text{ (radians)}$$
$$s = R\theta/57.3 \text{ (degrees)} , \qquad (7.8)$$

where R is the radius of the arc and θ is the angle of the arc. The natural units for θ in this equation are radians; the second form of the equation is used for degrees ($2\pi = 6.28$ radians $= 360°$). For small angles, the arc length approaches the same length as the "chord" (the line cutting across the circular arc with length *c* in figure 7-16). For very small angles, the following approximations are useful, provided that θ is measured in radians:

$$\theta = s/R \simeq c/R \simeq \tan\theta \simeq \sin\theta . \qquad (7.9)$$

Only in polar coordinates are some arc lengths easy to calculate, and then in only a very few cases. Another procedure is to use a flexible ruler on an elevation view of the curve of interest and mark out equal spacings. The perspective transformation is done only after the grid coordinates are determined.

Whether curvilinear or projected, the preceding grids were compatible with normal perspective. Unnatural perspectives can also be created. The possibilities are best illustrated with grids. The result is a perspective of a "curved" space—that is, of a non-Euclidean space. A *curved space* is not the

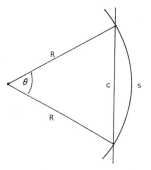

7-16. Basic definition of an angle

same as a space curve. Space curves are a normal part of three-dimensional Euclidean space where coordinate axes are at right angles to one another. A curved space either has the axes at nonright angles or has the units of length varying in different directions (or both). According to Einstein's special theory of relativity, high-speed travel changes space, opening the way for new explorations in perspective. As three-dimensional beings brought up in (apparently) Euclidean space, human beings cannot easily visualize other kinds of spaces. At the scale of planets and larger, real space is noticeably curved (Einstein's theory of general relativity). The type and amount of curvature can be measured by its manifestation as gravity, by the paths of light rays, and by comparing the calculated angles in large triangles with the results of triangles in "flat" space.

The most salient distinction of non-Euclidean space is that parallel lines may not be defined. The PP itself is a non-Euclidean two-dimensional space where "parallel" lines meet. The common analogies for imagining curved space are made with the surface of a sphere and with the surface of the hyperbolic paraboloid. On the sphere's surface, the angles of a triangle always add to more than 180°; how much more determines the radius of the sphere. Also, "parallel" lines such as the lines of longitude on the earth's surface meet (at the poles). On the hyperbolic paraboloid's surface, the angles of a triangle add to less than 180° and "parallel" lines diverge—hence, the apparent failure of the grid to have VPs in plate 5.

An example of a possible approach for the artist was given in figure 4-23. There, a grid with an unorthodox convergence of diagonals was constructed directly in the PP. In general, it should be decided what behavior the diagonals should have. The list of basic functions should be examined for one that curves as wanted for the diagonals. Symmetry and how the plane is to be covered uniformly should be considered. Parameters can be adjusted to fit the desired size and shape of picture. Drawing can be done by making templates or by plotting calculated points. The eye may perceive the resulting grid as a curved space.

Q7-7. Try to derive the ordinary perspective equations by requiring that the diagonals of a grid in PP be straight lines converging to VPs in the proper position.

A type of transformation of space that has received revived interest in recent years is the one used for anamorphic art (art requiring the viewer to "re-form" it). In past centuries, artists used the grid method to construct transformations of pictures that appear distorted unless viewed in the appropriate direction, at an extreme slant, or with a special mirror (conical or cylindrical). The anamorphic picture represents a curved space. Whether the anamorphic transformation gives a perspective in the usual sense may be arguable, but certainly perspective can be included in the overall operation. Anamorphic art is even more dependent on a special location of the viewer for an undistorted view than perspective is. The artist can study nonmathematical sources on anamorphic art and architecture[4] but would have to apply methods introduced in this book to arrive at a mathematical treatment.

Perspective enters into many anamorphic illusions that artists and architects have long used. For example, a tall sign or a mural high on a wall can be viewed only at a slant. The subject matter can be made more intelligible by being constructed in a predistorted manner so that, when viewed at an angle from the floor, its proper proportions are perceived. In figure 7-17 the q coordinates of the picture are stretched farther apart near the top of the picture so that the angular size α seen for grid spacings is the same all over the picture. The grid spacing needed can be calculated easily. For a situation in which the bottom of the picture is at eye level, the first grid spacing a is seen essentially head-on. For small values of a, it is seen with angular size $\alpha \simeq a/d$. All grid lines farther up the q axis should be seen with the same angular spacing. The nth grid line q_n should be at location $q_n = d \tan n\alpha$ for the triangle shown. Since $\alpha \simeq a/d$, the result is that the grid lines must be drawn at these vertical locations on the wall:

$$q_n \simeq d \tan (na/d) . \qquad (7.10)$$

The "tan" function must use radians, and the equation becomes inaccurate when the total angle approaches 90° and q_n approaches ∞. For accuracy, a should be such that α is no greater than a few degrees.

The illusion is preserved only for narrow, tall pictures whose sides cannot be seen at a severe angle. Otherwise, a similar scheme of changing the spacing of grid lines along the p axis must be used.

The resulting picture makes sense only to a viewer near a certain location. In this example, a "cylindrical" perspective has been created by drawing the picture as if it were arched over the viewer's head. The simulated cylindrical picture is represented in edge view by the angular arc in figure 7-17. A limit exists to how much a flat picture can be modified in this way. The mathematical method given is limited to a largest angle of view of less than 90°. For panoramic views, other mathematical methods are available. The possibilities, the methods, and other aspects of perspective illusion are covered in the next chapter.

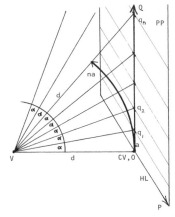

7-17. Tall anamorphic picture using a distorted grid

Notes

1. At an intermediate level, see Thomas, *Calculus;* Taylor, *Calculus;* or Purcell, *Calculus.* At an elementary level, see Jacobs, *Mathematics* or Land, *Language of Mathematics.*

2. On the mathematical and physical behavior of curving rivers, see Luna Leopold and W. B. Langbein, "River Meanders."

3. On superellipses (ovals), see Martin Gardner, "The Superellipse: A Curve That Lies between an Ellipse and a Rectangle."

4. On anamorphic transformations, see Fred Leeman, *Hidden Images* and Martin Gardner, "The Curious Magic of Anamorphic Art."

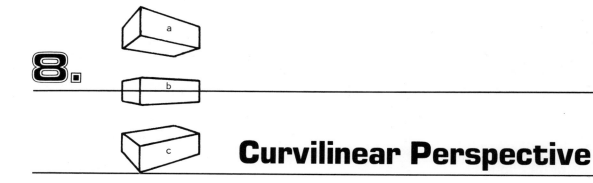

8.

Curvilinear Perspective

The Limitations of Rectilinear Perspective

Earlier chapters show many ways in which rectilinear perspective, constructed on a flat picture plane with the viewer in a certain fixed position, leads to distortions at picture locations away from the center of vision. Not only do squares, circles, and spheres appear more out of shape than they should, but the distortion differs at different viewing positions. At one viewing position in particular, features that are drawn properly but seem distorted in PP appear correct, but this position is usually too close, at least for illustrations in books.

There are three basic causes for the distortion, even if the viewer does not move the line of sight away from CV. First, the distances between viewer and PP and between PP and subject matter both vary. Second, the angle at which an object in the picture is seen varies. Third, the picture of an object does not become smaller as the object is moved to the side, although the angular size becomes smaller. A fourth defect occurs if the objects have width and depth.

Figure 8-1, a plan view, shows light rays from equal line segments $\overline{A}$, $\overline{B}$, and $\overline{C}$ coming from progressively farther distances and steeper angles. While the viewer might expect $\overline{C}$ to appear smaller than $\overline{A}$ because distance $\overline{CV}$ is greater than distance $\overline{AV}$, the size in the picture is unchanged. Moreover, the viewer is not prepared for the image of $\overline{C}$ on PP to be farther away than the image of $\overline{A}$. Distance $\overline{CC'}$—the distance from $\overline{C}$ to PP, as seen by the viewer—is greater than distance $\overline{AA'}$, as expected,

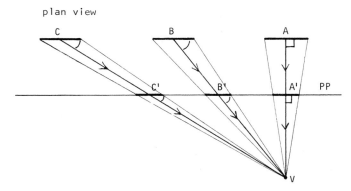

plan view

8-1. Shortcomings in rectilinear perspective

but not enough greater. Regardless of the angle at which light rays come from the objects, the angle at which they come from the picture of each object changes in the same way; they do not leave the picture surface normally. The farther to the side the viewer perceives the picture, the worse these three errors are. If the line of sight is shifted to an object at the side, the errors are compounded. If the line segments are the fronts, for example, of squares, the comparative size of the more distant squares to the side will seem unnaturally large.

The problems have been recognized for a long time in both art and architecture, but the solutions have rarely received detailed examination or been applied. The columns and steps of Greek temples have their shapes altered from straight lines to make them appear straighter. Fifteenth-century French paintings by Jean Fouquet show streets tiled in a curved grid.[1] Flat paintings based on curved grids trade one viewing problem for another. Features may become less distorted and the viewer freer to

look around, but the interpretation of a curved perspective can raise new confusion.

The Case for Curvilinear Perspectives

The term *curvilinear perspective* can be defined as a perspective viewed on a curved surface. The surface can no longer be called PP, which is a plane, but PS, for *picture surface*. Necessarily, there must be a transformation of a rectilinear grid or lattice to a curved one in the picture. A more natural coordinate system for the transformation may exist, such as polar or spherical. While the most common forms of curvilinear perspective are cylindrical and spherical, there are numerous other possibilities (elliptical and toroidal, for example). Some of the errors of rectilinear perspective can be relieved by curving PS to remain at a constant distance from the viewer. The viewer is then permitted to look in a variety of directions and see PS normally. A curved PS can match the way human eyes scan the world, but it may be necessary to distinguish vertical and horizontal scans.

When a curvilinear perspective is presented flat, an additional transformation has been done from the curved PS to the flat one (still called PS). The curved PS can be "ironed" flat or simply unrolled. A transformation can also be done from an orthogonal grid in space to a curved grid in the picture. Curvilinear perspectives have been explored by recent artists such as M. C. Escher and Albert Flocon.[2] Since these perspectives were used in prints that were to be displayed flat, the effect is more ingenious and technical than natural and convincing. Nonetheless, the general methods of curvilinear perspective—both graphic and mathematical—may open new areas of discovery and new options for the artist.

For curvilinear perspectives, the behavior of parallel lines must be reexamined. If the viewer is imagined to be lying on the ground looking up at two infinitely long, unsagging, parallel wires (figure 8-2a), the paradox of the perspective of parallel lines becomes apparent.[3] If the viewer could see to the horizon in both directions (a bit difficult, given the limitation to the angle of view for the eye), a vanishing point for the pair of wires would be seen in each direction. The viewer may be permitted to scan the scene visually, but a central point C for the line of sight—defined as the fixed point straight ahead (overhead, in this case)—exists in all cases.

Several distinct options are available for what is seen. Either the wires converge as straight lines to each VP, requiring a "kink" or *discontinuity* directly overhead, as in figure 8-2b, or the wires must appear to curve toward each VP, as in figure 8-2c. A discontinuity is defined as an abrupt change in direction or slope. No one has observed parallel wires to appear to kink in this way. Therefore, the slope of the parallel wires must smoothly change from one value near C to another at the VPs. Another, slightly more complex way in which the slope could change is shown in figure 8-2d. There, the slopes approach each other, which is to say that the wires curve asymptotically toward each other near the VPs. Since the curvature reverses somewhere in the distance, inflection points occur at I. Whichever case holds, the exact curve can be calculated, and a new perspective can be found that avoids the

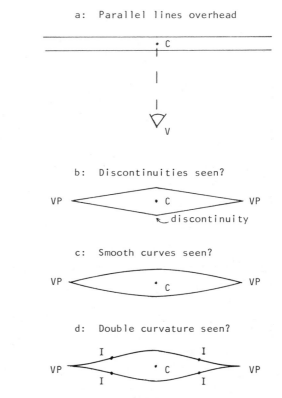

8-2. Looking at parallel lines [after Escher]

paradox. The mathematical proof for parallel lines is given later.

The preceding study for horizontal parallel wires can be turned and applied to any vertical parallel lines, such as the edges of a very tall pole or building. If situated next to the indefinitely tall object, the viewer would see that its edges curve together both below and above. In the third dimension (depth) the viewer should see, for example, that railroad tracks curve together toward VPs in the distance, both in front and behind. Parallel lines that seem to curve toward VPs are implicated for all three dimensions by this simple and symmetric argument.

Cylindrical Perspective by the Graphic Method

The procedure for constructing a cylindrical perspective can be done with a grid to illustrate the nature of the perspective. PS is the wall of a cylinder, with the cylinder's axis vertical and viewer V on the axis. The plan of figure 8-3 shows PS in edge view as a semicircle. This perspective is called a "horizontal pan" because V can scan PS as a horizontal panorama. The grid is a square xy grid located in GP. The grid must be plotted point by point until the needed amount of pattern appears. A double projection method is used. The picture is constructed on flat paper, and therefore the perspective is converted to flat form. The normal or resting position for the eye is at C in the picture, and it lies on HL as usual. The many steps that follow can be readily generalized for any object:

1. Decide the radius of the cylinder, which is the constant distance of V from the curved PS. Draw it in plan.
2. Decide the height of V above GP and show in elevation. V must be a distance equal to the radius from the element of PS at O. (For simplicity, figure 8-3 is arranged with V for both views at the same point, which also becomes the central point C of the picture.)

3. Place the grid with its origin O touching the back of PS on the central axis CA. The grid points should be labeled in an orderly manner, for example by the use of (x,y) coordinates as shown.
4. Show the grid in elevation, marking the y coordinates.
5. Starting with the first row of grid points, construct lines from V to each point, finding the pierce points in PS. Each pierce point is labeled $S(x_n, y_m)$, according to the grid point to which it corresponds. The complete construction lines are shown for points (1,0) and (5,2) in figure 8-3.
6. From centerline CL, which goes through V, measure vertically in the plan to the pierce points, obtaining the distances—for example, $v(1,0)$ to $S(1,0)$ and $v(5,2)$ to $S(5,2)$. Lay out each distance horizontally in the elevation view from CA, and draw a vertical line. The vertical lines can be labeled—for example, $\overline{PS}(1,0)$ and $\overline{PS}(5,2)$—to show that they are elements of PS as seen in elevation corresponding to the pierce points in plan. The central PS element passing through O is called $\overline{PS}_0$. Note how the spacing of PS elements varies as larger x coordinates are plotted.
7. Find the pierce point through each PS element in elevation for lines from V to y coordinates of grid points. Construct horizontal lines in the picture from each pierce point and label them—for example, $\overline{H}(1,0)$ and $\overline{H}(5,2)$.
8. Measure (with a flexible ruler) along the

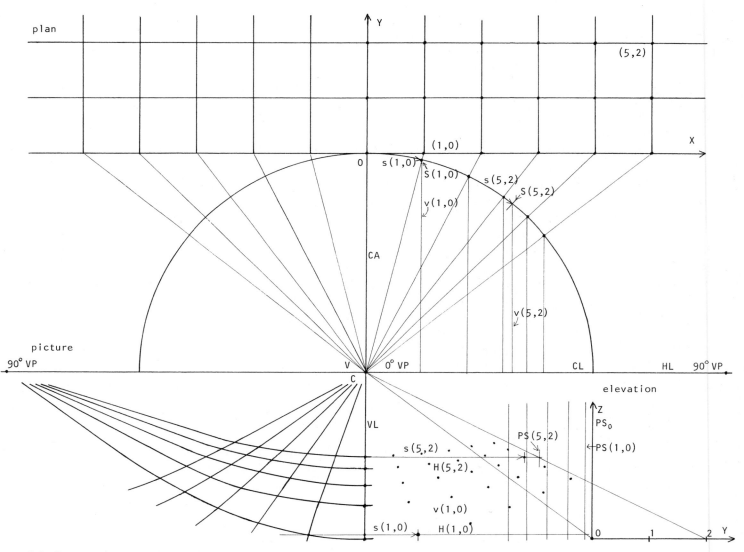

8-3. Constructing a grid in cylindrical perspective (the picture shows part of the grid and is flattened)

curved PS in plan from O to the points S, obtaining arc lengths—for example, $s(1,0)$ and $s(5,2)$.

9. Lay out the distances s in the picture along the lines $\overline{\overline{H}}$. For a grid, s is measured the same in both directions from VL.

10. Measure ¼ circular arc from O. Lay out this distance along HL to get a 90° VP on each side of O. C is the 0° VP.

11. Connect the points to form part of the curvilinear grid. Near the VPs, the grid lines become nearly straight. A good French curve for connecting the points would be one having a long and very gradual change in curvature, approaching straightness at one end. Note that the grid lines intersect at what seem to be right angles in perspective, as they should.

More grid can be added in the neglected areas behind PS if needed. Grid can even be placed in front of PP and plotted. The 90° VPs are 180° apart and represent the two ends of what was a straight line. The diagonals of the grid approach 45° VPs, which can be located by measuring ⅛ circular arc from O (45° from CA) and laying it out on HL. In the same way, any other VP can be found. The artist may wish to restrict the total field of view to less than 90°, causing one or both 90° VPs not to appear in the picture. Because of the necessity of plotting each grid point, the construction work can be very crowded.

If rectangular objects are to be located in cylindrical perspective, their horizontal edges have the same VPs and curve the same way as the underlying grid curves. Diagonal lines, like any other features, can be plotted point by point. In the mathematical section that follows some of the behavior of lines in general is discussed. Vertical parallel lines remain parallel because this perspective corrects distortion only horizontally. Vertical distortion remains, and tall objects should be avoided.

A new distortion seems to have been introduced in the form of the curvature of the grid; it disappears completely if the flat picture is rolled to the correct radius. The eyes can scan around the curved picture and see each feature normally; that is, the line of sight intersects PS perpendicularly. The view is designed for one viewing point at a certain distance (the radius), but the once-curved grid appears quite straight inside the curved surface even if the viewing position is altered.

Q8-1. Test the diagonals of the front center squares in figure 8-3. Lay out the 45° VPs, and see how well the diagonals are aimed at these VPs.

Q8-2. Roll figure 8-3 to a radius equal to that shown in plan, and position your eye at the same distance from C. Although the viewing is rather close, a 180° panorama of a perfectly square grid should result. It would be better to practice constructing the perspective of a large grid, with a radius of at least 30 cm.

Calculating Cylindrical Perspective

If PS is a cylindrical wall, three general orientations for it are possible. The axis of the cylinder can be vertical, parallel to but not identical with the z axis, as shown for the preceding graphic construction of a "horizontal pan." The cylinder axis can be horizontal, parallel to the x axis, giving a "vertical pan." The cylinder axis can be horizontal but parallel to the y axis; the viewer looks out the end of the cylinder, and it becomes useless for perspective.

Regardless of the orientation of the cylinder, certain lines visible in the picture can continue to have the same labels. An HL still lies horizontal with respect to the standing viewer. For convenience, VL is defined as a vertical line through C and perpendicular to HL. In vertical pan, VL wraps around the viewer and HL is straight. The opposite occurs for horizontal pans, and a GL may be visible. The calculation of the perspective for a general object point is done mathematically for both vertical and horizontal pans. The main distinction between the two sets of results is the inclusion of the distance h of the viewer above GP for the horizontal pan.

In figure 8-4, plan and elevation views are given for a viewer facing a horizontal, half-cylindrical wall for a vertical pan. The radius of the cylinder is R— the only needed picture parameter. The xy plane here is at eye level, although it could be elsewhere. The origin O of the xyz coordinates used for describing the subject matter is placed at C, touching the back of PS. The general point P has coordinates (x,y,z). The line $\overline{VP}$ pierces PS at P'. The vertical coordinate, measured along the curved surface from O, is called s. An alternative way to locate vertical positions is by using the ϕ, with positive values measured upward from centerline CA. The horizontal coordinate is p, measured as usual from CA in plan. The coordinate ϕ is most useful if PS remains curved. When PS is flattened, values of s, which are arc lengths, are easily measured, and s is the pre-

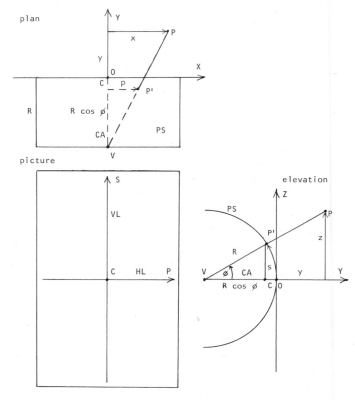

8-4. Calculating cylindrical perspective for a vertical panorama

ferred coordinate. By the definition of angle, s and ϕ are related by:

$$s = R\phi . \qquad (8.1)$$

At this time all angular measurements must be in radians or must be converted to radians. The conversion is most easily remembered from the fact that $2\pi = 6.2832$ radians $= 360°$.

For the elevation view of figure 8-4, the angular location of P is given by:

$$\tan \phi = z/(R + y) . \qquad (8.2)$$

The s coordinate of P on PS is found by combining equations 8.1 and 8.2:

$$s = R \tan^{-1} [z/(R + y)] . \qquad (8.3)$$

The inverse tangent "$\tan^{-1}$" is a function that calculates the angle from the ratio that expresses the tangent. It is found on most trigonometric calculators.

For the plan view, the p coordinate of point P is found by considering the ratios of the sides of similar triangles. The location p is measured to the pierce point P', which is on an element of PS somewhere between V and P. From the elevation, the pierce point can be seen to be at distance R cos ϕ from V. In the plan, the ratio of the sides of the triangles gives $p/(R \cos \phi) = x/(R + y)$. For calculation, the function of ϕ must be eliminated. Again from the elevation at which the properties of ϕ are visible, it can be seen that:

$$\cos \phi = (R + y)/\sqrt{z^2 + (R + y)^2} . \qquad (8.4)$$

Using equation 8.4 in the ratio, the expression for p becomes:

$$p = Rx/\sqrt{z^2 + (R + y)^2} . \qquad (8.5)$$

The horizontal pan for cylindrical perspective may be more useful. Figure 8-5 shows the plan and elevation views needed to obtain similar expres-

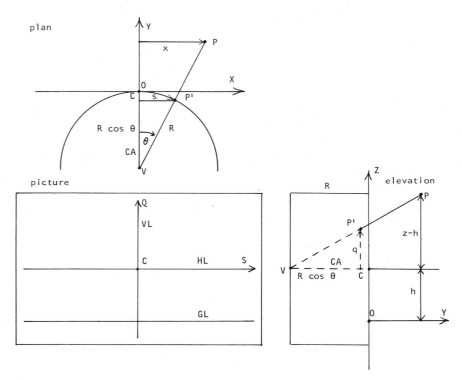

8-5. Calculating cylindrical perspective for a horizontal panorama

sions for the PS coordinates of a point P(x,y,z). In this case, the arc coordinate s is measured horizontally around PS from C. The equivalent angular location is given by θ, measured clockwise from CA to make positive θ agree with positive x. The familiar coordinate q is measured vertically from HL. The xy plane, GP, is placed a distance h below the viewer. From the definition of angle, s and θ are related by:

$$s = R\theta . \qquad (8.6)$$

From the plan the angular location is given by:

$$\tan \theta = x/(R + y) . \qquad (8.7)$$

The *s* coordinate on PS is found by combining equations 8.6 and 8.7 to give:

$$s = R \tan^{-1} [x/(R + y)] . \qquad (8.8)$$

The position of the PS element containing the pierce point for P is found in plan as distance R cos θ from V, with cos θ given by:

$$\cos \theta = (R + y)/\sqrt{x^2 + (R + y)^2} . \qquad (8.9)$$

Therefore, from the elevation view, the *q* coordinate of the pierce point can be found by means of similar triangles to be:

$$q = (z - h)R/\sqrt{x^2 + (R + y)^2} . \qquad (8.10)$$

As was seen for the graphic construction, the VPs are on HL for any lines in a plane parallel to GP. All lines except vertical ones curve toward their VPs. The location *d* of a VP on HL for a line at angle θ from CA is given by:

$$d(\theta) = R\theta \text{ (radians)} = 2\pi R\theta/360 \text{ (degrees)}, \quad (8.11)$$

where θ must be measured in radians or degrees according to which form of the equation is used. Location *d* is laid out along HL from C. Although the names of principal VPs are referred to in degrees—for example, 90° VP—the calculation must be done in radians if no conversion is made as indicated. For a line with a VP above or below HL, the vertical location (a *q* coordinate) is found by rectilinear procedures described previously. When the cylindrical perspective is a vertical pan, the preceding considerations must be changed accordingly.

It is necessary to calculate and plot more than the eight corner points of a rectangular box in order to illustrate curvilinear perspective. Otherwise, the box would seem to have straight sides rather than curved ones. Additional points along the edges of an object must be plotted to see the cylindrical or other curved perspective.

As an example, the cylindrical perspective of a simple tall building with square cross section is calculated in vertical pan. The viewer is located above the top, as shown in elevation in figure 8-6. The building is oriented angularly and symmetrically, as shown in the plan. The tall sides of the building are handled in four sections, so five *z* coordinates are used for the building (see elevation). For this simple situation, only eleven points need to be calculated. Others are found by symmetry, and a total of sixteen points are plotted, including four showing the top of the building.

After some trigonometry is used for a 4-unit-square cross section, the coordinates of the top (or any level, with an appropriate change in the value of *z*) are found to be as shown in the table below. The radius R of the PS is 10 units. The viewer is 5 units above the top, and the building is 20 units tall. Although its base is 25 units below GP, *h* = 0 in this arrangement and does not enter into the calculations. Equations 8.3 and 8.5 are used to calculate PS coordinates *s* and *p*, respectively. The calculations for the top four points, in the same arbitrary units, are given in the accompanying table.

Point	x	y	z	p	s
front corner	0	0	−5	0	−4.64
right corner	2.83	2.83	−5	2.05	−3.72
back corner	0	5.66	−5	0	−3.09
left corner	−2.83	2.83	−5	−2.05	−3.72

These and the remaining points are plotted in the flattened PS shown in figure 8-6. The 90° VP for the vertical edges of the building is located at $s = -15.71$. The locations of the VPs for the horizontal edges are the same for all levels. Since all levels are parallel to GP, the VPs are on HL. In the plan, they appear as ordinary 45° VPs given by $d \tan 45°$. In this case, V is distance $d = R = 10$ from PS, so the VPs are 10 units from C. However, the edges curve toward these VPs, as the perspectives of all lines except those parallel to the x axis must.

Q8-3. Calculate more values for the above table, and check the calculation of the 90° VPs. If you plot points, they may need scaling to fit the picture as printed.

Q8-4. At each level of the building in the picture of figure 8-6, test the directions in which the "horizontal" edges seem to point. Locate and compare these with the 45° VPs.

Q8-5. Why is the picture of figure 8-6 reminiscent of oblique perspective?

Now the behavior of parallel lines can be analyzed, using as an example the edges of a tall narrow object such as a pole. A vertical line in the

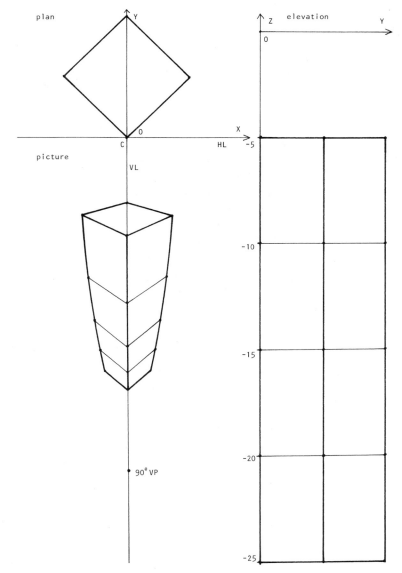

8-6. Cylindrical perspective of a tall building (vertical panorama shown flattened)

xz plane has the equations $\{x = x_0; y = 0\}$, where x_0 is a constant. This line and a symmetrically placed companion are shown in front view in figure 8-7. The perspective is to be a vertical pan on a cylindrical PS; VPs therefore fall on VL, the straight vertical line in PS that is the transformation of the *z* axis. The problem is to find the equation of the curve in the picture, representing the straight vertical line. The curve should be expressed in the form *s* as a function of *p*. The ratio preceding equation 8.4, $p = Rx \cos \phi/(R + y)$, is sufficient to start with. Angle ϕ can be eliminated in favor of *s* by means of equation 8.1. *y* is set equal to 0, and *x* is set equal to x_0, thus satisfying the conditions for a vertical straight line. *z* can be any value along the line, and transformations involving *z* can be avoided. The result is $p = x_0 \cos (s/R)$. This can be rearranged using an inverse cosine function to obtain:

$$s = R \cos^{-1} (p/x_0) . \qquad (8.12)$$

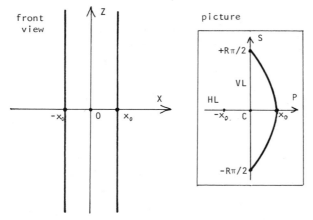

8-7. Calculating the cylindrical perspective of vertical lines (vertical panorama)

The "$\cos^{-1}$" function has a standard graph, as shown in figure 8-7. When *p* is zero, $\cos^{-1}$ has the values $\pm\pi/2$, so *s* is $\pm R\pi/2$. When *p* has the maximum value x_0, $\cos^{-1}$ goes to zero and *s* is zero. The graph shows part of a cosine function turned sideways, which is the way a $\cos^{-1}$ function appears. The x_0 is the amplitude and the expected location of the line at the center on HL. The companion line would share the same VPs and pass through $p = -x_0$ on HL. Similar results would be obtained if the straight line were moved back to some position $y = y_0$.

The behavior of the line can also be examined with equation 8.2. As *z* approaches $\pm\infty$, ϕ approaches $\pm\pi/2$ and *s* approaches $\pm R\pi/2$. Simultaneously, by equation 8.5, *p* approaches zero. At the center, *z* is zero and equation 8.5 gives $p = x_0$. All vertical lines would act the same way in perspective, curving sinusoidally (as required by equation 8.12) and differing only in amplitude. A similar analysis holds for horizontal lines in horizontal pan.

General Remarks on Cylindrical Perspective

If the picture is to be viewed flat, distortion can only be avoided by keeping the angular field of view reasonably small—90° or less. At most, just one of the 90° VPs should appear. Objects far from the circumferential line through C (HL for horizontal pans, VL for vertical pans) should be avoided. For experimentation, however, the cylindrical PS can be as long and as wide as wanted. The angle of pan can be as large as 360° for a complete wrap around the viewer.

When panoramas greater than 180° are considered, more VPs occur for a grid. Theoretically the entire 360° curve of the cylinder can be unrolled, showing five VPs at 90° intervals. A single once-straight grid line weaves back and forth in a sinusoidal pattern on each side of the circumferential line, passing through VPs. Beyond 360° of view, the scene should repeat itself, although no one may notice the difference if the artist creates a much longer flat mural. M. C. Escher's print "House of Stairs" exploits almost 270° of space, showing what might be called floor, three walls, and ceiling of a tiled interior. This picture illustrates how the grid is used in cylindrical perspective to present the several sides of a complex but originally rectilinear interior. Escher's print "High and Low" is also based on cylindrical perspective, but in it some other illusions are added.[4]

To be properly displayed, a cylindrical perspective should be rolled to the radius for which it was designed.[5] Then the viewer stands at the center and has up to 360° of view. Plate 9 shows the display of a pan of over 180°, with grid lines on GP. The picture is rolled to the correct radius, but the camera does not have a 180° lens and cannot be placed at the viewing center. The artist should consider the practical problems of display before completing many cylindrical works. New approaches to framing are needed. Cylindrical perspective could be well suited for large murals on curved walls.

The mathematics for this perspective has a singularity at the center. When $y = -R$, the transformation fails. The transformation for particular objects, such as circles, is left to the reader to test. The simplest approach is usually to calculate the transformation numerically for points established in the xyz system. A circle does not transform to an ellipse on PS. Probably no transformations other than for certain straight lines can be carried out analytically. The transformation (equations 8.3 and 8.5 or equations 8.8 and 8.10) is too nonlinear to preserve straight lines in general. Computer programs for calculating cylindrical perspectives can be modeled after those in the appendix.

Spherical Perspective

An improvement on cylindrical perspective can be obtained with *spherical perspective,* at the cost of greater complexity in mathematics, graphics, and practical construction. While the term "spherical" has been used to refer to almost any curvilinear perspective, it is reserved here for the case when PS is a sphere. The perspective is also known as a "fish-eye" view. Putting the viewer at the center of a spherical shell provides an equal distance from the viewer to all points of the picture. Moreover, all parts are seen normally (rays of light leave the surface at right angles). For cylindrical perspective, distortion was introduced at regions not near the circumferential line that passed through C. For spherical perspective, the eye can scan in any direction and is not limited to certain "pans." In fact, the spherical surface, or a part of it, imitates the approximately spherical surface of the retina, and the compatibility of eye and picture is as complete as possible. Photography would be done on spherically shaped film if it were technically possible. For artistic purposes, the use of spherical perspective may be limited to large permanent installations where part or much of a dome is built. A spherical theater is desirable but it is difficult to project the proper images from film, even in sections.

The problem of showing a sphere in perspective has been to make the cone of light rays from its edge intersect PP or PS as needed to give a circular image. Finding a PS that permits this under all conditions results in the use of a spherical PS. Another observation pertaining to spherical perspective is that the only straight line that appears straight to a viewer is the one being directly gazed at. All other lines appear curved, and none is parallel. If the viewer's gaze is directed at another line, that one appears straight and its neighbors appear curved toward it. Additional discussion of these and other aspects of spherical perspective may be found in other sources.[6]

The main practical problem with spherical perspective is that a real picture can never be flattened. It must be constructed directly on spherically shaped material and viewed, or it must be constructed on flat paper and remain flat. Even a small section of a very large sphere wrinkles when flattened, and, in any case, a small section loses the advantages afforded by the perspective. The long history of map-making for the spheroidal earth illustrates the difficulties of representing spheres on flat paper. Several kinds of distortion are unavoidable. When a high level of accuracy is required, the problems appear for regions as small as a county.

If distortion is acceptable, a spherical perspective can be constructed on flat paper with the same graphic double-projection methods already used. However, the construction is so complicated that the calculation method of spherical perspective is much more attractive. The graphic method is not attempted here. The main difficulty arises from trying to locate PS elements (which are no longer lines but simply points) in orthographic views. In the process of locating pierce points, the artist is led to a mathematical approach much like the following.

Spherical coordinates are natural for spherical perspective. In figure 8-8a, both the xyz system and the spherical system are centered at V (and O), for simplification of the calculations. The standard spherical coordinate system (ρ, ϕ, θ) is not the simplest form suitable for this perspective. The general point P at (x,y,z) is best located spherically in terms of a new system (ρ, σ, τ). Greek letter ρ, the radial distance from O and V to P, is the same. But the new angles σ and τ, are chosen to provide the simplest correspondence with a new pair of orthogonal PS coordinates s and t. For the angles to be measured, reference planes must be defined. The xyz system is aligned so that the central axis CA, where V looks when the eyes are at rest, is identical with the y axis. The yz plane is vertical and is called the central plane (CP). The edge where CP cuts the spherical PS is seen as VL, a straight line in the picture (figure 8-8b). The xy plane is horizontal and is called the central horizontal plane (HP). Where HP cuts PS is seen as the usual straight horizon line (HL). VL and HL can appear straight even though they may be wrapped around V. VL and HL intersect at C, where CA pierces PS.

The radial line from V to P pierces the spherical PS at P', a point with coordinates (x',y',z') or (R, σ, τ). R is the radius of the spherical PS. Angle τ is measured from HP up (or down) to P'. Angle τ is defined in a vertical triangle with opposite side z' and hypotenuse R. This triangle also defines a plane rotated (left or right) an angle σ from CP and CA. Angle σ is defined in another triangle with opposite side x' and hypotenuse R. The triangle containing σ

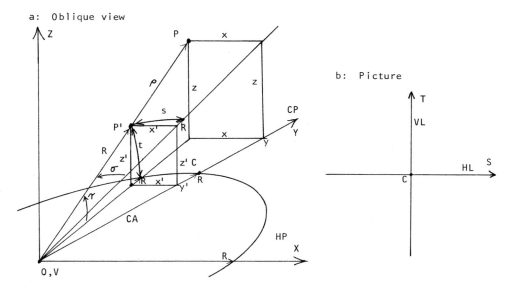

a: Oblique view

b: Picture

8-8. Calculating spherical perspective

happens to be titled up (or down) from HP by angle τ. Since an opposite side divided by a hypotenuse defines the sine of an angle, the inverse function "$\sin^{-1}$" is very useful for calculating the angle. Angle σ is given by $\sigma = \sin^{-1}(x'/R)$, and τ is given by $\tau = \sin^{-1}(z'/R)$. Because P lies radially outward from P', the same angles can be used to locate P in terms of its coordinates (x,y,z) by means of similar triangles. P lies a distance from V and O equal to:

$$\rho = \sqrt{x^2 + y^2 + z^2} \,. \qquad (8.13)$$

The angular locations of P are then:

$$\sigma = \sin^{-1}[x/\sqrt{x^2 + y^2 + z^2}] \qquad (8.14)$$

$$\tau = \sin^{-1}[z/\sqrt{x^2 + y^2 + z^2}] \,. \qquad (8.15)$$

With the definition of angle, σ and τ can be converted to curvilinear coordinates that can be measured with a ruler on a flat or curved PS. Figure 8-8b shows the PS coordinates s and t flattened on paper. Coordinates s and t were parts of great circles in figure 8-8a. Assuming that measurements of the inside (or outside) of a spherical shell of radius R are wanted, the horizontal measurement s is given by:

$$s = R\sigma = R \sin^{-1}[x/\sqrt{x^2 + y^2 + z^2}] \,, \qquad (8.16)$$

and the vertical measurement t is given by:

$$t = R\tau = R \sin^{-1}[z/\sqrt{x^2 + y^2 + z^2}] \,. \qquad (8.17)$$

If used explicitly, σ and τ are found in radians or degrees, depending on the calculator setting, by "sin⁻¹." They must be in radians on a computer unless appropriate conversions to degrees are made. Equations 8.16 and 8.17, when used to calculate s and t directly, do not involve measuring any angles. A graph of the "sin⁻¹" function is simply part of the graph of the "sin" function turned sideways. Angles σ and τ do not appear true size in any orthographic view for figure 8-8a. They have been chosen to give s and t as orthogonal coordinates on the flattened PS (which is not the same as the front view). Angle τ has a simple relation to the spherical coordinate ϕ but σ cannot be found readily from θ.

These are rather simple equations for calculating spherical perspective. They are completely symmetric in x and z; that is, identical results are obtained if x and z are traded. Nevertheless, these equations constitute a nonlinear transformation, and only certain straight lines to which they are applied remain straight.

Figure 8-9 shows the spherical perspective calculated for a part of a grid in an xz plane, the plane $y = R$. The grid is located symmetrically at $y = R$ so that $(x,z) = (0,0)$ just touches PS at C. The grid spacing is expressed in terms of R as 0.2R, avoiding problems of scaling in the printed illustration. Because of the four-way symmetry, only twelve distinct nonzero calculations are needed to find the forty-nine points shown. The calculation is done by setting up the usual table listing values of $x, y,$ and z, and then calculating values of s and t for each grid point. The symmetry is preserved in calculation because squaring a coordinate gives the same result whether the coordinate is positive or negative, and because "sin⁻¹" preserves signs. A computer program for calculating certain grids in spherical perspective is given in the appendix.

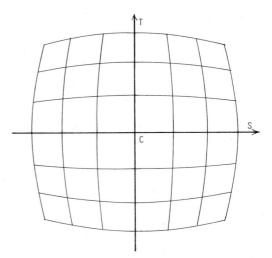

8-9. Spherical perspective of a grid in the xz plane (shown flattened)

The curved grid lines in figure 8-9 approach 90° VPs (not shown), calculated as before from $R\pi/2$. These VPs can also be deduced from equations 8.15 and 8.16, by letting x and z respectively go to zero while holding other coordinates fixed. In the limit, $\sin^{-1}(x/x)$ is obtained for equation 8.15, allowing large x values to cancel. The property of $\sin^{-1}$ is that $\pi/2 = \sin^{-1}(1)$. Ninety-degree VPs appear along both the s and t axes.

Figure 8-10 shows the spherical perspective calculated for a part of a grid in an xy plane, the plane $z = -0.6R$. The plane is below HP and HL and is seen from above. The y values are used from 0.8R to 1.6R. The grid spacing is 0.2R. The frontmost point calculated happens to touch PS at $(x,y,z) = (0, 0.8R, -0.6R)$. Thirty distinct calculations are required to obtain the thirty-five points shown. The left and right edges of the grid shown happen to represent the lines $\{x = \pm 0.6R; z = -0.6R\}$, producing in the picture the lines $t = \pm s$, which are

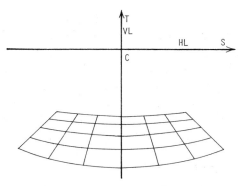

8-10. Spherical perspective of a grid in an *xy* plane (shown flattened)

also straight with slopes of ± 1. The lines represent the intersections of the vertical planes $x = \pm 0.6R$ with the plane $z = -0.6R$. These are among the few grid lines that do not curve in the picture. The boundary between lines that curve inward and lines that curve outward from C (the 0° VP) are shown by the $t = \pm s$ lines. Again, 90° VPs exist for all the grid lines.

Q8-6. Show that the frontmost point described above is on the spherical PS.

For the spherical perspective of a grid in figure 8-10, grid lines near HL are nearly straight and parallel to HL. The center grid line along the *t* axis is necessarily straight, by symmetry. The apparent straightness of certain lines in perspective can also be established by considering their projections on the sphere. Any line in space is in a plane containing O, the center of the sphere. Such a plane intersects the sphere in a great circle. All segments of great circles, and therefore all perspectives of straight lines, appear straight to the viewer at V when observed on the spherical PS. Only certain ones remain straight when PS is flattened; these are horizontal lines in HP (which appear as HL) and vertical lines in CP (which appear as VL). Also, lines formed by the intersection of the planes $x = \pm z = c$ (*c* being constant) are preserved as straight by the spherical transformation to a flattened PS. (These lines are not the same as the diagonal lines $x = \pm z$.)

In general, curved grid lines on the flattened PS are sinusoidal in shape. A sinusoidal curve seen in a plane at any angle still has that shape, although its amplitude varies. The spherical transformation (equations 8.16 and 8.17) can be used for any three-dimensional object. Because the transformation is nonlinear, no features except certain straight lines are preserved. Calculations are easy to carry out and plot for simple objects using a few points. Needless to say, curved edges are not apparent if just the eight corners of a rectangular box are plotted. Additional points along each edge must be used.

Q8-7. Set up the coordinates for a rectangular box, including several points you expect to be visible along each edge. Calculate and plot the spherical perspective for a suitable location and PS.

Q8-8. Postulate a row of circles in the *xy* plane as objects, and calculate and plot the spherical perspective to see if distortion is improved or worsened for these objects. Are elliptical shapes to be expected?

M. C. Escher's only evident use of spherical perspective was in the print "Balcony." There, a portion of a village is seen expanded—as if painted on a part of a spherical bubble. The effect is similar to one of looking at part of the scene with a strong magnifying lens. According to Escher's biographers, he did not use mathematics in drawing the spherically distorted grid on which the illusion is based. Another modern user of spherical perspective is Albert Flocon.

Flattening Spherical Perspective by Mapping

A complete familiarity with spherical perspective includes acquaintance with ways of transferring one surface to another. In particular, the coordinates plotted on a sphere to represent the perspective of an object can be transferred to a flat surface in other ways than those discussed above. These procedures are likely to be of interest only to experimentalists. The objective is to "map" points or small regions that are on the sphere onto the plane without grossly distorting the regions. "Mapping" can be defined as a one-to-one, point-by-point relation of one surface to another. The mathematics for mapping can be found in texts on the calculus of complex variables. Constructing a square grid on a spherical surface remains impossible.

Suppose the spherical PS is resting on the plane that is to receive the mapped picture (figure 8-11a). One way is to "peel" the sphere, unfolding petal-shaped sections from its top and pressing them to the surface. Much distortion occurs, however, because considerable empty area is introduced between each petal. One petal is πR long when pulled from a sphere of radius R. If the area of the sphere is $4\pi R^2$, the area to be covered with petals is $\pi^3 R^2$—about 2.5 times bigger. The distortion is worse in some regions than in others. Regions mapped from

near the pole where the peeling started spread farther from one another than regions near the other end of the sphere.

Another mapping is called "stereographic." If a bright light were positioned at the top pole of the sphere, rays would shine in all directions through points on a transparent sphere and land on the plane. Each ray would map a point P to P', as shown in figure 8-11b. Points near the bottom are mapped with little distortion, but points near the top are again mapped far apart. The top point is spread out to infinity everywhere on the plane!

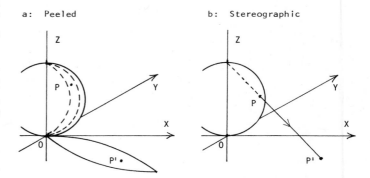

8-11. Mapping points from a spherical surface onto a flat surface

A variation of this mapping could confine the results to a circle of any chosen radius, with much distortion near the circumference. Some artistic results are shown in M. C. Escher's "Circle Limit" series, although mapping was not used for these. There is little to be gained mathematically because distortion is always severe away from the bottom pole. The artist is led back to spherical perspective drawn on a flat surface. The mathematics would be the same for situations involving small regions and a large radius.

Ideal Perspective and Horizons

For pictures representing a relatively small angle of view—so that little metaphorical crumpling is involved if the associated portion of a spherical surface is flattened—spherical perspective might be the ideal way to obtain flat pictures with less distortion. Necessarily, a large radius for PS must be used, causing "straight" lines to have rather gentle curvature on the flattened PS. Ninety-degree VPs are likely to be far outside the frame of the picture.

Suppose a fresh approach to obtain a more accurate flat picture is to be made. An underlying curved grid is implicated. Such a corrected perspective can be deduced by considering the behavior of an xy grid. The grid lines parallel to the y axis should —in the picture—approach the viewer from CV and curve gently inward. The grid lines parallel to the x axis must bulge slightly toward the viewer at the center and must approach the straight HL on the sides. Such an arrangement of grid lines must seem to intersect orthogonally; there is no other way to arrange curved lines to satisfy all these conditions.

What has been described seems identical to spherical perspective. A large radius gives gently curving lines in the directions described. Furthermore, the gentle curvature fits the spherical mathematical model, as well as any other curved model. Any gradual curve can be approximated with a portion of an arc; this holds for the sinusoidal shapes characteristic of spherical perspective.

A well known optical illusion[7] consists of a

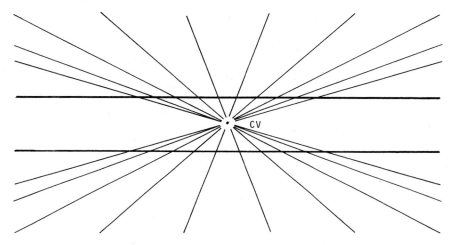

8-12. Illusion: straight lines seem to curve

straight horizontal line drawn across several lines converging to a point (CV), as in figure 8-12. The horizontal line appears slightly curved around CV, in accordance with spherical perspective. If this line is to appear straight, it must be drawn curved the opposite way. Greek temple designers combated the illusion by curving the temple base downward.

The horizon of the earth curves very slightly. This can be visualized by analogy to the cone of light rays coming from the circumferential horizon toward a viewer standing at the "top" of a perfectly spherical planet. The tangent points of the rays are on a circle lying in a plane below the feet of the viewer. The circle appears only in edge view (giving a straight line) to a viewer located in its plane. To a viewer above its plane, it presents a downward curvature. Therefore, some conflict exists between an "ideal" perspective based on rectilinear or curvilinear methods using a straight HL and the curved HL a viewer might observe on a small planet.

The distance to the (curving) horizon of a planet can be calculated with the aid of figure 8-13a. The viewer of height h sees the surface tangentially at distance j. Using the Pythagorean theorem with the right triangle thus formed permits calculation of the distance as:

$$j = \sqrt{2Rh + h^2} \simeq \sqrt{2Rh} . \qquad (8.18)$$

The approximation is good because h is usually much smaller than R, the radius of the planet. For the earth, j is approximately 4,370 m. If this value is used for a grid line in spherical perspective, calculation automatically produces the correct curved HL (although its difference from a straight HL is imperceptible).

The gently curving horizon is an arc and is closer to the viewer at the edges of a flat picture than at the center, as shown in figure 8-13b (a top view of figure 8-13a). For an angle of view α, the horizon at the edges—at $j \cos (\alpha/2)$—is closer. When this value is used numerically for y in a typical perspective calculation, the difference from a straight HL again is imperceptible in a picture.

Q8-9. Calculate $j \cos (\alpha/2)$ for the earth for a typical field of view, say 60°; compare q for this y against q for $y = j$, using $d = h = 1$ m.

General Remarks on Curvilinear Perspective

The fifteenth-century Fouquet paintings may be reexamined in light of curvilinear perspective. The curved grid of the street surface must have been

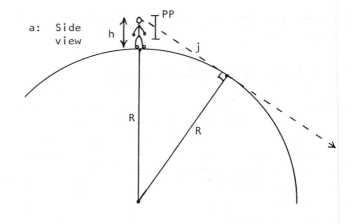

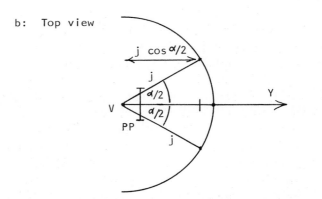

8-13. Calculating the horizon of a planet (exaggerated scale)

obtained by guesswork. The curves are exaggerated and erratic sinusoids, reminiscent of curves produced by either cylindrical or spherical perspective. The straight vertical lines of the buildings indicate that a form of cylindrical perspective was used. Leeman surmises that Fouquet used a convex mirror rather than perspective.

Reflections in spherical, cylindrical, and other curved mirrors do not create the corresponding curvilinear perspectives. The possibilities of mirrors and lenses for perspective are discussed briefly in chapter 9. Anamorphic pictures, showing an unusual kind of perspective, can be made or seen with cylindrical (or conical) mirrors, but the transformation is not the same as that for cylindrical perspective.

Curvilinear perspectives have been applied to Euclidean space. Spherical perspective should not be confused with non-Euclidean spherical space, a space analogous to the surface of a planet populated with two-dimensional beings.

The advent of space travel and "space art" has brought new kinds of pictures, such as those of life inside artificial worlds. NASA artist Don Davis and others have carried out the reverse of curvilinear perspective, using spherical, cylindrical, and toroidal subjects but rendering them in rectilinear perspective. The graphic challenge is substantial, but equations 5.3 and 5.4, together with the tools of chapter 7, can aid such work, bypassing the difficulty of locating VPs. Examples of the interiors of spherical, cylindrical, and toroidal "worlds" are presented elsewhere.[8] Plate 7 shows a cylindrical surface in rectilinear perspective. Earlier artists faced and solved the problem of rendering pictures so that they appear flat on curved surfaces such as domes.

Notes

1. For reproductions of Fouquet art, see Ernst, *Magic Mirror of Escher* and Leeman, *Hidden Images.*

2. For curvilinear perspectives by Escher, see Ernst, *Magic Mirror of Escher* and Locher, *World of Escher.* For curvilinear perspectives by Flocon, see Descargues, *Perspective History.*

3. The dilemma of parallel telegraph wires was explored by Escher, as discussed in Ernst, *Magic Mirror of Escher.*

4. Escher's curvilinear and other prints are analyzed in Ernst, *Magic Mirror of Escher* and are shown in Locher, *World of Escher.*

5. The method of cylindrical diorama was depicted by Adele le Breton, as shown in Descargues, *Perspective History,* plate 152.

6. For a good general discussion of spherical viewing, see Vero, *Understanding Perspective,* p. 122.

7. The usual psychological diagram uses diverging spacing for the "depth" lines to attain a stronger effect, but the illusion works for the equal spacing of lines in perspective (see figure 8-12). Using two straight parallel horizontal lines doubles the effect, but the reader can see it with half the diagram covered. Note that the effect works sideways, too. The illusions are discussed further in Gregory, "Visual Illusions."

8. On the art of artificial worlds, see Ron Chernow, "Colonies in Space May Turn out to be Nice Places to Live."

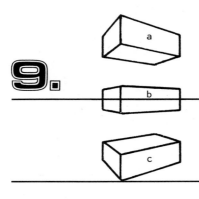

9.

Illumination and Reflection in Perspective

More than other aspects of perspective, lighting and shadowing raise many art-related topics not strictly in the realm of perspective. Illumination gives strong depth clues, especially when used with perspective. This chapter introduces only the physical and mathematical theories that bear directly on obtaining the perspective of subject matter. Many simplifying assumptions are needed, and artistic projects require substantial judgment, experience, and intuition. The graphic construction of shadows in perspective is well covered in various references. After a summary of the graphic methods, emphasis is placed on mathematical assistance. The discussion begins with the physical characteristics of light and light sources. The goal is to be able to find where shadows are, point-by-point if necessary, and to tell how dark they are. The coloration of

objects and their shadows, while providing important clues to depth, is not considered as part of perspective.

Light Sources and Light Intensity

Several distinct types of idealized light sources exist. Variations of them are encountered in real and hypothetical problems of art. The *point source* (both near and distant), the *line source,* and the *homogeneous source* are considered here. For practical purposes, a point source of light is a very distant source or one whose size is much smaller than the objects on which it is shining. Point sources of truly small size seldom need to be considered; the stars, for example, are too dim to cast shadows. "Extended" sources can be thought of, for purposes of analysis, as being composed of numerous point sources. Extended sources that are far enough away —the sun, for example—act as point sources.

Figure 9-1a shows a nearby point source, such as a naked light bulb, emitting rays of light radially in all directions. The rays impinge upon a flat surface with different angles of incidence, depending on whether the observer is looking directly beneath the source or some distance away. In figure 9-1b, the source is so far away that its rays are essentially parallel when received over a relatively small region. In this situation, every ray strikes a flat surface at the same angle. The sun provides essentially parallel rays, although the source clearly is not a point. The laser, which sends almost all its light in one direction, functions as a distant point source with parallel rays, no matter how close it is.

The line source of light is often seen but little studied. It can be thought of as a long fluorescent tube. Rays shine from it radially, but with a cylindrical pattern, as shown in figure 9-1c. Situations involving illumination with one long fluorescent bulb are rarely encountered, but illumination by a short fluorescent bulb or by several bulbs can be calculated. The illumination from a regular array of fluorescent tubes, or from an array of any other type of light source, can be understood by considering them one at a time, using a principle called "superposition."

A third distinct form of lighting is homogeneous (or uniform and diffuse) light. The source may not be discernible, and the light seems to come from everywhere. No shadows are visible if the illumination is completely homogeneous. Features, if not inherently colored, are invisible. With some forms

of what is commonly called "indirect" or "diffuse" lighting, the source seems to be the whole ceiling or the overlaying cloud layer (figure 9-1d). Technically, this source is called a sheet or plane source; it can cause shadows. Any source that provides illumination reflected from a direct or "primary" source can be called a "secondary" source.

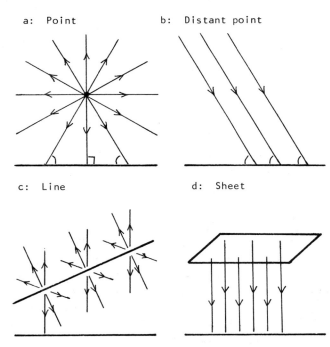

9-1. Sources of light

Many physical terms and many units of measure are used for discussing light intensity. *Luminance* (E) can be adapted to describe the amount of power being emitted by a unit section of a source. The direction in which light is emitted is important.

The light impinges on a surface at a certain angle, not necessarily normal to the surface. The light received normal to a surface of unit area is called the *illuminance,* the illumination, or simply the intensity (I or I′) and is expressed in units of power per unit area.

Several different physical models may help the artist to visualize light. The "ray" model is fairly obvious and illustrates the travel of light in straight lines—an accurate description for all practical purposes. The "wavefront" model shows the symmetry of the source in a different way and helps clarify the behavior of the intensity. The wavefront is always normal to the ray or direction of travel.

A point source is characterized by a total luminance E and has spherical wavefronts (shown in cross section in figure 9-2a). In any direction from a point source, at a given distance, the same intensity of light is received. As the light travels, its power is spread out over larger and larger spherical shells. Since the area of a spherical shell grows in proportion to the square of the radius, the light intensity must decrease by the same proportion in order for the total power emitted to equal the total power received at any distance. This is the origin of the "inverse square law," which governs the decrease of light intensity with distance from a point source. The law has the mathematical form:

$$I = E/4\pi r^2 , \qquad (9.1)$$

where r is the radial distance from the point source and I is the illuminance. (The law does not hold in so simple a form for other sources.) For very large distances, the spherical wavefront is so flat over small regions that the light is said to travel as "plane waves," a form complementary to parallel rays.

For a line source, the wavefronts are cylindrical shells surrounding the source (figure 9-2b); considerable complication is encountered at the ends of the source. The luminance must be described as E_L watts per unit length of the source. The total power is spread over an area that grows in direct proportion to the radius of the cylinder. Therefore, the intensity decreases in inverse proportion to the distance from the source. The exact expression is:

$$I = E_L/2\pi r , \qquad (9.2)$$

where r is the radial distance from the line source. Light does not weaken at increased distance as swiftly from a line source as from a point source; no matter how far away the viewer gets, an infinitely long source remains visible, stretching across the whole sky.

With the aid of calculus, the illuminance from a short or "finite" line source can be calculated. Light from the ends must be ignored—a safe procedure if the source is long or if the objects illuminated are close. The source is assumed to have length $a + b,$ with one end at distance a away from the origin O on the axis (see figure 9-2c) and the other end at distance b in the other direction. A radial line from O passes through P, the point at which the intensity is to be calculated. The result, which can be adapted to any orientation, is:

$$I = \left(\frac{E_L}{4\pi r}\right)\left(\frac{b}{\sqrt{b^2+r^2}} + \frac{a}{\sqrt{a^2+r^2}}\right) . \qquad (9.3)$$

The sheet source, if large enough, has plane wave fronts as shown in figure 9-2d. It must be characterized by a luminance E_S, expressed in power per unit area. If the sheet is very large or the objects are very close to it (which is usually not the case), the sheet is considered infinite. Otherwise, edge effects are substantial. The intensity law is very simple. Everywhere in front of the sheet, the illuminance on surfaces parallel to the sheet is:

$$I = E_S . \qquad (9.4)$$

As usual, illuminance must be expressed in units of power per unit area, the same units as for E_S. The intuitive way to understand this result is to realize

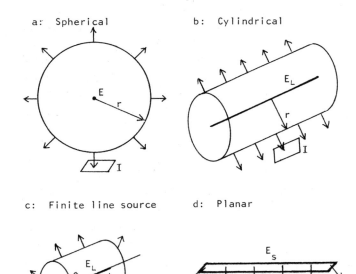

a: Spherical   b: Cylindrical

c: Finite line source   d: Planar

9-2. Luminance, wavefronts, and light intensities (illuminance)

that a viewer can never get far enough away from an infinite sheet to see its intensity diminish. Therefore, it stays constant. The illuminance is homogeneous but directed. A surface oriented perpendicular to the sheet would receive no light. As with the other sources, none is received behind an opaque surface oriented normal to the rays.

The illuminance or intensity received by a surface depends on the angle at which the rays (or wavefronts) impinge. In figure 9-3 rays of intensity I are shown at angle ι with respect to the normal N to the surface. This is the customary way of measuring the angle of light incidence, but the complementary σ measured from the surface is often used. The illuminance I' for that surface is given by:

$$I' = I \cos \iota . \qquad (9.5)$$

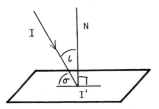

9-3. Illuminance normal to a surface

I' values remain the same for a surface regardless of whether the light is absorbed, reflected, or transmitted through the surface. The history of the light after it reaches a surface is discussed later.

One physical theory of light holds that light behaves as tiny particles, called photons, that travel in the same direction as light rays. No new discussion is needed for using this model for artistic purposes. Another, more complex model of light, the wave theory, has no consequences for perspective as such but does help explain many optical phenomena encountered in the visual arts. Occasionally, in regard to shadows, a situation might be arranged where "diffraction" occurs. Diffraction, briefly, is the bending of light around obstacles that have sharp edges. The wave nature of light provides an explanation for a series of narrow bands of light and shadow that appear at places where light passes by an obstacle. The effect is usually too small to see, or is obscured by other effects.

Illumination and Shadow

"Direct" illumination is the term applied to light rays from a source that reach an object without obstruction. "Indirect" or "diffuse" illumination reaches regions that would otherwise be quite dark, by means of the scattering and reflection of direct rays. Reflection can be diffuse (such as that from a rough surface scattering light in all directions), specular (such as from a mirror—discussed later), or a combination. What seems to be a smooth surface can be sufficiently rough to diffuse light, since the degree of roughness necessary for specular reflection to occur only requires very small irregularities—less than the size of the wavelength of light. Most common rough surfaces reflect 10 percent to 30 percent of the light falling on them. Surfaces painted with a light color can reflect up to 80 percent; such a surface is an ideal diffuser. The atmosphere, depending on dust and water content, provides about 10 percent to 15 percent of the total light on a sunny day as diffuse rays. On overcast days, about half the light is diffuse in all directions and the other half comes from the cloud layer. Surprisingly, the amount of diffuse light increases when the sun is covered; it is scattered from regions where the sun is uncovered.

The opposite of illumination is darkness or shadow. Shadows, in practical terms, never present the absolute absence of light but rather regions of diminished intensity. If the direct light from a source has a relative intensity of 100 percent, a perceptible shadow might receive anywhere from 95 percent—still quite bright—to 1 percent—characteristic of the darkest woods on a sunny day. If there were no air around us and no other diffuse sources of light, shadows would be totally dark. The partial illumination of shadowed regions results from the scattering of light by the atmosphere and nearby objects into the shadowed region; the shadowed surface then reflects some of this diffused light.

In some artistic problems, finding the shadow is hard but finding where the light passes is easy. A fundamental principle in artistic design is to pay special attention to the light-dark boundaries where illumination seems to reverse—a figure-ground approach. The boundary formed on a surface between directly and indirectly illuminated regions is called the *shadow line* or "line of separation." The darker, indirectly illuminated region is "in shade," and its coloration said to be "shaded." Generally, a shaded area is a shadow an object creates on itself; an example is the area presented by the side of a cube that lies opposite the sun. The term "shadow" is usually reserved for the dark region the object creates on another surface. The outline of the shadow is an image of the shadow line. The direction of the illumination must be known in order to find both the shading and the shadowing. Even without perspective, the proper depiction of shading and shadowing (either of which may imply more than one light source) gives strong depth clues.

Shadows are not sharp-edged, partly because of diffraction but more because of scattering and the use of extended sources of light. Each of several point sources creates its own shadow. An extended source then causes a profusion of shadows. A general description of the shadow structure is shown in figure 9-4. A round obstacle is placed in front of the sun or other source. Behind it lies the "umbra," where no direct rays impinge, and the "penumbra," where rays from part of the source can impinge. Beyond the penumbra is the region of direct illumination from all parts of the source. This shadow structure may be familiar from descriptions of solar and lunar eclipses, but it also applies to many sources and objects close at hand.

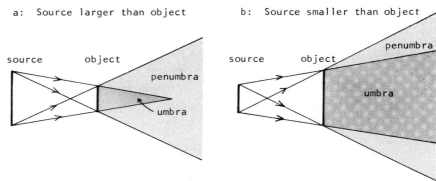

9-5. Extended source and different object sizes (top view of shadows cast on ground)

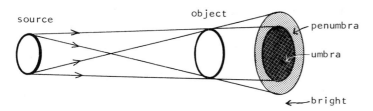

9-4. Shadow structure for an extended source (oblique view)

For similar reasons, shadows do not exactly imitate the shapes of the obstacles producing them. Close to the obstacle, the shadow is sharp-edged. Farther from the obstacle, the penumbra grows until the shadow fades out. In figure 9-5a in top view, a large source is shown near a smaller obstacle. The umbra cast on the ground vanishes a short distance behind the obstacle, while the penumbra grows and fades until indistinguishable from light scattered by the sky. If the source is smaller than the object (as in figure 9-5b), both the umbra and the penumbra grow and fade from view. This discussion has neglected the height of the object. The theory for finding the location and the "darkness" of shadows is covered later.

Q9-1. Sketch in top view a point source and an infinite sheet source, each shining on an object of a chosen width; show the shape and length of the umbra and penumbra, if any.

Small apertures in obstacles, such as the spaces among the leaves of a tree, do not necessarily create negative shadows—small regions of brightness imitating the shape of the apertures. Far from an aperture, the ability of rays to pass through various parts of the hole results in illumination corresponding to the shape of the source, not the hole. Sunlight shining through a small hole of any shape creates a small round image of the sun—the pinhole effect. Excellent general books are available that cover a wide variety of light and shadow phenomena of potential use to the artist.[1]

Q9-2. In top view, sketch a small aperture and a point source. Use rays to find the size and resolution of the image on nearby and distant screens.

This is shadow work in reverse. Try for an extended source.

The Perception of Light

Physically, illumination is measured in terms of illuminance, color (wavelength or frequency), and color purity. Human-oriented perceptual measures known as the psychophysical variables correspond to these. *Brightness,* the only perceptual measure to be considered here, corresponds to illuminance. Color is gauged in terms of *hue;* color purity is gauged in terms of saturation or *chroma.* Illumination can be measured with instruments directly. Brightness (also known as *value*) is of principal concern to the artist and has a strong subjective element. It must be discussed as a perceptual experience. Only from variations in the brightness of light reflected from surfaces can the features of surfaces be distinguished.

The eye is extremely sensitive to the absolute intensity of light. It can perceive the brightness of some scenes that have a billion times the illuminance of other scenes. Because the eye has adaptive mechanisms, the perceived range of brightness is not nearly as great. At a given level of illumination, the range of perceived brightness is relatively small. Although its performance is much better than that of film, the retina cannot simultaneously see outdoor features normally in a sunlit scene and see indoor features clearly through the window of a darkened room.

For small variations in brightness, the eye is very sensitive to contrast. Sometimes the eye creates contrast where none exists. The Chinese knew how to darken the boundary between two regions of equal brightness in order to make them appear to have different brightnesses.[2] A uniformly illuminated surface of an object may appear to have a different brightness near its edges, making its shape more apparent. For realism, the brightness (or "darkness"), orientation, and length of shadows must be depicted quite accurately.

A "gray scale," such as a photographic one, can be used to compare brightness in ten or more seemingly equal steps from black to white. Pictures with a wide range of contrast, whether photographs or paintings, can have more than a hundred distinguishable levels of gray. Shading material is available in densities that are measured percentages of total black (a black that still reflects some light). The densities are calculated from the proportion of the area occupied by the dot or other pattern. Near either of the extremes (10 percent or 90 percent), the eye perceives brightness in a nonlinear manner, so that the gray scale becomes approximate.

Locating Light Sources

A terrestrial light source usually has a known location that can be expressed either with orthographic views (plan and elevation) or with mathematical coordinates. This description can be accomplished for idealized sources—point, line, or sheet—but is difficult for natural sources, especially secondary ones such as reflections from objects, clouds, or water. For either graphic or mathematical work, the direction in which light rays strike parts of the object can be found by considering the location of the source with respect to the object points.

Much art and architecture depends on solar illumination. Since the sun is a very distant source, effectively parallel rays are received. Any part of a small scene receives light at the same angle at a given time. The location of the sun in the sky and therefore the angle of its rays can be described for any time of day or year. During the day, the sun seems to follow the path of a great circle in the sky as the earth rotates (figure 9-6). This path is inclined at an angle called the *declination,* and the declination varies seasonally.

Two angles are needed to specify the sun's position—*altitude* and *azimuth*. These angular loca-

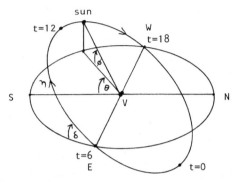

9-6. Locating the sun in the sky

tions resemble spherical coordinates and can be used for the rays from any source. The altitude ϕ is now defined to be measured vertically from a local plane on the surface of the earth to wherever the sun is. Solar rays strike any horizontal surfaces at the angle ϕ (measured from the surface, not the normal). The azimuth tells in which compass direction the sun is located. Azimuth θ is usually measured from due south and is measured in the horizontal plane to the point "under" the sun. (A person must be located below latitude 23.45° ever to be directly under the sun.) Altitude can vary from 0° to as much as 90° (not all in one day). Azimuth varies from about −90° to about +90°—more in summer, less in winter. Unless these angles are

given, guessed, or measured in the field, they must be calculated before shadows in perspective can be found. For describing rays other than solar ones, the range of the azimuth can be extended to 360°.

Calculating altitude and azimuth requires knowing the hour angle, the declination, and the latitude. The time of year can be used to find the declination because the sun swings back and forth in the sky sinusoidally for any given time of day. Using the tilt of the earth's axis, 23.45°, the declination δ is given by:

$$\delta = 23.45° \sin [360°(D - 81)/365] . \quad (9.6)$$

D is the number of the day in question, counted from January 1. The summer solstice, the day on which the sun is at its highest, is June 21, or D = 172, in the northern hemisphere. All calculations for angles for light sources are shown in degrees.

The *hour angle* specifies the location of the sun on its daily great circle. The hour angle η is calculated from the time of day as:

$$\eta = 360°t/24 , \quad (9.7)$$

where t is measured in decimal hours from midnight preceding the day in question. Noon is $t = 12$, for example, and 6:30 P.M. is $t = 18.5$.

The solar location at a given latitude λ, hour angle η (for time of day), and declination δ (for day of the year) is given by:

altitude: $\phi = -\cos \lambda \cos \delta \cos \eta + \sin \lambda \sin \delta$

azimuth: $\theta = -\cos \delta \sin \eta/\cos \phi . \quad (9.8)$

If great accuracy is not needed, solar and architectural design books have charts for finding the solar angles at given times.[3]

The time of day used is solar time, measured so that the sun is at its greatest altitude at $t = 12$ (solar noon). This arrangement should be the most useful to artists and architects. Obtaining t from local clock time is more challenging than it might appear. The clock time must be corrected if "daylight savings" time is in use. It must also be corrected for longitude; solar noon agrees with clock time only at longitudes that are multiples of 15° from Greenwich (0°). A small correction, no more than ¼ hour, is needed for the "equation of time"—an expression of the variation of solar angle over the year due to the earth's elliptical orbit.

The azimuthal location of the sun is expressed as an angle from due south, a direction not easy to find accurately. Compass readings alone would be in substantial error in some parts of the United States, and an architect seeking a high degree of accuracy must use surveys, an isogonic chart (a map of corrections), or the sun itself to find south. The matching of due south to the coordinate system for the subject matter to be pictured is discussed later.

Q9-3. Calculate the altitude and azimuth for the sun at 3:00 P.M. on June 21 at 40° North. The results of this question are used in a later example.

Graphic Location of Shadows

The graphic method, with the aid of considerable thought and ingenuity, can solve very impressive and challenging shadow problems. It cannot tell how dark the shadows are. (The next section will show how mathematical analysis can help with both aspects.) Graphic methods have been covered well in other sources.[4] The discussion below focuses primarily on point sources. The extension to other sources involves superposition, or repeating the work for each new point of the source. For the most part, shadows are found on horizontal planes, usually GP.

Finding the shadow thrown by a point source illuminating one point of an object requires having the source S (or a ray from it) and the point P located in plan and elevation, as shown in figure 9-7. The shadow point P' is found by extending the line from S to P in elevation view until the intersection with GP is obtained. After P' is plotted in both views, the perspective of P and P' is constructed in the picture, using VPs and/or the double projection method. This exercise seems rather futile until P is defined as the top of a vertical line segment. P' then shows both the length and direction of its shadow.

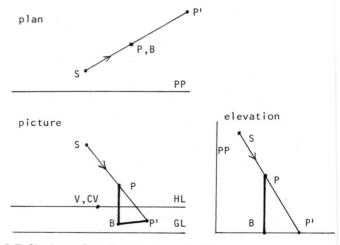

9-7. Shadows of a point and of a vertical line

The base B of the line segment must also be plotted in perspective, as in figure 9-7, to establish the picture of the shadow. In the simplest case, B must be on GP. If the line $\overline{BP}$ represents an object that has width, such as a pole, the width of the shadow is the same only if the source is very far away. For a nearby point source, the shadow width is larger than the object width, as shown earlier.

Q9-4. In perspective, sketch or draw the shadow for a point source near a pole, showing how the shadow grows (and fades) with distance.

Q9-5. Calculate or estimate the sun's altitude for the first three hours after sunrise, and draw the relative lengths of the shadows thrown by a vertical stick. Try to include the change in azimuth as well. At what time of day do sun shadows change length most rapidly?

For more complex objects, the procedure is repeated for each point that seems likely to help locate the shadow. Shadows of lines are obtained by using the end points of the lines. Shadows of surfaces are found by considering points around the perimeter. If two or more sources exist, the procedure is repeated again for each source direction. The darkest shadows occur at places where no sources penetrate. The relative luminance of the sources must also be considered. If the source is the sun or some other inaccessible source, its altitude and azimuth must somehow be obtained. Rays at the azimuth angle are drawn in plan, with due south defined as desired. Rays at the altitude angle are drawn in elevation, measured from GP.

Following is a summary of the rules for obtaining shadows directly in perspective for parallel light rays (distant sources) after the perspective of the objects has been drawn by any means:

1. The light rays drawn in perspective are not parallel lines (unless the source is directly behind V on the vision axis).
2. The source is the VP for its rays in perspective and is called VVPS because it is usually a vertical vanishing point.
3. The source does not appear in the picture if it is behind V. In that case an "antisource" exists at VVPS' and can be used to draw rays. Rays of light appear to converge to VVPS'.
4. The source or antisource can be located in perspective by the usual method of finding the VP for a given line (a light ray).
5. The straight edge of a shadow has the same VP as the edge causing the shadow, if the object edge is parallel to the plane on which the shadow falls.
6. The VP of a straight shadow edge is in the plane on which the shadow falls.

In figure 9-8, these rules for working with shadows in perspective, in concert with the double projection method, are used to find the shadow of a simple rectangular building so situated that the shadow falls partly on a vertical wall. Either procedure could have been used alone to accomplish the same result. The use of a vertical wall at an angle with the building introduces some complication. V is placed at the same point for both plan and elevation for figure 9-8, but this is not required for the construction. A typical light ray is shown in both

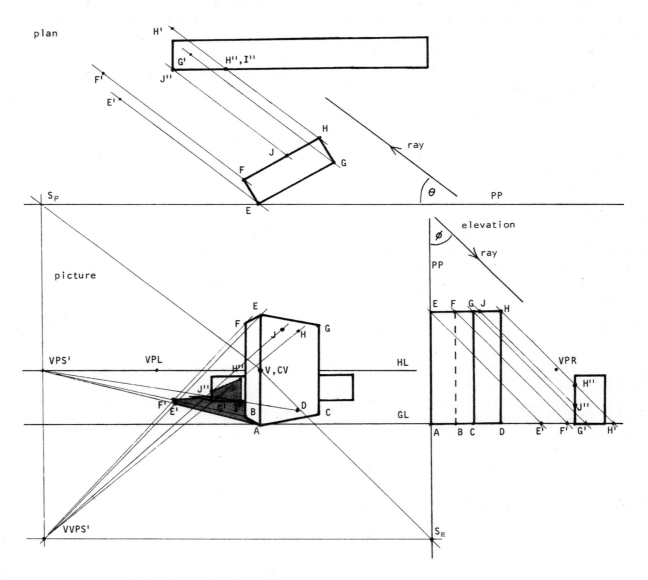

9-8. Two graphic methods for finding the shadow of a building

180

plan and elevation. If altitude ϕ and azimuth θ are known, the ray can be drawn as shown at those angles. Finding this ray in perspective is useless because no other rays have the same direction. But all rays in plan and elevation are parallel to it, and the location of shadow points on GP can be found for any points of the object. In elevation, for example, a ray through the top front corner point E strikes the ground at E'. In plan, E' is on the same ray through E, and E' is as far from PP in plan as it was in elevation.

The usual double projection method allows point E' to be plotted in perspective. The shadow points F' and H' for other top points F and H of the building can also be found and plotted. Point G does not contribute to the shadow line, and G' is useless. The shadow edges can now be drawn on the ground, starting from the bottom point A. However, part of the shadow falls on the wall. Point H'' is plotted where the original ray intersects the wall. To find the rest of the shadow of the edge $\overline{HF}$ on the wall, another point is needed, such as J'' where the shadow reaches the corner of the wall. Parallel rays can be used to find J and plot J'' on the corner. Point I'', where the shadow of edge $\overline{DH}$ on the ground reaches the wall, can also be plotted. The shadow of the wall itself should not be forgotten.

Examination of the rays postulated shows that the source must be behind the viewer, to the right. The other procedure starts with finding VVPS' for the source. All construction lines shown in the picture for figure 9-8 are for this procedure. In elevation, V looks in the direction of the ray, determining point S_E on PP. In plan, V looks in the direction of the ray, determining S_P. VVPS' is at the intersection of the projections of these points. This is the point

toward which any ray in the picture converges. The shadow points of E and F are found by means of rays drawn from E and F to VVPS'. The rays intersect lines in GP from the base points A and B to VPS', giving E' and F' and agreeing with the previous method. The ray from H first meets the wall at H'', where the vertical shadow edge for $\overline{DH}$ falls on the wall. The ray from J to VVPS' can be plotted after J is located in the picture. After some shadow points are plotted in this way, shadow edges can be drawn toward appropriate vanishing points. The edge from A to E' is aimed at VPS'. VPS' is on HL, since edge $\overline{EF}$ is parallel to GP. The shadow edge $\overline{E'F'}$ belongs to a building edge aimed at VPL; therefore this shadow edge is aimed at VPL. The edge from F' toward H' should aim at VPR. The shadow of edge $\overline{FH}$ on the wall (segment $\overline{J''H''}$) has a VP not easy to find.

The rays from a nearby point source are not parallel. The source (or properly drawn diverging rays) must be available in plan and elevation. Alternatively, the source with diverging rays can be drawn directly in the picture. An antisource can be used if the source is behind the viewer. The shadows of line segments appear to diverge from a vanishing point VPS' associated with the source. If the source is throwing shadows on a surface, VPS' is on the surface directly beneath the source. Other rules remain the same as for parallel rays.

In figure 9-9, a point source S is shown in a box in perspective. The shadow for the pole projecting from the left wall aims at VPS'_1, located perpendicularly "beneath" the source on the wall. The shadows for the vertical edges of the small wall aim at VPS'_2, directly beneath S. The lengths of the shadows are determined by rays. Other shadow edges

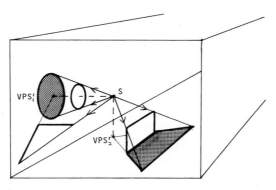

9-9. Shadows from a point source in a box (in perspective)

aim at the appropriate VPs, as before. The shadow for the circular shade to the left of the source appears larger and elliptical on the wall.

The shadow of a circular object can be found by enclosing it in the usual square and finding the outline of the shadow of the square. The elliptical shadow can then be constructed as before. For a sphere, the shadow line is a great circle in a plane perpendicular to the central light ray. This circle must be found in plan and elevation and drawn in the picture.[5] The shading of a sphere or cylinder can be complex and is thoroughly discussed in art books.[6] To avoid the labor of drawing cross-hatching, stipples, and so on to show shadows, the artist can purchase, cut, and apply stick-on or rub-on materials with various patterns to shadowed regions.

Calculation of Shadows in Perspective

Calculating shadow points is not much more difficult than finding the altitude and azimuth of the point source. Since the image of the shadow line is sought, judgment is needed in choosing the points to use for calculation of the shadow. Otherwise, numerous points might be plotted that lie within the shadow and provide no information. The method is shown here mainly for shadows on an xy plane. For solar illumination, the xyz system is oriented with the negative y axis pointing south (V faces north). Many other arrangements are possible, leading to slightly different equations. If, as is likely, PP is to be aligned in some direction not dictated by the source direction, a rotation of the xyz system around the z axis should be done before locating PP and calculating the perspective.

For the simplest case—the shadow of a vertical pole of height b—the length s of the shadow is given by:

$$s = b/\tan \phi . \qquad (9.9)$$

Angle ϕ is the altitude of the light ray used. The shadow aims opposite the direction of the source, regardless of how that angle is expressed. While formulas can be developed for calculating the length and direction of any point or line shadow on any surface, the number of possible arrangements is too large for specialized equations.

The general calculation of the shadow of a point on an xy plane can be done with the aid of figure 9-10. For this case, parallel rays are used. The work is shown in an oblique view of the three-dimensional arrangement. The source is not shown, since all rays are determined by altitude ϕ and azimuth θ. Angle θ is measured from the y axis, and ϕ is measured from the xy plane. The point P at (x,y,z)

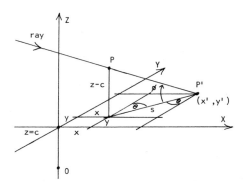

9-10. Calculating the shadow of a point (parallel rays, oblique view)

has shadow P' at (x',y',z') on a plane $z = c$ above the xy plane. The location of P' with respect to P is found, by means of trigonometry, to be:

$$x' = x + s \sin \theta$$

$$y' = y + s \cos \theta$$

$$z' = c . \tag{9.10}$$

The s is found from equation 9.9 to be $s = (z - c)/\tan \phi$.

The perspectives of P and P' are then found using the usual transformation (equations 5.3 and 5.4) and plotting the picture. Plotting the perspective of the point (x,y,c) gives the base of the vertical line segment under P and therefore shows the shadow of the vertical line. If the shadow of P is to be found at P' on any specified surface $z' = f(x,y)$, the constant c is replaced with the appropriate value of z for each case in which x and y are used for calculation. Even the equation for a vertical wall could be used for the surface. Several sets of over-lapping calculations must be done if several surfaces are involved.

When the point source is nearby, the altitude and azimuth for the ray passing through P must be found from the coordinates of the source. In figure 9-11, source S is at (u,v,w) in an oblique view. No

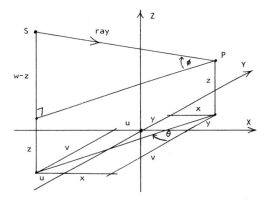

9-11. Calculating the altitude and azimuth for a ray from a point course (oblique view)

advantage results from putting the origin of the xyz system at S. Trigonometry in the xy plane gives:

altitude: $\theta = \tan^{-1} [(x + u)/(y + v)]$

azimuth: $\phi = \tan^{-1} [(w - z) \div$
$$\sqrt{(u + x)^2 + (v + y)^2}] . \tag{9.11}$$

Equation 9.10 can be used to find the shadow point.

In figure 9-12, the shadow of the catenary for a rope hung between two poles has been calculated and plotted. The catenary is nearly in the yz plane $(x \approx 0)$, and the sun has altitude 50°. The y axis

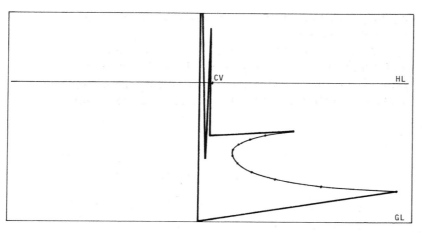

9-12. Calculated perspective of the shadow of a catenary

points north and the azimuth of the sun is $+80°$, indicating a summer afternoon (recall *Q9-3*). The perspective parameters are $d = 6$ and $h = 6$ units. The poles must be 12.26 units high for a catenary with $a = 2$ (a dip to $z = 2$ at the center) and spanning 10 units. The catenary is seen nearly edge-on. Eleven points for its shadow are plotted in perspective, as are the bases of the poles. The calculations for the first two points are shown in the accompanying table.

SPACE COORDINATES						PERSPECTIVE			
catenary				shadow		catenary		shadow	
x	y	z	s	x'	y'	p	q	p'	q'
~0	0	12.26	10.29	10.13	1.79	~0	6.26	7.80	−4.62
~0	1	7.52	6.31	6.22	2.09	~0	1.30	4.60	−4.45

The *xyz* coordinates of the catenary were found with equation 7.3 translated for a center at $y = 5$. Since the shadow is on the ground, $z' = 0$ is used.

Shadow points (p', q') are measured with respect to the same p and q axes. CV in the picture shows the location of the q axis. It is helpful to record intermediate quantities such as s in the table. Only half an hour is required to calculate and plot the shadow by hand; the graphic method requires more work and much construction. Plate 10 is a photograph of a hanging chain with a similar shadow.

Brightness of Surfaces and Shadows

The work of defining a gray scale and calculating and showing light intensities at each part of an illuminated scene is very difficult (without a computer) and requires many assumptions. A compromise approach is to use the mathematical theories for intensity from various light sources and their reflections as guides for estimating brightness.

If only a single point source is present—for example, a streetlight on a dark night—the light intensity or illuminance must decrease as the square of the distance from the source. (Nearby, this should not be measured on the ground but radially to the source itself.) How can the decrease in perceived brightness be shown? Doubling the distance and thus decreasing the intensity by four could not be duplicated in any simple way on a gray scale. The resulting decrease in brightness cannot be so easily quantified. Judgment must be used in determining how many steps down the gray scale corresponds to one-fourth of the intensity. Once this guidepost is established, doubling the distance again results in going down a similar number of steps. Attempts to quantify the gray scale result in a logarithmic scale that has the property just described.

If the original brightness is shown by using

shading with a density of 20 percent dark, is one-fourth of the brightness represented by shading that is 80 percent dark? Such a literal interpretation, although mathematically correct, is not advisable because a rather small range of illuminance has consumed most of the available gray scale. If it is any consolation, the need to compress or modify the brightness scale plagues photographers as well as artists.

Adding the effects of two or more point sources requires still more complex judgments as to what regions are dominated by each source and how the brightnesses due to two or three sources are combined. Two equal sources almost double the intensity at any point, but the brightness cannot be said to double. It only moves up the gray scale a step or two. On a given surface, two different sources may shine from different directions. The intensity received is the sum of the components normal to the surface, an amount that is less than the total intensity possible. The artist trying to show the illumination in a perspective of a long row of streetlights should notice some regularity in the application of these ideas. The lights should not appear too bright in the distance (contrary to reality), as a consequence of decreasing brightness at the wrong rate.

Similar considerations apply to the brightness of shadows and shading. A shadow is not "pitch dark" because nearby objects (and the atmosphere) serve as secondary sources of light. The light intensity reflected from an object follows approximately the inverse square law. Closer objects have a much stronger effect in back-lighting a region. The relative reflective ability of the objects must be considered. Light, glossy objects retain their stronger effect at considerable distances and may dominate the light reflected by dark, dull objects nearby. The

orientation of reflecting surfaces is also important. (The laws for reflection are discussed in the next section.)

As shown in figure 9-13, shadows resulting from a local source of light fade faster than shadows caused by a bright distant source such as the sun, also present. An incandescent light bulb's illumination decreases by 75 percent when the distance from it is increased from 1 m to 2 m, whereas it would be necessary to travel hundreds of millions of kilometers to see the solar intensity diminish similarly. A shadow due to a source is perceptible only to the extent that other sources do not replace the lost

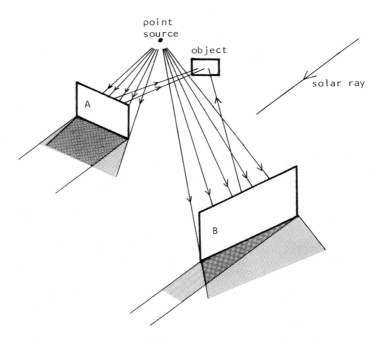

9-13. Relative brightness and shadows for near and distant surfaces reflecting light from two sources onto an object (in approximate perspective)

light. Accompanying the fading of the shadow is a decrease in brightness of the surrounding region illuminated by that particular source.

The viewer makes assumptions about the properties of the light source from the shadowing provided. Bright sources are assumed when strong contrasts are present. A distant source (probably the sun) is assumed when shadows are parallel. A close point source is assumed when shadows diverge. An extended source (possibly the sun) is assumed when shadows lack sharp edges. No shadows implies a uniform diffuse light.

Q9-6. At this point, you should be able to construct the shadow of a simple object illuminated by a line source and show that it is different from shadows due to other sources. What can be said about the decrease of brightness with distance? (Ignore end effects.)

One phenomenon noticed in outdoor scenes and often carried into perspectives is the increase in brightness for distant regions. A large area, uniformly lighted, appears brighter near HL because the scattering of light from more and more regions is presented to the viewer in a smaller and smaller portion of the picture. As in the case of any illuminated sheet, the inverse square law does not apply. The illumination does not become dimmer with distance; it stays constant and becomes concentrated in the perspective. Less contrast is evident, as well.

Illuminance cannot be calculated in perspective because the true distance information is lost. Illuminance must be calculated in orthographic views and then transferred to the appropriate points in the picture by showing relative brightness in accordance with a gray scale.

Reflection

Enough of the optics of reflection are covered here to aid the artist who needs to study illumination for perspective. A basic law of reflection states that the angle of incidence of light rays on a flat surface is equal to the angle of reflection. While these angles (ι) are defined so as to be measured with respect to the normal, they may also be measured from the surface (σ) for most artistic purposes, as shown in figure 9-14a. The practical consequence of this law is that the viewer must be in a certain location in order to see maximum reflected light from a given source and surface. For specular reflection, the surface must be so smooth that it reflects light in an ordered way, allowing a clear image to form. The ordered reflection diminishes as the surface is made rougher, but more light is sent in the direction determined by the reflection law than in other directions. Relatively rough surfaces show no preferred direction of reflection and reflect diffusely in all directions, as shown in figure 9-14b. An ordinary, painted, smooth surface reflects light in a combina-

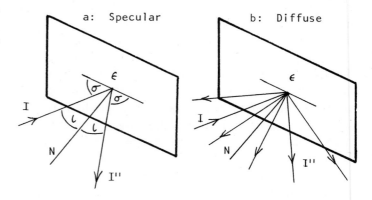

9-14. Laws of reflection for smooth (shiny) and rough (dull) surfaces

tion of specular and diffuse modes.

The laws for specular and diffuse reflection can be stated in forms that show what happens to the intensity. The incident intensity is symbolized by I, the component normal to the surface by I′, and the reflected intensity by I″ (now in the role of a luminance). I′ is always found by equation 9.5. The surface can be characterized by a *reflectance* ε—a number between 0 and 1 (corresponding to the percentage of reflectivity). Not all the incident light is reflected; ε measures the part that is not absorbed (or transmitted through a transparent material) but reflected. The intensity law for specular reflection is:

$$I'' = \epsilon I' = \epsilon I \cos \iota . \qquad (9.12)$$

Reflectance ε is nearly 1 for a mirror and is a significant 0.04 for each surface of glass. A window pane has at least 8 percent reflectance, and more at steep angles (large values of ι).

For diffuse reflection, the law (called Lambert's law) is:

$$I'' = \epsilon I . \qquad (9.13)$$

With no dependence on angle, this law indicates that light is scattered more or less equally in all directions (figure 9-14b). Although I″ can be calculated for the reflection of any source from any surface at a given orientation, the labor is too great without a computer. Further levels of reality can be incorporated (as mentioned in chapter 10) by a theory for highlights, with coefficients for glossiness and with selective reflection of colors.[7] The artist may be able to judge the depiction of surface brightnesses better by knowing the laws involved.

Q9-7. Consider how these theories can help you show transparency. A transparent material necessarily transmits most of the light it receives in an ordered way so that images are intelligible (otherwise, it might appear translucent). The material therefore must have very smooth surfaces. Which laws of reflection hold, and what must be assumed for the reflectance?

Figure 9-13 illustrates in an approximate way that the intensity of light received by a surface and reflected to an object depends on the distance of the reflecting surfaces from the source and from the object. Surface B is shown as larger than A, but twice as far away. B has the same angular size as A with respect to one source, so it receives about the same amount of light (depicted by the number of rays). Both A and B then scatter the light (mostly diffusely). Because B is farther from the object than A is, less of the light scattered from B is in the direction of the object. At twice the distance, B reflects an amount of light to the object as little as one-quarter of the amount reflected to the object by A. Greater reflection occurs, as shown, if the relative angles favor it; in this case, B sends half as much light as A to the object.

Q9-8. What shadows and shading are omitted from figure 9-13, and what should their relative amounts be, considering reflections?

The laws of reflection apply to any surface. Specular reflection occurs for quite rough surfaces if the angle of view is low enough. A rough sheet of cardboard appears as shiny as a mirror if the eye is situated very near the surface and strong light is available at a similar low angle from the other direction.

Curved surfaces illustrate the laws in a special way because they have portions of their surfaces available at almost any angle. Some part of the curved surface usually has the alignment needed to reflect a "highlight"—a spot of high intensity—to the viewer. Figure 9-15 shows in cross section a cylindrical reflecting surface. Light rays impinge at all possible angles from normal ("head-on," 0°) to just grazing the surface (90°). The specular law of reflection is most easily applied by measuring the angles of incidence and reflection with respect to the radii. Uniform illumination, depicted by a uniformly spaced set of rays, is spread out in direction and intensity by reflection. The viewer, looking toward one of the reflected rays, sees the cylinder as bright in that direction. The brightest highlight occurs when it is viewed from the left because more rays are reflected to the right.

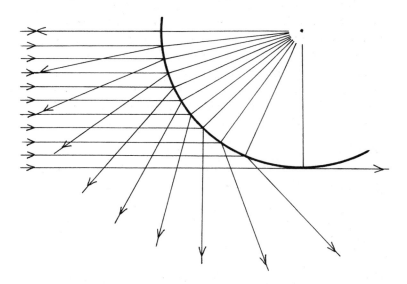

9-15. Reflection from a shiny cylindrical surface (cross section)

Any curved surface may show varying brightness because of reflections from sources and other nearby objects; highlights appear as stripes or spots if the surface is shiny. Plate 8 shows a sinusoidal surface with a grid (an abstract rolling landscape); it has uniform reflectance but varying brightness according to the angle at which the viewer sees the surface.

Q9-9. Sketch an elevation view (a sine curve) for plate 8. Assume solar rays incident at a suitable angle, and identify the parts of the "hills" that reflect (specularly) toward the viewer. Part of the reflection must be diffuse—why? Which parts reflect the least to V? Into how many valleys can V see before the hills get in the way?

To settle the question of whether reflection in curved surfaces produces perspective, the image for a convex spherical mirror is calculated below. In figure 9-16, the cross section of part of a polished spherical surface is shown. The source of light is at S; it can be a point on an object that scatters light. The center of curvature is at C, and the radius is R. The source can be given a general location (x,y,z), and the figure shows the xy plane. All locations must remain near the y axis. S might be distance z above the xy plane. The origin of the xyz system touches the mirror at O on the y axis of symmetry through C. Light rays from S reflect from the curved surface and go in many directions. They appear to diverge from a "virtual image" of the source, located at I. Optical theory provides that a spherical mirror has a focus F located at R/2 from the center. Geometric construction using the law of reflection establishes that rays from S parallel to the axis are

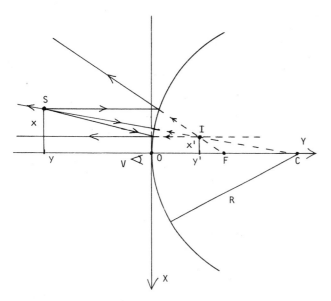

9-16. Image formed by a spherical convex mirror (cross section, xy plane)

reflected away from F. Rays from S toward C head back toward S after reflection. Rays from S toward F are reflected parallel to the axis. All appear to have come from I. By reference to the triangles involving these rays, equations can be calculated giving the location (x',y',z') of I:

$$x' = -xR/2y$$

$$y' = +R^2/4y$$

$$z' = -zR/2y .\qquad\qquad(9.14)$$

In their dependence on y (which is negative and identifies the distance of the source or object point), these equations resemble the perspective transformation. But they do not compress three dimensions

to two, and they are only good near the y axis. The image seems to be in the space behind the mirror, not on the surface. If the y' coordinate is ignored, giving a projection of the image to an xz plane, a form of perspective transformation is obtained that has the viewer at O ($d = h = 0$), looking at PP. If the light rays were not blocked, the viewer could look into the mirror and see the image of S, diminished in size but not inverted. A CV would lie on the axis, and the perspective is rectilinear very near the axis. An examination of the advanced optical equations for an image far from the axis would show a spherically distorted image that is not a spherical perspective. Not only is the PS curved the wrong way, but z' is different from $z' = t$ (the expected identity from equation 8.17).

The same calculations and results would follow for a concave mirror that produces a real image or for any lens. Although the image can be focused on paper, perspective is not produced because only one plane of the spatial image can be focused at a time. If all parts of the spatial image could be projected to a screen, then an approximately rectilinear perspective would be produced. A lens can show a scene in perspective on a screen or film as long as depth of field is not needed. Cameras do take pictures that are perspectives.

The calculations above were done with a convex mirror because this form of reflecting surface appears in several other applications. Some anamorphic art is designed to be viewed in a convex cylindrical or conical mirror.[8] So far, no one seems to have constructed a piece of art for a spherical mirror. Nature and man produce convex and concave reflecting surfaces, notably waves on a body of water, globes, bottles, and so forth. M. C. Escher created several prints showing scenes as reflected in a shiny globe.[9] His "Hand with Reflecting Sphere" does not show a spherical perspective. Rippled water produces interesting effects in perspective.[10] Another property of curved shiny surfaces is that they produce "caustics"—bright points and lines of light, not just from reflection but from concentration. Some part of such a surface always has the right curvature to enable light to concentrate in the direction of the viewer.[11]

The coverage of reflection in perspective here is limited to the perspective of the image of a point in a flat vertical mirror. The artist can extend the methods to any of the complex situations mentioned. Graphically, the method is shown in figure 9-17. In the plan, the law of reflection must be used to construct the ray of light from source S that is reflected by the vertical mirror M toward V. The light reflects at point P. If the mirror is clean, P cannot be seen. The light appears instead to come from S', the image of the source, which is located along the line of the reflected ray as far behind the mirror as S was in front. The positions of S and S' are measured with respect to point T, between them on the mirror. The mirror plane can be extended as far as is needed. The reflected ray pierces PP at point R. Finding R may aid in finding S', since R, P, and S' are in a straight line. Once S' is found in plan, and its height is found in elevation, the perspective of the image point is easily constructed. Of course S is also plotted in the picture if it fits within the frame.

When VPs are involved, they are treated the same as any other object points and are reflected in the mirror. The apparent ray from S' has a VPS' if needed, located with R. The line from S to S' van-

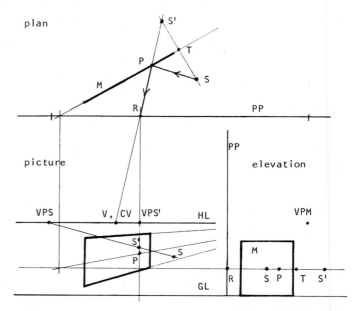

9-17. Perspective view of a point seen reflected in a mirror

ishes at a VPS located 90° from the VPM for the mirror. The VP of a line segment differs from its image (unless it is parallel to the mirror). These various observations summarize the special properties of reflection in perspective. The reflected image is not identical to the real picture because of these changes caused by perspective. Also, the usual property of mirrors holds: some image points can be seen, but not the corresponding real points, and vice versa. If the mirror is inclined, a view must be obtained showing its edge before the image can be found.[12]

Mathematically, the location of S' is found by reversing its coordinates with respect to the reflecting surface. This is not simple if the mirror is not parallel to any of the coordinate planes. As usual,

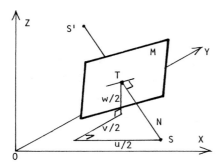

9-18. Calculating the mirror image of a point (oblique view)

the viewer looks along the *y* axis for purposes of this discussion. One method is to find what translation by *u, v,* and *w* produces point S′ from S, as shown in the oblique view of figure 9-18. The coordinates of S′ are $(x - u, y - v, z - w)$. The point T where the normal $\overline{N}$ through S intersects the mirror is at $([x - u]/2, [y - v]/2, [z - w]/2)$, providing a possible way to find *u, v,* and *w*. Another procedure is to obtain the equation of the plane for the mirror. Then, $\overline{N}$ through S can be found, and the coordinates of T or S′ can be calculated because they are points on the line $\overline{N}$.

An optical effect related to reflection but involving a different law is "refraction," the bending of light rays as they pass from one transparent material to another. Artists can obtain interesting if rarely used perspective effects—for example, depicting a stick extending from water to air—but the subject goes beyond the scope of this book.

Notes

1. For nontechnical coverage of light and shadow, see M. Minnaert, *The Nature of Light and Color in the Open Air.*

2. On contrasts at boundaries, see Floyd Ratliff, "Contour and Contrast."

3. The solar location formulas used here are adapted from Bruce Anderson and Michael Riordan, *The Solar Home Book.*

4. On graphic methods for shadows, see Gill, *Creative Perspective;* Vero, *Understanding Perspective;* Rex Vicat Cole, *Perspective for Artists.*

5. On shading the sphere, see Gill, *Creative Perspective.*

6. On the shading of cylinders and spheres, see Vero, *Understanding Perspective.*

7. On illumination in computer graphics, see Joan Scott, *Introduction to Interactive Computer Graphics* and Donald Greenberg, et al., *The Computer Image.*

8. On anamorphic art using reflection, see Leeman, *Hidden Images* and Gardner, "Anamorphic Art."

9. For Escher prints of reflecting globes, see Ernst, *Magic Mirror of Escher* and Locher, *World of Escher.*

10. On reflections and refractions in water for perspective, see Cole, *Perspective for Artists.*

11. On caustics, see Jearl Walker, "Caustics: Mathematical Curves Generated by Light Shined through Rippled Plastic."

12. On reflection in perspective, see Cole, *Perspective for Artists* and Gill, *Creative Perspective.*

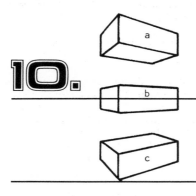

10.

Mechanical and Electronic Assistance for Perspective

Mechanical instruments (and possibly a calculator) are necessary for drawing (as opposed to sketching) perspective by hand. For further assistance in the mathematical approach to perspective, the computer is available—the greatest of modern tools for art. The computer does nothing more than a prodigious quantity of calculations according to very sophisticated programs or direct user input. It can convert its calculations into highly accurate pictures, producing visible results that are impressively complicated, very beautiful, or worthless. Everything depends on the understanding and vision of the human user. To guide that vision, some new concepts conceived by mathematical minds and made more comprehensible by the computer are discussed here.

Drawing Lines—Straightedges and Other Tools

This review of drawing techniques and tools emphasizes problems that arise in perspective drawing. It is by no means complete, and good engineering drawing texts should be consulted for more general practices in drawing.[1]

Some parts of a perspective require extreme accuracy of line placement; otherwise, the eye notices the lack of alignment of certain features. Intersections of grid lines tend to lose their regularity in "distant" parts of the picture. The "straightedge" should be sight-tested for straightness before it is purchased. A warp of 1 mm in 1 m is enough to cause frustration in laying out a precision drawing.

Straightness can be tested by drawing a long line and then turning the tool over and retracing the same line. This procedure magnifies any curve in the straightedge by a factor of two, and the direction of curve can be ascertained. T squares can be tested for accuracy similarly, assuming that the two edges of the drawing table are perfectly parallel (easily measured).

Since the straightedge or ruler is often slid across drawings, it should not be made of aluminum or any other material that leaves marks or smears pencil. An aluminum ruler can be covered with thin plastic tape to solve the problem. Rulers, triangles, French curves, and templates with raised edges to avoid ink smears may not be available. Having raised edges also raises their price considerably. The problem is easily solved by sticking strips of thick clear tape under a standard tool, near the working edges. Tape strips can be put on both sides if the template or curve must be turned over. The tape should not have residual adhesive that might injure the drawing.

Drawing pencils should be sharpened to a conical point with sandpaper. For construction lines, the pencil's hardness should be sufficient to leave a faintly visible line at moderate pressure. Tests should be made as to whether erasure of construction lines is necessary or feasible. On very hard surfaces such as gesso, very hard pencils are needed. A 9H pencil acts like a 1H on gesso and must be resharpened after only one or two long lines are drawn. It is better to make trial drawings on cheap paper than to try to erase lines repeatedly from a rough or expensive material because the drawing is not coming out as expected.

For least error in drawing lines, the straightedge is first placed against the sharp pencil point at a point of the picture (such as the viewer point V) and aligned with some other feature. Then the pencil point is moved to some other point (such as a pierce point on PP), and the straightedge is pivoted around the pencil point. When one point (such as a VP) is used repeatedly to determine many lines, a pin can be inserted through the point into a suitable material beneath to serve as a pivot. Alternatively, a sharp wedge of wood can be taped at the point.

For lines that must be drawn to distant VPs not located on the paper, several procedures are possible. If the VP is less than 1 m outside the picture edge, a strip of wood or cardboard can be taped or glued to the back of the drawing sheet or board to provide a pivot point at the needed position. The actual position must be obtained either by alignment with large rulers and squares, by extrapolation from a small-scale drawing, or by calculation. Straightedge rulers as long as 8 ft (over 2 m) can be obtained. Beyond that, a very straight piece of lumber can be used. For very large work, a wire can be stretched and fastened at a distant VP located at the proper place in the room. It then serves as a self-pivoting straightedge.

A device called the *linead* can aid in drawing lines to an inaccessible VP or any other point. Such lines represent parallel lines in perspective. A linead can be difficult to locate for purchase, but it can be simply made from three straight flat pieces of molding from 1 m to 2 m long. As shown in figure 10-1, a sheet of aluminum or other thin stiff metal, plastic, or wood is cut any suitable shape to form a plate to connect the three wooden arms. The center arm is

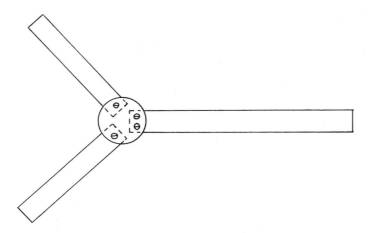

10-1. Making a linead

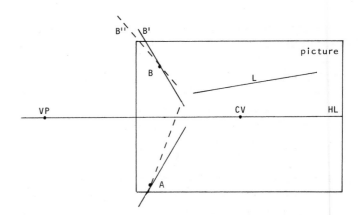

10-2. Setting the linead for drawing lines to a distant vanishing point

the longest and should act as a straightedge for fin-ished drawing. It is fastened in fixed position to the center plate. The other arms are fastened with screws or wing nuts so that they can be pivoted and clamped in the desired position. The fasteners should be recessed underneath to avoid injuring the drawing. The smaller the plate and the narrower the arms, the less interference likely with the drawing.

Before the linead can be used, a small-scale drawing is needed to show the "inaccessible" VP on paper. Figure 10-2 shows the whole preparatory drawing, including picture location and VP. Any line $\overline{L}$ (except HL) is drawn toward the VP, and whatever part of it fits is transferred to the full-scale picture. Other means can be used to obtain $\overline{L}$, such as measuring the location of the VP outside the pic-ture and sighting toward it with a straightedge. The angle between $\overline{L}$ and HL can be calculated or used for the transfer. The center arm is then placed along HL, and both other arms are locked at trial angles

of about 60° from HL. The particular angles may need modification to fit the application, but once set they must not be changed.

Any pont A is located near the bottom left cor-ner of the picture (for a VP off the left side), and the lower arm is placed against A. A test line $\overline{B'}$ is drawn along the upper arm. Next, the center arm is swung into alignment with line $\overline{L}$, carrying the other fixed arms with it to the dashed position shown. The lower arm is again placed against A, and another test line $\overline{B''}$ is drawn along the upper arm. The inter-section of $\overline{B'}$ and $\overline{B''}$ determines point B for all fur-ther use of the linead for the given VP. If $\overline{B'}$ and $\overline{B''}$ are not long enough to intersect, or if B should not occur in the upper left of the picture, the arms should be readjusted and the process repeated. For accuracy, A and B should be far apart. The more distant VPs require the arms to be opened to larger angles. The linead is used by placing the center arm on the point through which a line is wanted, and then moving the whole instrument to touch points A and B. The line can then be drawn. For efficiency, pins or wedges should be placed at A and B. The linead and related tools are described in some drawing texts. Calculating the line locations is likely to be more efficient.

A line parallel to another line can be drawn by using two 30°-60° triangles together, giving two parallel edges with adjustable spacing. Many parallel lines, closely spaced, can be drawn with an adjustable lettering guide. Some clear plastic rulers have several parallel lines along their length that are useful for making a quick alignment with a line on the drawing, prior to drawing a parallel line by visual estimation. This practice can be quite accurate when the spacing is less than 1 cm. A drafting machine, although expensive, enables the artist to draw parallel lines accurately and quickly in any orientation.

Plotting Coordinates

A ruler is an instrument with regular markings for laying out distances, usually in metric or English units. It may also serve as a suitable straightedge. As discussed in chapter 2, a meterstick marked in millimeters is the best available tool for extreme accuracy on large pictures. None seems to be available with a beveled edge, so it must be set on its edge for marking. A metric "scale" (a ruler with triangular cross section and built-in scaling) is only about 30 cm long and is good for smaller work. The beveled edges are not suitable for drawing lines but are fine for marking coordinates. A flat, clear, inexpensive, 30-cm ruler with an edge tested for straightness and squareness is excellent for the majority of layout and drawing. Straight rulers can be obtained as long as 8 ft (over 2 m). Beyond that, a tape measure can be used; metric ones are available.

Plotting picture coordinates (p,q) often involves measuring many values of q from HL (the p axis). A straightedge can be fastened temporarily along HL so that the ruler for marking values of q can be butted against it. As discussed earlier, problems of accuracy are most noticeable near HL, so that careful measurement of all values of q from HL is essential. Another straightedge can be fastened along the q axis for marking values of p.

Sometimes the greatest accuracy is obtained by plotting angles when lines are to be drawn to a VP. The largest possible protractor should be used to ensure accuracy in marking angles, since protractors are difficult to read and use accurately. A small protractor is also needed for measuring and marking angles on small features. Drafting machines can be used to measure and draw angles.

Rapid plotting of coordinates requires two or more rulers. An artist with access to a woodshop can make a "plotter" like the one shown in figure 10-3. A piece of wood is cut so that one meterstick is guided to slide beneath another at a right angle. Care is needed to avoid jamming instead of sliding. The x locator is slid along the x ruler, carrying the y stick with it. A pencil slot is cut into another piece of wood that slides along the y ruler. Latches can be arranged to lock either locator to its stick for cases in which one coordinate is fixed. In use, the y ruler is fixed somewhere to the picture, out of the way. The two locators are slid until their index

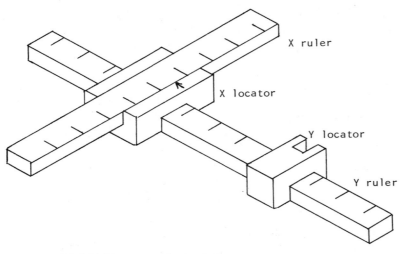

10-3. Making a coordinate plotter

marks match the coordinates; a pencil mark is then made in the slot.

Some other tools have been or could be invented for working with more esoteric forms of perspective. Extensive use of stretched strings and grids was needed for the old anamorphic paintings and the "trompe-l'oeil" illusions painted on curved ceilings. Descargues and Leeman show tools and methods used by various artists for anamorphic art, cylindrical perspective, and other forms.[2]

Sometimes, the artist is able to obtain a complicated plot of coordinates on paper, but the final medium is to be canvas, masonite, or another thick medium. Perhaps a computer was used to plot points on paper with a printer or plotter. The transfer of the points would be very laborious. The simple trick, assuming that the paper plot is full size, is to prick through the paper with a sharp hard pencil onto the final medium at each point. If the paper is not full size, perhaps it should have been, or perhaps a "pantograph" can be used to change the scale. The plotting work can also be shortened by buying or assembling large sheets of metric graph paper on which coordinate axes can be numbered and points plotted.

Hand Calculation and Pocket Calculators

For large projects, a pocket calculator is essential. It should be chosen for efficiency of use; the RPN-logic calculators are recommended. Several memories, "trig" functions, squares, and square roots are essential. Inverse "trig" functions, angle capability in radians, and a choice of rounding off decimals are very useful. Other functions to match the artist's plans should be included, as well. Some programs for architectural use are available for certain programmable calculators,[3] but the number of steps to be entered can be very large (many hundred). A printing calculator enables the artist to avoid having to write down a large number of results.

Forming a table is essential for calculation, as discussed in earlier chapters. It should show any intermediate calculations that are needed several times or that are not easily stored in memories. Working on a large project causes the artist to seek maximum efficiency in using the calculator. After trial runs to check that points plot in the places wanted, a careful plan of calculation should be made to avoid all unnecessary entries of numbers or repetitions of work. All possible symmetries should be used to advantage. For example, positive and negative coordinates may be the same, or both sides of a circle may be found by the same square root. RPN logic allows the least use of keystrokes to enter data or functions. Some work can be calculated mentally—for example, adding $d = 6$ automatically to every y value before entering it. Trigonometric and exponential functions usually involve some time waiting for the calculator's internal program to run to completion, and their use should be minimized. If only a few angles are involved, their "trig" functions should be stored in memories. Numbers should be rounded off by the calculator display to the least accuracy needed for plotting (usually 0.1 mm for fine work, and 1 mm for coarse work).

Survey of Computer Graphics

It is beyond the scope of this book to cover computer calculation of perspective and all the prior preparation in computer graphics implied thereby. But it may help the artist to know what types of computer assistance are available. Seeing in what ways computer systems have been enlisted to do the methods previously discussed (there are similarities and differences) may also be edifying. Many general nontechnical surveys of computer graphics are now available.[4] Most discuss and illustrate applications for visual arts as well as for science and technology, but few computer artists seem to be using perspective. The general treatments describe available computer hardware and software (programs) briefly, without being very specific. The field continues to change rapidly as new developments occur. Technical descriptions of computer graphics can be harder to find.[5] To a large extent, the artist must rely on the manuals and software available for the particular system at hand. Few industry standards exist for hardware and software, and the technical books have something of a reputation for obscure description. The graphics market is growing rapidly, however, and the situation should improve.

Developments in computer graphics are in part due to the practical requirements of computer-assisted design and computer-assisted manufacture (known as CAD and CAM). References on CAD might be useful to the computer artist. For artists who are interested in mathematical methods and new procedures but do not intend to use the computer, exploring the computer graphics literature can still be helpful. For example, the article "The Perspective Representation of Functions of Two Variables" and other general mathematical articles can be found in the Freeman collection. The practical areas currently making the most use of perspective are flight-simulation graphics, films, and architectural design. These naturally involve large distances.

The input to a computer graphics system can be made with a variety of hardware. Available are plotting boards on which a stylus or the finger marks points, screens to be used with light pens or finger touches, a "mouse" that causes a point to move on the screen as the mouse is rolled on a flat surface, and more. All plotting is seen first on a video *monitor,* also known as a cathode-ray tube (CRT) or screen. Points, lines, other features, and changes can be entered with a keyboard. If picture information is not entered directly, it must be entered mathematically (as functions to be calculated) or numerically (as a string of data).

Computer systems can be obtained with monitors that display in either monochrome (white, green, or amber on black) or color in various-sized palettes. The brightness of monochrome can be varied through sixteen or more levels of "gray," but this capability often is not made available. The most common color video monitor has separate red, green, and blue (RGB) shadow-masked electron beams; the picture is painted with scanning lines and is called a "raster scan." A commercial television uses one beam, producing less color control and more flicker. Most frequently, computer-generated art is photographed directly from an RGB monitor.

For detailed and accurate artistic work, high resolution is needed for pictorial input and output. *Resolution* can be defined as the smallest features in a picture that can be distinguished, either by the eye or by a particular technology. Levels of resolution taken for granted by artists, photographers, and filmmakers are currently much finer than those available on commercially available computer systems. Picture resolution is measured in terms of pixels for video technology and in terms of granularity for film-based technology. A *pixel,* from the term "picture element," is a single dot of light whose location in the picture is established by one pair of coordinates. 35-mm film (still or motion) is capable of resolving 10 million to 100 million pixels per frame. No viewer takes these all in at one time, but as the high-resolution part of the retina (at the fovea) scans the picture, any lesser resolution becomes apparent as a grainy structure. The eye is capable of resolving one part in about 4,000 in a 50° view, both horizontally and vertically, implying a potential picture content of almost 20 million pixels in a 50° field of view.

A standard television screen with 512 visible scan lines and about 400 pixels per line provides about 200,000 pixels. The better general video monitors resolve about 700 pixels horizontally and 500 vertically, or 350,000 pixels. Systems that give less than 300 scan lines vertically are suitable only for coarse work. A new industry standard of 1 million pixels is anticipated—barely enough for fine work. This corresponds to a 1-m-square picture with 1 mm resolution. Because of the speed, computer time, and large equipment required, the 1-million-pixel picture may remain expensive to attain. While few artists want to be personally responsible for each of 1 million pixels in a picture, some straight lines and curves at this resolution become noticeably jagged. This problem is known as "aliasing."

If the screen is not to be photographed, the resolution provided by the output device (printer or plotter) becomes critical. Dot matrix printers can at least match the resolution of monitors; plotters can easily exceed the resolution of monitors while providing larger pictures (at considerable expense). Color monitors can usually provide better color range and quality than color plotters. Color printers still provide color of limited hue and saturation. Perspective can be done without gradations of color, but a monochrome output with a gray-scale (halftone) capability is desirable to show lines and surfaces as shaded or fading in the distance. This is not possible on current printers without substantial loss of resolution.

Since printers and plotters provide paper of limited size, the artist wanting a very big plot could direct the computer to provide the picture in sections—four, six, eight, or more, depending on what is compatible with printout format and final picture size. The mathematical approach to perspective provides that any part of any picture can be viewed in any way. The viewer can temporarily be postulated as viewing just one section of the picture on the monitor, as shown in figure 10-4. If another section is to be shown, V remains fixed but the monitor is assumed to be at the new section.

At least four different levels of realism are possible with a computer picture. As complexity is increased, the amount of computation time increases rapidly. Each picture can be done as an orthographic view or as a perspective, with more realism achieved by means of perspective. Simplest is the "wire-frame," in which lines delineating the objects are shown as if the objects were made of wire and their surfaces were transparent. This view is the same as a line drawing in which all lines are visible. A refinement is obtained if hidden lines (and surfaces) are suppressed, producing an outline drawing. The third step toward realism is to show surfaces by shading them according to the illumination. A fourth level of sophistication occurs when the color and reflectance of surfaces are calculated, including highlights and the properties of the intended light sources. All of these stages can be treated graphically or mathematically, but the computer carries some of them out differently. A fifth level is achieved when motion is included.

A computer can (theoretically) be made to present almost anything pictorially; its results are

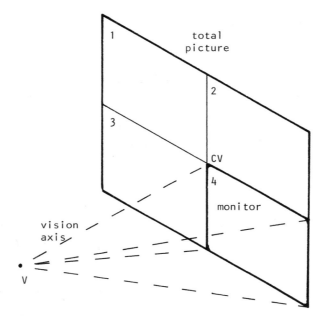

10-4. Constructing a picture in four sections (by computer)

limited only by time, programming, and human imagination and understanding. But the visible results are only as good as the display device can make them. The screen or other output gives a relatively flat picture, although cylindrical solid-state or plasma displays are feasible. The viewer must be assumed to be looking at the center of the screen unless some feature causes CV to move elsewhere. The subject matter provided for computation and display may entail a larger angle of view than that defined by the location of the viewer and the width of the screen (typically about 60°). The picture computation must remove or "clip" unwanted regions, saving computer time as well as reducing confusion.

Computer Calculation
of Perspective

As far as the computer is concerned, all pictures must be reduced to mathematically described parts —points, lines, polygons, and vertices. The computer cannot truly envision a mathematical function but must have it expressed as a table of numbers. Curves are problematic, since the only graphs possible from numerical descriptions of curves involve approximations consisting of discrete, straight-line segments. The artist must either enter a picture with the graphic input devices previously described, after which the computer digitizes the input to numerical form, or the artist must have mathematically described subject matter. The numerical basis of the subject matter does allow analysis for slopes, curvatures, and other features, in imitation of what calculus can do analytically with functions.

The computations are done with respect to coordinate systems, usually rectilinear ones defined slightly differently from the way they are in this book. Often, the horizontal and vertical scales of the pixels—and therefore of the screen, printer, or plotter—are not the same. In other words, the pixels are not shaped as tiny circles or squares but as tiny ellipses or rectangles. The scaling behavior of the output device must be found, usually by experiment, and then allowed for in programming by means of an inverse scaling. Most graphic languages assume that the screen coordinates have their origin at the upper left corner, so all coordinates must be translated to this system. Some graphic languages provide for the automatic specification of simple features such as lines, rectangles, circles, and shad-ing, but modifications of these must be programmed.

The computation can be programmed and carried out almost exactly as discussed heretofore, including the perspective view and the illumination and shading. The computer equivalent to filling in a table with numbers calculated by a repetitive procedure is "iteration" with an *algorithm*. An algorithm is a logical procedure instructing the computer as to the exact order for doing the specified calculations. Iteration is the process of repetition in which the computer works in a "loop." Calculations are made with an independent variable set at one value. Then that variable is increased by a suitably small increment, and the process is repeated. Examples of iterations for the coordinates of simple functions appear in the BASIC programs in the appendix. Usually everything possible, including printout or plotting, is done in one step before the next step is begun.

The actual mathematical method for most graphic programs is one using "matrix" calculation. The transformations (linear, scaling, rotational, perspective, even illumination) can be expressed as three-by-three (or four-by-four, for technical reasons) arrays of numbers. The arrays or matrices for a series of transformations, often done in the order just listed, can be combined into a single matrix. It is applied to each set of coordinates for each object point. The matrix does the transformations "all at once" for the three coordinates. This process may be more efficient for a properly programmed computer than the methods of this book, or it may require more computation. The artist could learn and use the matrix transformation method by hand, but much more work is involved and confusion is likely.

If the picture is to consist merely of a perspective line drawing on the screen, the computations are few and fast. Milliseconds are required for calculation (after possibly laborious programming), but the hardware for video graphics may require several seconds to "paint" the simplest picture. If colored surfaces are included, the computer must carry out the procedure for every pixel of every surface to be shown. The running time can be many seconds for a single picture, without shading.

The use of matrix calculation saves much time because only adding and multiplying are involved. Any use of division, trigonometry, or other special functions slows down the computer considerably. A computer said to cycle (typically) at 5 million times per second does an addition analogous to $1 + 1 = 2$ in several cycles. Other seemingly simple calculations may take 10 to 100 microseconds, and general "housekeeping" takes additional time. If the calculations are repeated for 300,000 pixels, the running time is many seconds for one frame.

Efficiency is gained by obtaining efficient programs in fast languages, by incorporating special hardware dedicated to graphics, and by using the fact that calculations need not be repeated for every nearby pixel in the same situation. Even so, "real-time" moving pictures are feasible only on very expensive specialized systems capable of making thirty new and slightly different pictures every second.

A more difficult part of the computation problem has not been mentioned yet—the "recognition" and suppression of hidden lines and surfaces. This process, which a human can do intuitively without evident expenditure of thinking time, can require a vast number of computations by computer, occupying minutes of work. Research continues on the best way to carry out the work, and many approaches have been developed. One set of approaches works with the geometric description of the subject matter and is done before the perspective transformation. Each polygon (region bounded by lines) is considered as a surface. The outward normal to it is found and the angle between the vision axis and the normal is examined to find whether the surface can be seen or not. Other routines test every polygon to determine what polygons might be overlapping. The computer cannot "see" anything geometrically but can only work by algebraic rules that at best serve to identify alleged surfaces by points defining their flattened outlines. Tests must be undertaken to determine if one polygon is in front of or behind another, using the available depth information. The operations are done in an order that presents the fewest cases for testing at each stage, to reduce computation time.

Another general approach makes use of the fact that screen graphic information is stored in a large ordered memory from which each "byte" of numerical data is "mapped" to a pixel on the screen. The information has already been transformed to perspective, and the illumination, if any, has been calculated. To start the determination of hidden surfaces, a feature (such as a polygon) is sent first to this memory (called a "frame buffer") and then to the screen for display. Then another polygon is sent to the buffer, and calculations determine what parts of the second polygon should appear in front of the first. If any parts fit this description, they are displayed and the affected part of the previous polygon is removed. This method can be fast, but it is limited to exactly what is displayed. The previously described method provides more generally useful information on visibility, applicable to other viewpoints. For technical help with programming for hidden line removal, the reader must turn to computer graphics journals and texts.

Another large computational load is incurred when calculations for surface reflections are wanted. The method requires surface reflectance to be described with several parameters for every point of every surface. The reflectance may depend on the color of the illumination; glossy surfaces require a special highlight description. All sources of light, including reflections from other objects, must be specified. Some degree of texture can be implied by means of the glossiness of the surface. Shiny surfaces that reflect light directly to the viewer are identified. Shadows are automatically created by these procedures, and coloring is as realistic as the optical knowledge that is supplied.

Although some of the physical laws were introduced independently in chapter 9, an artist cannot possibly calculate illumination without a computer. However, the traditional way of producing art resembles the mathematical process. In regard to technique alone, talented artists can still outperform computers at showing coloration and shadowing. Computers cannot yet depict mists, trees, and other ''soft'' features well, but some progress is being made.

The graphics transformations reviewed in chapter 6 should all be part of any graphics program. To that list of point and line transformations should be added these pertaining to the appearance of surfaces: shading, coloring, and highlighting.

General Remarks on Computers and Art

Many computer languages have been developed for graphics. The programs provided in the appendix are in the most common language, BASIC. Different systems use slightly different versions of BASIC. The programs in the appendix are only for computation of specific objects; BASIC programs for a variety of other particular applications (such as for drawing a circle through three given points, or for drawing a parabola) have also been published.[6] The immense variety of graphics commands and hardware make it impossible to provide sample programs that can tell every computer how to show the result. Learning to program, learning particular languages, and becoming acquainted with specific graphics hardware are tasks that must be left to the artist. Very few microcomputer programs for computing perspective are commercially available. Those that are available may provide no significant advantage over what the artist with a simple graphics computer can learn to do (however slowly): they either lack hidden line suppression and surface shading or lack versatility or are very expensive and slow.

Factors to consider in acquiring a graphics computer are its speed, memory, and versatility, and the availability of compatible hardware and software (programs). A medium-priced personal computer is fast enough. Large amounts of memory

(256 kilobytes to 512 kilobytes) may be necessary for advanced work. Even this much can store only one or two full-screen pictures. A reasonable amount of screen buffer memory is provided with the graphics circuit card that forms a necessary part of the system, but it cannot be used for computation or unrestricted storage. All hardware must be tested before purchase to ensure compatibility, as must all software. Software is not a major issue, in the sense that no firm is likely to develop the particular software needed by the specialized or advanced artist; the artist probably has to learn to develop it to match the particular system. Graphics cards usually come with limited supporting programs whose versatility can be judged only after real use. If a printer is to be used, some searching will be necessary to find one that has both fine resolution and available hardware and software for copying the picture developed on the screen.

The art of creating natural-looking objects through numerical calculation was advanced significantly by the invention of "fractals," a mathematical way of describing the raggedness of edges and surfaces. A randomness with the proper type of order can be imposed on surfaces to mimic natural mountains, trees, and so on. Examples by various artists appear in the works cited in note 4 and in other articles.[7] The connection of the fractal approach to perspective is likely to be of increasing importance. Fractals are closely related to the depiction of scale and depth in nature. For more information, the artist is referred to the beautiful book by Mandelbrot, who has found a new way to see order in chaos.[8] Plate 2 shows an approximation of a fractal object.

A new development for the computer—good for graphics, for teaching children, and even for generating fractals—is called "turtle geometry."[9] Drawing is done in a local manner from one point to the next (an approach sometimes known as the "differential," as opposed to "integrative" or global). The mathematical artist can gain new insights, and the methods can be done graphically on paper, as well as on the computer. Turtle geometry's relevance to perspective may lie in the new way of envisioning and using spaces it encourages.

A technical trick made more feasible with the computer is the calculation of stereoscopic views. A stereoscopic view is necessarily a perspective—actually, two perspectives of the same subject matter constructed for two slightly different viewpoints. The artist can also calculate or construct them by hand. The two perspectives are meant to be seen by the two different eyes of the same viewer; the positions of V can be spaced apart by the distance between the eyes, or by a wider distance. The two views are useless without a means of displaying them such that each eye sees the picture meant for it. Computed stereographics are precise and impressive, but at present they are used mainly in scientific and technical applications.[10] The curious artist might want to explore the work done with random dot stereograms.[11] Two pictures of dots with apparently random patterns are made (by computer) with a certain relation between the two patterns. Only when each eye views its proper picture is a recognizable feature—for example, a stack of squares—seen in depth. The reference in note 11 demonstrates the effect with the aid of red-green "3-D" glasses, and the reader might speculate whether a new kind of perspective is being demonstrated.

The development of methods for computer graphics has stimulated further research into human vision, in hopes of discovering what methods used by the eye can be employed technologically. The goal of computer vision is intricately linked with questions of how human beings see depth and interpret perspective.[12] The best indications are that we interpret scenes by means of disparities (from our stereoscopic vision) and from shading.

The loop is now closed with regard to the history and use of perspective. The earliest experimenters with perspective did not attempt curves.[13] The symbol of highest competence in perspective art was the drawing of a "mazzocchio"—a sort of large torus made entirely of polygons (about 160 of them) to form a polyhedron with a hole. In ensuing centuries, perspective as a graphic art was refined but relegated to the status of a technique. The computer (and other recent developments) may contribute to its revival. Computer graphics can now be used to depict the same torus, necessarily made of polygons because shading and other operations can only be calculated for flat surfaces, however many and however small they may be. One result, using 841 polygons, can be seen in the article by Whitted cited in note 4. Further computer operations are needed to show the surface smoother, as a curved surface. In the age of relativity and indeterminacy, room has been found for the classical viewpoint of perspective, though with some new variations.

Notes

1. For general technical drawing methods, see references listed in chapter 3, note 1.

2. For various historical tools and methods, see Descargues, *Perspective History* and Leeman, *Hidden Images*.

3. On calculator programs, see Yue, *Drawings by Calculator*.

4. For nontechnical coverage of computer graphics, see Greenberg, *Computer Image;* Scott, *Interactive Computer Graphics;* Dale Peterson, *Genesis II: Creation and Recreation with Computers;* Joseph Deken, *Computer Images;* Ruth Leavitt, ed., *Artist and Computer;* Jasia Reichardt, ed., *Cybernetic Serendipity;* and Turner Whitted, "Some Recent Advances in Computer Graphics."

5. For technical coverage of computer graphics, see David Rogers and J. Adams, *Mathematical Elements for Computer Graphics;* Herbert Freeman, ed., *Interactive Computer Graphics;* Donald Hearn and M. Pauline Baker, *Computer Graphics for the IBM Personal Computer;* and William Newmann and Robert Sproull, *Principles of Interactive Computer Graphics*.

6. Many BASIC programs for graphics are given in Rogers, *Mathematical Elements*.

7. For brief illustration and discussion of fractals, see Jeanne McDermott, "Geometrical Forms Known as Fractals Find Sense in Chaos."

8. For broad and thorough coverage of fractals, see Benoit Mandelbrot, *The Fractal Geometry of Nature*.

9. On turtle geometry, see Harold Abelson and Andrea Disessa, *Turtle Geometry: The Computer as a Medium for Exploring Mathematics* and Brian Hayes, "Turning Turtle Gives One a View of Geometry from the Inside Out."

10. For new ways of showing surfaces, perspective, and fast hidden-line removal, see Paul Bash, et al., "Van der Waals Surfaces in Molecular Modeling: Implementation with Realtime Computer Graphics" and Robert Langridge, et al., "Realtime Color Graphics in Studies of Molecular Interactions."

11. On random dot stereograms, see Bela Julesz, *Foundations of Cyclopean Perception*.

12. On advances in computer and human vision, see C. M. Brown, "Computer Vision and Natural Constraints."

13. On early uses of perspective (such as for making the mazzocchio), see Tormey, "Renaissance Intarsia."

The Lower-case Greek Alphabet

alpha	α
beta	β
gamma	γ
delta	δ
epsilon	ϵ
zeta	ζ
eta	η
theta	θ
iota	ι
kappa	κ
lambda	λ
mu	μ
nu	ν
xi	ξ
omicron	o
pi	π
rho	ρ
sigma	σ
tau	τ
upsilon	υ
phi	ϕ
chi	χ
psi	ψ
omega	ω

Appendix: Six BASIC Programs for Perspective

BASIC Program for Dividing Any Line into Equal Parts in Perspective

```
10 PRINT"Calculation of division marks Q1...Qn on a line in perspective"
20 PRINT"For equally-spaced unit marks seen to converge to VP in perspective."
30 PRINT"a' must be unit size as seen in front projection.  If unit size a is"
40 PRINT"given, front projection a' must be found first."
45 PRINT"For line at angle theta to PP, a'=a cos (theta)."
50 PRINT"Reference point Q0 for measurement is at the beginning of the line."
60 PRINT"Line length in perspective is h', measured from Q0 to VP on PP."
70 PRINT"Either d and a' must be known, or the first mark Q1 must be known."
80 PRINT"If d/a' is not known, calculate it from Q1, the first mark."
90 PRINT"The equation is Q1=1h'/(1+d/a'), or d/a' = (h'/Q1) - 1 ."
100 INPUT"ratio of viewer distance to unit size d/a'";DA
110 INPUT"total line length h'";H
120 INPUT"number of marks to calculate n";N
130 DIM Q(N)
140 PRINT
150 PRINT"Locations of unit marks in perspective"
160 PRINT USING"\          \";"n";"Qn"
170 FOR I=1 TO N
180 Q(I)=I*H/(I+DA)
190 PRINT USING"####.##   ";I;Q(I)
200 NEXT I
210 END
```

BASIC Program for Perspective of a Rectangular Box

```
10 PRINT "Calculation of rectilinear perspective for rectangular box, any"
15 PRINT"orientation, 8 corners"
20 PRINT"For square in xy-plane, use a=b, c=0. For cube, use a=b=c."
30 PRINT"Rotation angles are in degrees.  If no rotation, use zero for angle."
40 PRINT"Rotations leave the reference point (x,y,z)=(0,0,0) fixed."
50 PRINT"It is recommended that the reference point of box be at (0,0,0),"
60 PRINT"if the box rather than its location is the principal object of study."
70 PRINT"If bottom left front corner is not be to reference point, use"
80 PRINT"negative values for a, b, or c to move reference point."
90 INPUT"viewer distance d to picture plane";D
100 INPUT"viewer height h above ground plane (z=0, the xy-plane)";H
110 INPUT"bottom left front corner coordinates x,y,z";X(1),Y(1),Z(1)
120 INPUT"angle of rotation in xy-plane, ccw around z-axis from PP, theta";TH
130 INPUT"angle of tilt ccw around x-axis from ground plane, phi";TI
140 INPUT"angle of roll cw around y-axis as seen in front view, psi";TS
150 INPUT"width a, depth b, height c";A,B,C
160 'calculation of remaining seven corners of box
170 X(2)=X(1)+A: Y(2)=Y(1): Z(2)=Z(1)
180 X(3)=X(1)+A: Y(3)=Y(1)+B: Z(3)=Z(2)
190 X(4)=X(1): Y(4)=Y(1)+B: Z(4)=Z(1)
200 X(5)=X(1): Y(5)=Y(1): Z(5)=Z(1)+C
210 X(6)=X(1)+A: Y(6)=Y(1): Z(6)=Z(1)+C
220 X(7)=X(1)+A: Y(7)=Y(1)+B: Z(7)=Z(1)+C
230 X(8)=X(1): Y(8)=Y(1)+B: Z(8)=Z(1)+C
240 PRINT
250 PRINT"Verification of coordinates of box corners:"
260 PRINT "corner","x","y","z"
270 FOR I=1 TO 8
280 PRINT I, X(I), Y(I), Z(I)
290 NEXT I
300 TH=.0174533*TH:TI=.0174533*TI:TS=.0174533*TS    'convert degrees to radians
310 'accelerate trig calculations
```

```
320 STH=SIN(TH):CTH=COS(TH):STI=SIN(TI):CTI=COS(TI):STS=SIN(TS):CTS=COS(TS)
330 PRINT
340 PRINT"Rotated box coordinates, and perspective coordinates:"
350 PRINT USING "\          \";"corner";"x (rot)";"y (rot)";"z (rot)";"p";"q"
360 FOR I=1 TO 8
370 XR(I)=X(I)*CTH-Y(I)*STH    'rotation by theta around z-axis
380 YR(I)=X(I)*STH+Y(I)*CTH
390 YRR(I)=YR(I)*CTI-Z(I)*STI    'rotation by phi around x-axis
400 ZR(I)=YR(I)*STI+Z(I)*CTI
410 ZRR(I)=ZR(I)*CTS-XR(I)*STS    'rotation by psi around z-axis
420 XRR(I)=ZR(I)*STS+XR(I)*CTS
430 Q(I)=(ZRR(I)-H)*D/(YRR(I)+D):P(I)=XRR(I)*D/(YRR(I)+D)    'perspective
440 PRINT USING "###.###   ";I;XRR(I);YRR(I);ZRR(I);P(I);Q(I)
450 NEXT I
460 END
```

BASIC Program for Perspective of a Circle

```
10 PRINT"Calculation of circle in rectlinear perspective, any orientation"
20 PRINT"Caution: be sure circle radius and center do not cause it to approach"
30 PRINT"viewer position."
40 PRINT"Program starts with circle in an xy-plane.  To re-orient, use angles"
50 PRINT"to rotate this plane about x-axis and/or y-axis."
60 PRINT"Rotation angles in degrees.  If no rotation, use zero for angle."
70 PRINT"Number of iterations to obtain points is limited to 100."
80 INPUT"viewer distance d to picture plane";D
90 INPUT"viewer height h above ground plane";H
100 INPUT"center of circle at x0,y0,z0";X0,Y0,Z0
110 INPUT"circle radius r";R
120 INPUT"angle of tilt ccw around x-axis from ground plane, phi";TI
130 INPUT"angle of roll cw around y-axis as seen in front view, psi";TS
140 INPUT"number of points n, less than 100";N
150 DIM X(100),Y(100),XR(100),YR(100),ZR(100),ZRR(100),P(100),Q(100)
160 W=2*R/N  'calculate interval size
170 X(0)=X0-R  'set coordinates for center
180 TI=.0174533*TI:TS=.0174533*TS    'convert degrees to radians
190 STI=SIN(TI):CTI=COS(TI):STS=SIN(TS):CTS=COS(TS)   'calculate trig
200 PRINT
210 PRINT"Re-oriented circle coordinates, and perspective coordinates:"
220 PRINT USING "\          \";"index";"x (rot)";"y (rot)";"z (rot)";"p";"q"
230 FOR L=1 TO -1 STEP -2
240 FOR I=0 TO N
250 X(I)=X(0)+I*W
260 Y2=R*R-(X(I)-X0)*(X(I)-X0)
270 IF Y2<0 THEN 350
280 Y(I)=L*SQR(Y2)+Y0
290 YR(I)=Y(I)*CTI-Z0*STI   'rotation by phi around x-axis
300 ZR(I)=Y(I)*STI+Z0*CTI
310 ZRR(I)=ZR(I)*CTS-X(I)*STS   'rotation by psi around y-axis
320 XR(I)=ZR(I)*STS+X(I)*CTS
330 P(I)=XR(I)*D/(YR(I)+D):Q(I)=(ZRR(I)-H)*D/(YR(I)+D)   'perspective
340 PRINT USING "###.###   ";I;XR(I);YR(I);ZRR(I);P(I);Q(I)
350 NEXT
360 NEXT L
370 END
```

BASIC Program for Perspective of a Sphere

```
10 PRINT"Calculation of a Sphere in Rectlinear Perspective"
20 PRINT"Caution:  be sure sphere radius and center do not cause it to"
30 PRINT"approach viewer position."
40 PRINT"Number of iterations to obtain points is limited to 100."
50 INPUT"viewer distance d to picture plane";D
60 INPUT"viewer height h above ground plane";H
70 INPUT"center of sphere at x0,y0,z0";X0,Y0,Z0
80 INPUT"sphere radius r";R
90 INPUT"calculation interval w (use 1/integer not less than 1/100)";W
100 DIM X(100),Y(100),Z(100),V2(100),V(100),P(100),Q(100)
110 X(0)=X0-R   'set x-coordinate for center
120 M=2*R/W    'calculate number of intervals for x
130 PRINT
140 PRINT"Verification of sphere coordinates, and perspective coordinates:"
150 PRINT USING "\         \";"x";"y";"z";"p";"q"
160 FOR L=1 TO -1 STEP -2    'for top and bottom halves of sphere
170 FOR I=0 TO M    'sweep x values
180 X(I)=X(0)+I*W     'calculate x-values
190 V2(I)=R*R-(X(I)-X0)*(X(I)-X0)   'intermediate square
200 V(I)=SQR(V2(I))    'distance in xy-plane from center, along y
210 N=INT(2*V(I)/W)   'calculate number of intervals for y
220 Y(0)=-V(I)+Y0    'set y-coordinate for center
230 FOR J=0 TO N    'sweep y values
240 Y(J)=Y(0)+J*W
250 Y2=(Y(J)-Y0)*(Y(J)-Y0)    'temporary square
260 IF V2(I)<Y2 GOTO 300    'avoid negative square root, crashes
270 Z(J)=L*SQR(V2(I)-Y2)+Z0  'points of sphere surface
280 P(J)=X(I)*D/(Y(J)+D):Q(J)=(Z(J)-H)*D/(Y(J)+D)
290 PRINT USING "###.###   ";X(I);Y(J);Z(J);P(J);Q(J)
300 NEXT J
310 NEXT I
320 NEXT L
330 END
```

BASIC Program for Perspective of a Log Spiral in Polar Coordinates

```
10 PRINT"Calculation of Polar Curve in Rectilinear Perspective"
20 PRINT"Example done with log spiral r=a exp(b theta)."
30 PRINT"Polar function can be modified in program to any other function."
40 PRINT"Curve assumed in xy-plane.  Add rotation transformations to program"
50 PRINT"to obtain perspective of curve in other orientations."
60 PRINT"Polar origin should be translated behind PP, using x0 and y0."
70 PRINT"Number of iterations to obtain points is limited to 100."
80 PRINT"Enter any angular parameters in degrees; program changes to radians."
90 PRINT"Caution: be sure curve does not pass thru viewer position."
100 INPUT"viewer distance d to picture plane";D
110 INPUT"viewer height h above ground plane";H
120 INPUT"Polar origin x0,y0";X0,Y0
130 INPUT"parameter a";A
140 INPUT"parameter b (b=.4 increases r 12 times in 1 revolution)";B
150 INPUT"calculation interval w for theta (any integer number of degrees)";W
160 INPUT"number of interations n (less than 100)";N
170 DIM X(100),Y(100),R(100),TH(100),P(100),Q(100)
180 W=W*.0174533  'convert to radians
190 PRINT
200 PRINT "Polar, rectilinear, and perspective coordinates:"
210 PRINT USING"\          \";"r";"theta";"x";"y";"p";"q"
220 FOR I=0 TO N  'sweep theta values
230 TH(I)=I*W    'steps in theta (in radians)
240 R(I)=A*EXP(B*TH(I))    'calculate the function
250 'convert polar to rectilinear coordinates and translate center to x0,y0
260 X(I)=R(I)*COS(TH(I))+X0: Y(I)=R(I)*SIN(TH(I))+Y0
270 Z=0    'set in xy-plane
280 P(I)=X(I)*D/(Y(I)+D): Q(I)=(Z-H)*D/(Y(I)+D)   'perspective transform
290 PRINT USING "###.###   ";R(I);TH(I)*57.29578;X(I);Y(I);P(I);Q(I)
300 NEXT I
310 END
```

BASIC Program for Spherical Perspective of a Grid

```
10 PRINT"Calculation of Grid in Spherical Perspective"
20 PRINT"Number of iterations is limited to 100."
30 PRINT"Spherical perspective coordinates s & t can be plotted horizontally"
40 PRINT"and vertically, respectively, on flat paper."
50 PRINT"Choice of xy, yz, or xz grids.  Use zero for one axis or program"
60 PRINT"produces perspective of lattice, confusing to plot."
70 PRINT"Origin of xyz coordinates same as center of sphere, at viewer.  Grid"
80 PRINT"will start with points farther than R.  Viewer looks along y-axis."
90 INPUT"radius of picture surface R";R
100 INPUT"grid unit interval a";A
110 INPUT"number of grid lines for each axis wanted in order x,y,z";L1,L2,L3
120 INPUT"enter 0 or location of plane (e.g.0,0,5 for the xy-plane z=5)";
C1,C2,C3
130 DIM X(100),Y(100),Z(100),S(100),T(100)
140 PRINT
150 PRINT"Grid coordinates, and spherical perspective coordinates:"
160 PRINT USING "\       \";"x";"y";"z";"s";"t"
170 FOR M1=1 TO -1 STEP -2
180 FOR I=0 TO L1   'sweep x values +&-
190 X(I)=M1*I*A+C1    'calculate grid coordinates
200 FOR J=0 TO L2   'sweep y values
210 Y(J)=R+J*A+C2
220 FOR K=0 TO L3   'sweep z values +&-
230 Z(K)=K*A+C3
240 VYZ=SQR(Y(J)*Y(J)+Z(K)*Z(K)): VXY=SQR(X(I)*X(I)+Y(J)*Y(J))   'temp.sq.root
250 S(K)=R*ATN(X(I)/VYZ): T(K)=R*ATN(Z(K)/VXY)   'spherical perspective
260 PRINT USING "####.##   ";X(I);Y(J);Z(K);S(K);T(K)
270 NEXT K
280 NEXT J
290 NEXT I
300 NEXT M1
310 END
```

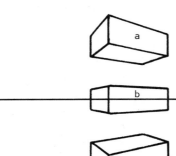

References

Abelson, Harold, and Disessa, Andrea. *Turtle Geometry: The Computer As a Medium for Exploring Mathematics*. Cambridge, MA: Massachusetts Institute of Technology Press, 1981.

Anderson, Bruce, and Riordan, Michael. *The Solar Home Book*. Harrisville, NH: Cheshire Books, 1976.

Bash, Paul, et al. "Van der Waals Surfaces in Molecular Modeling: Implementation with Real-time Computer Graphics." *Science,* 23 December 1983, pp. 1325–27.

Beakley, George. *Introduction to Engineering Graphics*. New York: Macmillan Co., 1975.

Brown, C. M. "Computer Vision and Natural Constraints." *Science,* 22 June 1984, pp. 1299–1305.

Burington, Richard. *Handbook of Mathematical Tables and Formulas*. 5th ed. New York: McGraw-Hill, 1973.

Chernow, Ron. "Colonies in Space May Turn out to be Nice Places to Live." *Smithsonian,* February 1976, pp. 62–69.

Cole, Rex Vicat. *Perspective for Artists*. 1921. Reprint. New York: Dover Publications, 1976.

Coxeter, Harold. *Introduction to Geometry*. New York: John Wiley & Sons, 1969.

———. *Non-Euclidean Geometry*. 4th ed. Toronto: University of Toronto Press, 1961.

Deken, Joseph. *Computer Images*. New York: Stewart, Tabori & Chang, 1983.

Descargues, Pierre. *Perspective: History, Evolution, Techniques*. New York: Van Nostrand Reinhold, 1975.

Dubery, Fred, and Willats, John. *Perspective and Other Drawing Systems*. New York: Van Nostrand Reinhold, 1972.

Edgerton, Samuel, Jr. *The Renaissance Rediscovery of Linear Perspective*. New York: Basic Books, 1975.

Ernst, Bruno. *The Magic Mirror of M. C. Escher*. Westminster, MD: Ballantine Books, 1976.

Freeman, Herbert, ed. *Interactive Computer Graphics*. Silver Spring, MD: IEEE Computer Society Press, 1980.

French, T. E., and Vierck, C. J. *Engineering Drawing and Graphic Technology*. 12th ed. New York: McGraw-Hill, 1978.

Gardner, Martin. *The Ambidextrous Universe*. 2d ed. New York: Charles Scribner's Sons, 1979.

————. "Mathematical Games: The Curious Magic of Anamorphic Art." *Scientific American*, January 1975, pp. 110–16.

————. "Mathematical Games: Extraordinary Nonperiodic Tiling That Enriches the Theory of Tiles." *Scientific American*, January 1977, pp. 110–21.

————. "Mathematical Games: On Tessellating the Plane with Convex Polygon Tiles." *Scientific American*, July 1975, pp. 112–17.

————. "Mathematical Games: The Superellipse: A Curve That Lies between an Ellipse and a Rectangle." *Scientific American*, September 1965, pp. 222–36.

Giesecke, F. E., et al. *Engineering Graphics*. 3d ed. New York: Macmillan Co., 1981.

————. *Technical Drawing*. 6th ed. Revised by Henry Cecil Spenser and Ivan Leroy Hill. New York: Macmillan Co., 1974.

Gill, Robert W. *Creative Perspective*. London: Thames & Hudson, 1981.

Greenberg, Donald, et al. *The Computer Image*. Reading, MA: Addison-Wesley, 1982.

Gregory, Richard. "Visual Illusions." *Scientific American*, November 1968, pp. 66–76.

Hayes, Brian. "Computer Recreations: Turning Turtle Gives One a View of Geometry from the Inside Out." *Scientific American*, February 1984, pp. 14–20.

Hearn, Donald, and Baker, M. Pauline. *Computer Graphics for the IBM Personal Computer*. Englewood Cliffs, NJ: Prentice-Hall, 1983.

Holden, Alan. *Shapes, Space, and Symmetry*. New York: Columbia University Press, 1971.

Jacobs, Harold. *Mathematics: A Human Endeavor*. New York: W. H. Freeman, 1970.

Julesz, Bela. *Foundations of Cyclopean Perception*. Chicago: University of Chicago Press, 1971.

Kline, Morris. "Projective Geometry." *Scientific American*, January 1955, pp. 80–86.

Land, Frank. *The Language of Mathematics*. London: John Murray, 1960.

Langridge, Robert, et al. "Real-time Color Graphics in Studies of Molecular Interactions." *Science*, 13 February 1981, pp. 661–66.

Leavitt, Ruth, ed. *Artist and Computer*. New York: Harmony Books, 1976.

Leeman, Fred. *Hidden Images: Games of Perception, Anamorphic Art, Illusion*. New York: Harry Abrams, 1975.

Leopold, Luna B., and Langbein, W. B. "River Meanders." *Scientific American*, June 1966, pp. 60–70.

Levens, A. S., and Chalk, W. *Graphics in Engineering Design*. 3d ed. New York: John Wiley & Sons, 1980.

Locher, J. L., ed. *The World of M. C. Escher*. New York: New American Library, 1971.

McDermott, Jeanne. "Geometrical Forms Known As Fractals Find Sense in Chaos." *Smithsonian*, December 1983, pp. 110–17.

Mandelbrot, Benoit. *The Fractal Geometry of Nature*. New York: W. H. Freeman, 1982.

Minnaert, M. *The Nature of Light and Color in the Open Air*. New York: Dover Publications, 1954.

Newmann, William, and Sproull, Robert. *Principles of Interactive Computer Graphics*. 2d ed. New York: McGraw-Hill, 1979.

Peterson, Dale. *Genesis II: Creation and Recreation with Computers*. Reston, VA: Reston Publishing, 1983.

Pirenne, M. H. *Vision and the Eye*. 2d ed. London: Chapman & Hall, 1967.

Purcell, Edwin. *Calculus with Analytic Geometry*. East Norwalk, CT: Appleton-Century-Crofts, 1965.

Ratliff, Floyd. "Contour and Contrast." *Scientific American,* June 1972, pp. 90–101.

Reichardt, Jasia, ed. *Cybernetic Serendipity*. New York: Praeger Publishers, 1968.

Rogers, David, and Adams, J. *Mathematical Elements for Computer Graphics*. New York: McGraw-Hill, 1976.

Scott, Joan. *Introduction to Interactive Computer Graphics*. New York: John Wiley & Sons, 1982.

Smith, Cyril. "The Shape of Things." *Scientific American,* January 1954, pp. 58–64.

Springer, R. D., et al. *Basic Graphics*. Newton, MA: Allyn & Bacon, 1963.

Taylor, Angus. *Calculus with Analytic Geometry*. Englewood Cliffs, NJ: Prentice-Hall, 1959.

Thomas, George, Jr. *Calculus and Analytic Geometry*. 3d ed. Reading, MA: Addison-Wesley, 1960.

Tormey, Alan and Judith. "Renaissance Intarsia: The Art of Geometry." *Scientific American,* July 1982, pp. 136–43.

Vero, Radu. *Understanding Perspective*. New York: Van Nostrand Reinhold, 1980.

Walker, Jearl. "Caustics: Mathematical Curves Generated by Light Shined through Rippled Plastic." *Scientific American,* September 1983, pp. 190–91.

Wenninger, Magnus. *Polyhedron Models*. London: Cambridge University Press, 1971.

Weyl, Hermann. *Symmetry*. Princeton: Princeton University Press, 1952.

Whitted, Turner. "Some Recent Advances in Computer Graphics." *Science,* 12 February 1982, pp. 767–74.

Yue, David. *Perspective Drawings by Programmable Calculator*. New York: Van Nostrand Reinhold, 1984.

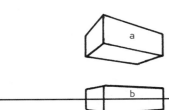
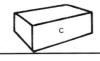

Index